PROFIT BY DESIGN

SECOND EDITION

Essays on Managing
a Profitable Architectural
& Engineering Practice

Steven Lawrence Biegel, AIA

Profit By Design
Essays On Managing a Profitable Architectural & Engineering Practice
Second Edition

Copyright ©2023 STEVEN LAWRENCE BIEGEL, AIA All rights reserved.

No part of this book may be reproduced in any form or by any mechanical means, including information storage and retrieval systems without permission in writing from the publisher or author, except by a reviewer who may quote passages in a review. All images, logos, quotes, and trademarks included in this book are subject to use according to trademark and copyright laws of the United States of America.

BIEGEL, STEVEN LAWRENCE, Author
PROFIT BY DESIGN
STEVEN LAWRENCE BIEGEL, AIA

Broadview Development Corporation
5050 Woodway Drive, Suite 3K
Houston, Texas 77056

Published by
ELITE ONLINE PUBLISHING
63 East 11400 South #230
Sandy, UT 84070
EliteOnlinePublishing.com

ISBN: 978-1-956642-82-7 (Hardback)
ISBN: 978-1-956642-85-8 (ePub)

Design & Editing by Philip Wanke

ARC015000
ARC017000

QUANTITY PURCHASES: Schools, companies, professional groups, clubs, and other organizations may qualify for special terms when ordering quantities of this title. Copies of this publication may be ordered from:
Broadview Development Corporation
5050 Woodway Drive, Suite 3K
Houston, Texas 77056
email: sbiegel@broadviewcorp.com

All rights reserved by STEVEN LAWRENCE BIEGEL, AIA and ELITE ONLINE PUBLISHING
This book is printed in the United States of America.

PROFIT BY DESIGN

Profit By Design

for:

Ashley A. Biegel
Jace M. Patton
Benjamin W. Biegel
Brittany A. Lawrence
Steven Hunter Lawrence
Lise M. Lawrence
Ben Ed Sepaugh
Paula Sepaugh
Teresa Sepaugh
Roger Sepaugh
N. Dale Biegel
Kurt R. Biegel

They endured and taught me to believe in the strength of family. They withstood and understood.

Dedicated to the memory of:

Donald J. Stephens, FAIA Architect & Mentor

and

John E. Biegel, PhD
Geraldine L. Biegel
M. Scott Lockard

PROFIT BY DESIGN

"The primary factor that separates management of design practice from management of a business is the fact that the professional's bottom line is not the same as the businessman's bottom line. The businessman is trained to measure the success of management in chiefly quantitative terms—usually units of money, or output, or the like. In contrast, the bottom line of the creative professional is most often qualitative—measured in terms of the professional's ultimate judgment about whether the output of the organization is as good as it can be. This single distinction is the most common reason why the many books and courses about business management don't ring quite true to the design professional.

For example, the quantitative manager will be inclined to deal with overruns in design budgets by imposing a design freeze as soon as the time allocation for design is used up. The qualitative manager, on the other hand, will frequently tolerate the overrun and justify it on the basis that it produced a better solution. Similarly, the quantitative manager will likely accept work in lean times or reject work in busy times simply on the basis of its contribution to volume and profit objectives. The qualitative manager in such cases will frequently select work to pursue solely on the basis of its professional interest, and may allow the firm to suffer severe ups and downs as a consequence. In the final analysis, the quantitative manager will usually measure a life's work by the size of the estate left behind; the qualitative manager's measurement will be in terms of the work accomplished and its impact on the society/profession left behind."

Weld Coxe

(Excerpt from Managing Architectural and Engineering Practice, by Weld Coxe, © 1980, Van Nostrand Reinhold Company, Inc.)

PROFIT BY DESIGN

PROFIT BY DESIGN

Acknowledgements

The single greatest debt of gratitude is owed to my adoptive father, John E. Biegel, Ph.D. who guided my early development and taught me the value of education. Along with my brothers, Dale and Kurt, we enjoyed a secure and instructive home life with summers spent traveling, camping and learning. Dr. Biegel's first book, Production Control was, in part, an inspiration for this text.

Many other friends and family members encouraged the writing of this book. Loudest among the voices was that of Medi Falsafi, loyal friend and business entrepreneur. Mr. Falsafi, as President & CEO of ABC Imaging of Washington, Inc., provided his personal time, encouragement, staff resources and graphic support to help produce the basic manuscript.

Other notable individuals who must be credited with enduring my banter for more than a year include Kerry Harding, Lise Lawrence, William Ryals, John Maudlin-Jeronimo, Jerri Biegel (my mother), David Nestleroth, Benny Pasqueriello, Tom Rohrbaugh, Kester Okhah, Michael Boomer and Ben & Paula Sepaugh. These people encouraged and inspired this work, whether they knew it or not at the time.

As a tribute to my first architect-employer and mentor, Donald J. Stephens, FAIA, this book builds on many concepts and business management tactics taught to me during my time at Donald J. Stephens & Associates, Architects, P.C. in Albany, New York. Don's attention to professional time management and profitability became the foundation on which I built a successful design management career.

Profit by Design is intended to help architects and engineers realize higher revenues, profits, personal income and professional satisfaction. I have endeavored here to describe the many elements of profitability in terms that may be understood by my professional colleagues. Thanks to everyone who helped and to everyone else who finds value in these pages.

PROFIT BY DESIGN

Profit by Design is intended to provoke thought, creativity and discipline about financial management among design professionals. Students of architecture and engineering who are immersed in courses entitled "Professional Practice" or "Practice Management" (or some permutation thereof) should derive a basic understanding of business concerns and strategies from these pages. Perhaps schools of architecture and engineering will pay greater attention to the void now existing in design curricula and place greater emphasis on business as an integral part of design education.

In this second edition of Profit By Design I must acknowledge the patience of my wife, Ashley Biegel. Over the last 15 years she has been a friend, colleague, supporter, and enthusiastic partner. This book updates many concepts and puts forward new expectations about managing sophisticated teams of architects & engineers. Many contributing designers and firms were involved in this manuscript. Ashley helped focus ideas and provided a sounding board as final edits were accomplished.

Credit is also due to Philip Wanke of PLACE designers, Inc. Philip helped with the design and editing for this updated book.

Steven Lawrence Biegel, AIA
Architect

PROFIT BY DESIGN

Preface

This book is vital to those who intend to offer architectural design services and achieve a profit.

In my experience over several decades of managing large development projects and banking investments, architects can be both visionary and creative. Architecture is a necessary component and service for clients; however, those wanting to hire an architect should be mindful of the give and take between cost and creativity. Likewise, architects must manage their business and learn to efficiently allocate their time and resources. This book provides a framework for both.

The decision to hire an architect is not based solely on cost. The decision to retain an architect should be based on their experience, talent, vision, track-record, efficiency, endorsements from prior clients, empathy, wisdom, communication skills, and a variety of technical considerations based upon building type and project location. Only once all of these aspects have been considered should cost and fees be examined. The litmus test for selecting a quality architect is first and foremost reputation in the marketplace.

I believe that students of architecture, practicing A&E professionals, real estate developers, land speculators, investors, clients with specific intentions, and/or owners who wish to renovate or re-purpose their property should read this book. It's easy to read with concise, well-presented content.

Steven Biegel's book is both instructive and compelling. The linear and sequential logic presented here is described in the simplest of terms for those interested in architecture and engineering services. Read this before you consider retaining an architect to understand the process and to recognize what it takes to manage and apply creative brainpower.

PROFIT BY DESIGN

The architectural design process is not simple. In fact it is enormously complex. Efficient management of the process will result in financial credibility and successful projects. With this book, readers will be able to learn about architecture and engineering services prior to engaging an architect, thereby setting themselves up for future success with their project.

Jennifer Hoff
Senior Vice President and Director of Public Affairs
IBC Bank

PROFIT BY DESIGN
Table of Contents

Update & Preamble 1
Introduction 2
The Future Today 5
Back to Basics 27
The Profit Paradigm 35
Attitude about Profit 43
Earning Revenue 49
Macro-Management 57
The Overhead Rate 71
Utilization 89
Creating Reserves 97
Estimates to Complete (ETCs) 105
Overtime versus "Comp Time" 109
Collections and DSOs 115
Relevance of Backlog 127
Break Even Analysis 133
Internal Audit/Internal Control 139
Profit through Cost Reduction 147
Facilities Management Outsourcing 157
Once Through Process 165
Planning for Negotiation 177
Profiting from Federal A&E Contracts 195
Federal Procurement Analysis Guide 205
Automation and Real Time Data 223
Building Delivery Process 235
Conclusion 285
Appendix 289
Bibliography 363
About the Author 365

PROFIT BY DESIGN

PROFIT BY DESIGN
Update & Preamble

In 2020 science fiction became reality and the world changed. The "normal world" became dangerous and hostile as we attempted to cope with a strange, invisible invader. Businesses collapsed, the stock market plunged, national borders were closed, and people died. The most unlikely world catastrophe surprised governments, health officials, scientists, militaries and the population at large. Millions of people became unemployed. The world economy went into an unanticipated tail spin with no visible horizon. Even gravity seemed unreliable. A pandemic showed us the newest form of chaos.

Former business management strategies are unreliable now. They were predicated on "business as usual" and the pulse of a well-organized and thriving economy. All of that has been irreparably altered by a ghostly pandemic with global tentacles and our global societal vulnerability has been revealed.

On the bright side, we have learned to work from the confines of our private homes. We have become socially distant by edict of our governments. We are learning to be self-reliant. People are taking their health more seriously. We have explored new past-times and other forms of home entertainment. We have found renewed joy in a 2000 piece jigsaw puzzle. We have learned to remotely operate the service industry with video calls and virtual conferences. We have discovered a new vanity in Facetime media and split-screen meetings resembling "Hollywood Squares" and "The Brady Bunch". Zoom and Teams are now household words. We have renewed our appreciation of time and mortality. We have greater respect for our fragile planet.

This 2nd Edition of "Profit By Design" brings forward the dynamic paradigm of achieving success and profits in a changing business environment. These chapters highlight an unshaken allegiance to a free enterprise economic system wherein supply and demand govern service delivery and pricing. This update to the original 2003 edition is both timely and necessary.

Steven L. Biegel, AIA, NCARB, LEED AP, Architect

PROFIT BY DESIGN

Introduction

The nature of a professional services organization can be viewed in narrow terms as an entity that provides intellectual services for a fee. Design services preformed by architects and engineers are intellectual works, illustrated with graphic and artistic skill.

Licensed architects and engineers are authorized to perform professional design services for clients and to sell their services for a reasonable fee. Granted the freedom to practice a distinguished profession, they are required to protect public health, safety and welfare in the process. Architects and engineers perform these services for a fee, but must accept the responsibility of protecting the public and their clients' interests. With this added responsibility of protecting the public good comes the obligation that design professionals have to educate their clients and teach the basic precepts of design and construction.

This book embraces the definition of Basic Design Services and distinguishes between basic and supplemental design services. This text also summarizes the many problems experienced by design and engineering professionals as they strive to perform services and produce documents for the benefit of their clients. There are many facets to performing "efficient" design services. Developing an efficient design and production process is essential to generating **"profit by design"**.

An important point repeated throughout this text is that architects and engineers must become good business people, in addition to good designers. The business of performing design services is complicated. Making money while endeavoring to solve design and engineering problems can be difficult (and nearly impossible) without imposing discipline on the design process and insisting on strong management of that process. One aspect of the design process that is difficult to control is the up front performance of schematic design services.

Schematic design can be and almost always is manifest as an iterative process of trial and error. Even with the most accurate programmatic data, designers have a tendency to interpret and reinterpret the design problem, with a variety of graphic ideas and solutions. Each iteration takes time and costs money. Controlling the schematic design process and achieving an early solution that responds well to the program and is supported by the client are important goals.

"Earned revenue" is a term that must be understood by architects and engineers. The idea that design professionals "market" professional services but "sell" time is not appreciated by most designers. Making money through the performance of design services requires careful management of the design process and the recognition that billable time should be charged to clients at rates that fully recover the cost of all services and expenses. Analysis of all costs associated with each hour of time devoted to a project is necessary in order to arrive at billable rates that capture all costs and assure a "reasonable profit". The basics of earning revenue and the many methods of deriving rates which reflect total cost will be presented in simple terms in this text.

Through the past century, the design professions have evolved and matured. Larger firms have organized around disciplines of "management", "design", "production", and "administrative support". The most profitable large firms tend to be the best managed firms, with clear sets of internal controls established to contain design and production efforts. Profits can be made or lost in an instant by a small shift in management style or the need to repeat some aspect of the design process. Strong management is necessary to prevent wasted time and "spinning" as services are being performed.

This book will reinforce the idea that the greatest assets in a professional services organization are people. The individual skill sets of employees that combine to allow an efficient and unique response to a design program are of highest value to the business of architecture and engineering. Other corporate assets including computers, software, drafting tables, office space, reference books and drafting supplies are nearly valueless in a design practice. Investing in people and improving their skill sets is key to a successful and sustainable architectural or engineering practice.

PROFIT BY DESIGN

Profit margins in professional services firms are usually small and vary only within a tight range. Design firms in particular tend to produce annual profits on net revenues of from 0% to around 22%. The best managed firms produce the highest profits. Although survey data concerning profit of A/E firms is difficult to obtain and usually subject to interpretation, the medium range for profits generated by well managed A/E firms is usually from 5% to 11% on net revenues, with the average around 6.1%. These percentages are all pre-tax and pre-bonus. (These statistics were compiled by Case and Company, Inc. management consultants and the Committee on Federal Procurement of A/E Services.) Even this level of profit generation requires strong management and careful control of the design and production process.

Although reliable sources of survey data on A/E firms are difficult to find, one of the most comprehensive surveys is conducted annually by Zweig White of Natick, Massachusetts. In the Zweig White 2001 "Successful Firm Survey" the average pre-tax, pre-bonus profit on gross revenues was calculated to be 7.9% and the average pre-tax, pre-bonus profit on net revenues was set at 10.6%. The number, type and composition of firms participating in the Zweig White 2001 survey is not clear. Compiling the raw list of "successful firms" to be invited to take part in the survey must be a daunting task. Therefore, only the most general of opinions can be derived from this data in support of this text.

Higher profits are derived from better project management, firm management and constant awareness of revenue generation goals. An A/E business can be enormously profitable and rewarding, if a positive attitude about profit is combined with qualitative design goals.

Conveying techniques and strategies to maximize the generation of profits from performing design services is the goal of this text. The many ways to accomplish this are outlined for the benefit of any architect or engineer who intends to be successful, both as a design professional and as a businessman. A/E practice should be profitable, satisfying and sustainable.

PROFIT BY DESIGN
The Future Today

This is our "site".
What we do with it next is important.
How we touch the earth must be both delicate and deliberate.

PROFIT BY DESIGN

WELCOME TO

Profit By Design

BUILDING THE FUTURE

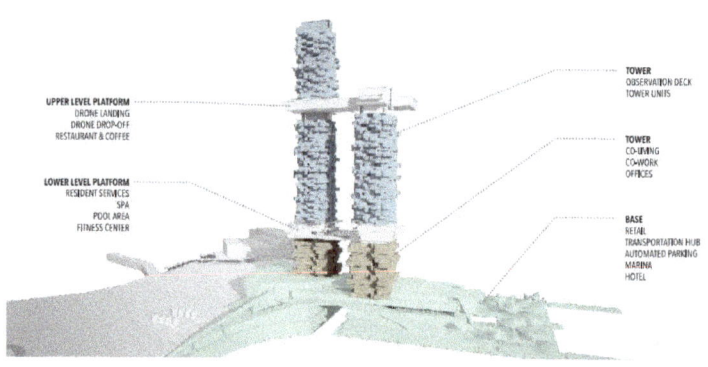

The Future Today

PROFIT BY DESIGN

TRENDS AND TECHNOLOGY AVAILABLE

TODAY

New technology + proven design methodologies

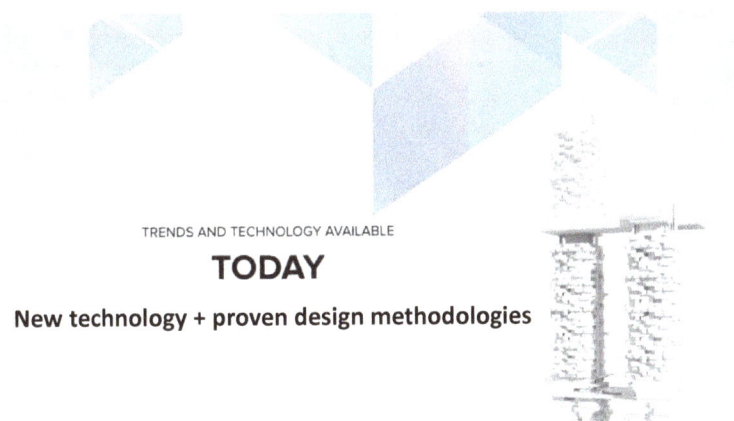

CO-WORKING
- 84% of users are more motivated
- 69% of users feel more successful
- 82% have expanded their networks
- 69% learned new skills

CO-LIVING
- Unique community feel
- Rapidly growing segment
- Small units, loaded with services
- One bill

The Future Today

PROFIT BY DESIGN

LOWER LEVEL PLATFORM
AMENITIES

- Cocktail bar
- Private dining room
- Cigar lounge
- Poker room
- Kids playroom
- Fitness Center
  - Rock climbing
  - Electro-magnetic bikes
  - Immersive fitness
  - Hydro training
  - Spa
  - Cryotherapy
- Hot & cold storage
- Package mail box
- Pet services

BASE / PROMENADE
ENTERTAINMENT

5G network, real time connection, LED lightning, food, music and people watching.

OBSCURA
- Immersive experience
- Inspire audiences

ECHO
- Huge virtual image from a small projector
- Captivating and memorable
- Image directly onto the viewer's eye

TOWER / OFFICE
DIGITAL TECHNOLOGY
INTERACTIVE GLASS

- Smart surface technology
- Transforms a variety of surfaces into functional touchscreens
- Watch TV shows in the kitchen while you cook
- Manage home appliances
- Bluetooth audio and online video
- Plan a bus trip on a interactive map

8   The Future Today   Copyright 2023, Steven L. Beigel, AIA

PROFIT BY DESIGN

VIRTUAL REALITY

- Selling projects yet to be built
- Eliminates need for model units
- Easy finish out showcase
- 24/7 robot assistance
- Variety of finishes at the touch of a button

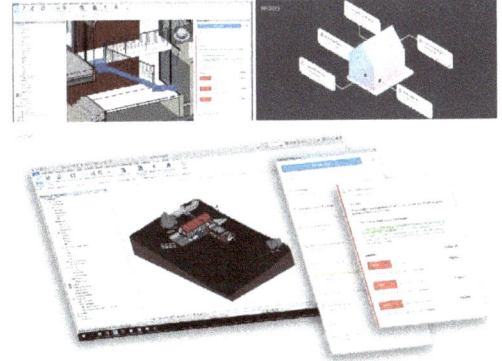

BUILDING CODE AUTOMATION

- For architects and engineers
- View code errors in Revit
- Accelerate project timelines
- Reduce errors

SMART SHOPPING

- Shoppers make 51% of their purchases online
- 44% of orders placed on smartphones
- E-commerce is growing 23% year over year
- In 2022 e-commerce sales are going to be $640,000 million US

AMAZON GO

Amazon Go is a new kind of store featuring the world's most advanced shopping technology.

The Future Today

PROFIT BY DESIGN

TOWER / HOME TECHNOLOGY
HOME ASSISTANTS

Google Home
- Hands-free help
- Control your smart home

Alexa
- Control your smart home
- Ask any question

Apple Home Kit
- Control your home kit

Hi, how can I help?

TOWER / HOME TECHNOLOGY
TECHNOLOGY

Nest
- Thermostat
  - Energy savings 10% to 15%
- Protect
  - Lets you know where smoke is coming from
- Hello
  - Lets you know who's there 24/7
  - Go back 3 hour snapshot history
- Cam
  - See your home 24/7
  - Alert when something happens
- Doorbell camera
- Multi-credential property acces control
- A.I. vacuum
- Glass cleaners

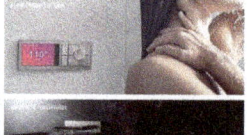

TOWER / HOME TECHNOLOGY
SMART BATHROOM

U BY MOEN
- Digital Shower
- Control by voice, phone and controller
- Avoid wasting water
- Set temperature, length, notificactions

SMART WATER
- Automatic bathtub filling
- Desire depth and temperature

NUMI HIGH TECH TOILET
- Motion-Activated cover and seat
- Deodrizer
- Heated seat
- Foot warmer
- Music

The Future Today

PROFIT BY DESIGN

TOWER / HOME TECHNOLOGY
SMART KITCHEN

INTERACTIVE COOKTOP
- Embedded induction surface
- Multi-touch counter

MOLEY CHEF ROBOT
- Reproduces the human hands
- Operated from a touch screen or via smartphone

SMART REFRIGERATOR
- Create shopping list
- Peek inside your refrigerator

FOOD RECYCLER
- Zera converts 95% of waste into ready-to-use fertilizer

SOLAR TRASH COMPACTOR
- Powered by solar energy

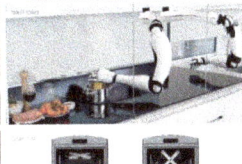
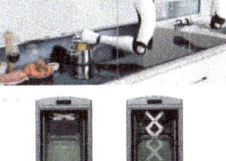

SUSTAINABILITY
DYNAMIC GLASS

COOLING
- Saves 34% in cooling loads

LIGHTING
- Saves 29% in electrical use

VISIBLE LIGHT
- Controls between 60%-1%

SOLAR HEAT
- Controls between 0.40-0.05

TOWER / UNITS
PREFAB

- Offsite construction
- Factory built
- Standard buildings chassis
- Mass production allows more time focused on delivering high quality and creative design solutions
- Fast construction
- Lower cost by buying in bulk
- Katerra

Right Now,
There are
20 Million Containers
Crossing The Seas

PROFIT BY DESIGN

TOWER / UNITS
MODULAR

EXCEPTIONAL QUALITY
. Reach superior results than traditonal techniques

SPEED
. Built in about 1/3 the time needed to construct a site-built building

COST SAVINGS
. Modular construction can save the consumer 10-20%

FLEXIBILITY OF DESIGN

ENERGY EFFICENCY
. 50% more energy efficient

'KASITA' CONCEPT
. Small package
. Delivered ready

TOWER / UNITS
ALL IN ONE FURNITURE

. Ori
. At the touch of a button, the full sized configuration transforms to offer a full scale bedroom, office and living room

. Versatility and mobility
. Cost savings
. Space savings

SUSTAINABILITY
WIND POWER

COST
. Less than 1 cent per kWh

ENERGY PER YEAR
. Small wind turbines could provide up to 1.5 TW.h

CARBON FOOTPRINT
. Yearly emissions eliminated

SOLAR POWER
. Double digit growth year after year

COST
. 3.7 cents per kWh

ENERGY PER YEAR
. 1 watt-peak of solar PV capacity generates 1 to 2 kWh

The Future Today

PROFIT BY DESIGN

SUSTAINABILITY
WATER
- Less than 5% of water is used for drinking and cooking
- Greywater makes up 65% of wastewater
- Reduces water bills 30%

VERTICAL FARMS
- 1 acre = 100 farmed acres
- 90% less waste

GREEN WALLS
- Reduces urban heat island effect
- Cleans air of pollutants

SUSTAINABILITY
TESLA ENERGY

SOLAR ROOF
- $21.85 per square feet
- Invisible solar cells
- Infinite tile warranty
- $5000 cost
- $2000 installation

POWERWALL
- Stores the excess solar energy

TESLA APP
- Monitor and manage your storage energy.

TRENDS AND TECHNOLOGY AVAILABLE BETWEEN NOW AND

5 YEARS

The Future Today

PROFIT BY DESIGN

TOWER / HOME TECHNOLOGY
A.I. PERSONAL ASSISTANT

TEMI
. Personal assistant

HONDA
. A18. Charming companion
. B18. Chair-type mobility
. C18. Multi-functional cargo
. D18. Autonomous off-road vehicle

CUTTI
. Elder autonomy help

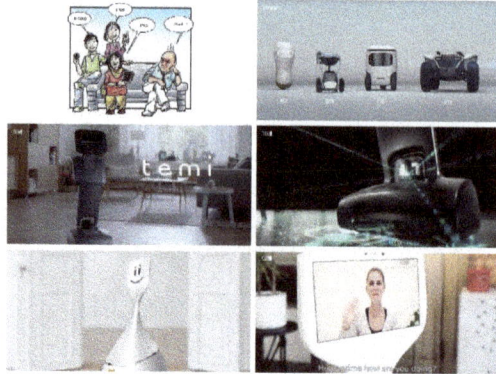

ROBOTIC CONSTRUCTION

TIMBER CONSTRUCTION
. Modules prefabricated by robots
. Robotic precision
. Computer-aided

3D PRINTING
. Computer controlled
. Enables almost any shape
. Fast and accurate construction
. Low labour costs
. Less material waste

PLATFORM'S CONNECTION
HORIZONTAL ELEVATORS

DIRECTION
. Vertical and horizontal

FOOT PRINT
. 50% less

CAPACITY
. 50% more

WEIGHT
. 50% less compared to standard technologies
. Allows for new building configurations

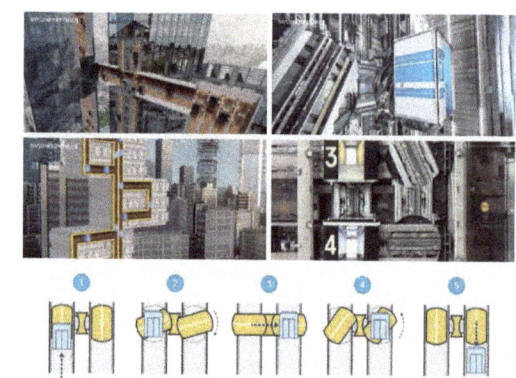

PROFIT BY DESIGN

UAV DELIVERY
UNMANNED AERIAL VEHICLE

. 60% reduction in delivery costs

AMAZON PRIME AIR
. Improves road safety
. Reduces delivery time, less than 30 minutes
. Package delivery up to 5 pounds

CONNECT ROBOTICS
. Drone delivery service wherever it is needed
. Don't have to buy any equipment
. Seller and customer connected
. Drone takes off after the payment is done in the app
. Fully automated, end-to-end

AVs DELIVERY
DRIVER LESS

KROGER GROCERY DELIVERY
. Vehicle for groceries
. Take up very little space on the road

ROBOMART
. Mobile grocery market
. "Grab and Go" technology
. Fresh fruit and vegetables stock

DOMINO'S PIZZA AV
. Ford and Domino's fusion
. Built-in pizza oven
. Customer will have a PIN number

BASE / MEANS OF TRANSPORTATION
AUTONOMOUS VEHICLES

CAR
. Tesla charger: 30 min charging your vehicle
. Prevents 90% of car accidents
. Increases road capacity by 273%

BUS
. 100% autonomous
. 15 passengers
. 25 km/h operating speed
. 9 hours autonomy

PROFIT BY DESIGN

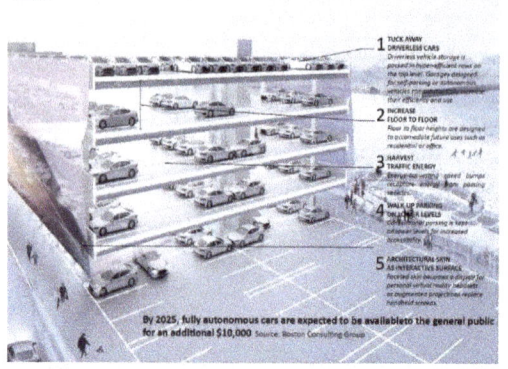

BASE / MEANS OF TRANSPORTATION
PARKING

CONVENTIONAL GARAGE DESIGNED TO ADAPT TO AUTONOMUS VEHICLES

- Today the typical car is used only 5% of the time
- 95% of the time it is parked at a house or on the street
- By the time today's garages are built, self parking cars and shared fleets will be a reality

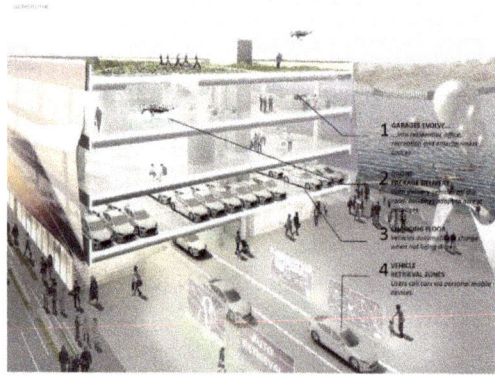

BASE / MEANS OF TRANSPORTATION
PARKING

PARKING GARAGE EVOLUTION

- Car ownership will evolve to a subscription service with intelligent fleets
- Less need for parking
- In 2035, the need for parking should decline by more than 5.7 billion square meters in the United States

SMART CITIES

SIDEWALK LABS

- Transformation from an ownership model to a mixed model of fleet-owned vehicles
- Opportunity to right-size the automobile itself
- Driverless shuttle buses replace private cars
- Will have some kind of spatial differentiation or universal time-of-day pricing
- Elimination of on-street parking and transforming that space into bike lanes, bus lanes, and loading/unloading spaces
- Traffic lights track the flow of pedestrians

PROFIT BY DESIGN

TRENDS AND TECHNOLOGY
AVAILABLE IN

10 YEARS

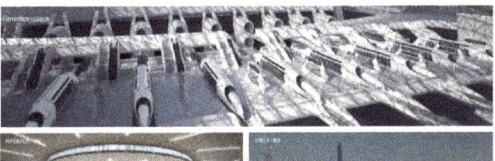

BASE / MEANS OF TRANSPORTATION
TRANSPORTATION

HYPERLOOP
- System of tubes through which a pod travels free of air resistance and friction
- Average speed of 600 mph
- Goal of being in service by 2021

SPACE X
- NYC to Shanghai in 39 minutes
- Elon Musk, imagines carrying people from any part of the world in less than 30 minutes

UBER
- Drone flying car
- Rideshare network
- Operational by 2023

TOP PLATFORM
DRONES

FLIGHT SPEED
- 100 km/h

CRUISING DURATION
- 25 min

CRUISING ALTITUDE
- 500 m

TOWER
PRIVATE DRONE PLATFORM

The private drone platforme can be used by penthouse owners.
- Called in via app

The Future Today

Copyright 2023, Steven L. Beigel, AIA

PROFIT BY DESIGN

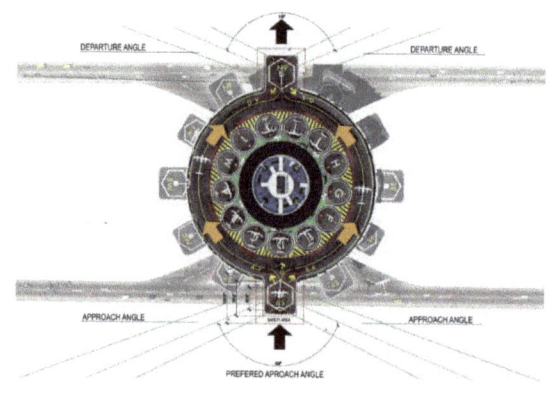

The Future Today

PROFIT BY DESIGN

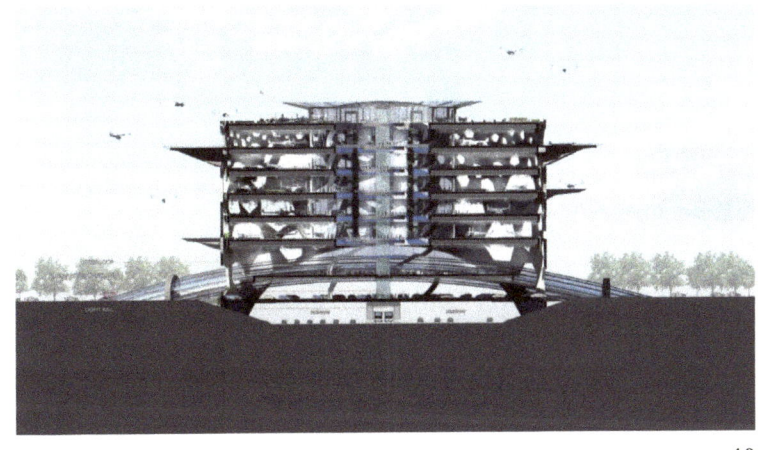

PROFIT BY DESIGN

MODULAR MULTIFAMILY / THE NAKED TRUTH

TODAY'S MODULAR CONSTRUCTION IS MUCH MORE THAN DOUBLEWIDES AND TRAILER PARKS.

The Future Today

PROFIT BY DESIGN

Minimum Number of Maximum-Sized Boxes

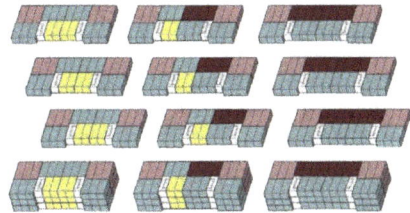

STRAIGHT, **FLAT**, RATIONAL

PROFIT BY DESIGN

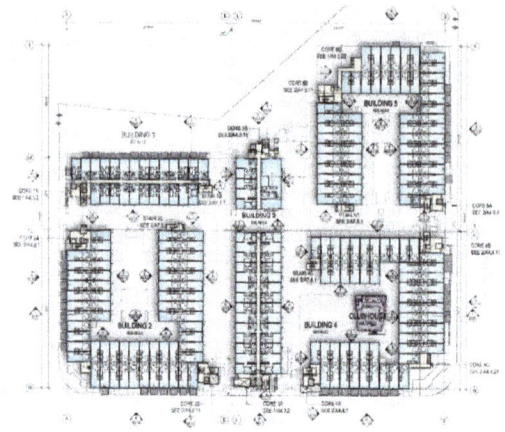

WHAT MODULAR WANTS TO DO

WHAT MODULAR WANTS TO DO

The Future Today

PROFIT BY DESIGN

WHAT MODULAR CAN DO

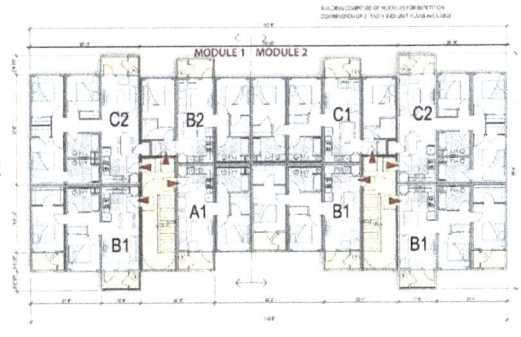

MODULAR PROS & CONS

Labor Rate Savings

Faster

Price Certainty

Better Quality

Safer, Security, Noise....

Transportation & Installation Costs

Early Decision Making

$$$ Front End Loaded

Uses 20% More Material

PROFIT BY DESIGN

WHAT MODULAR WILL DO

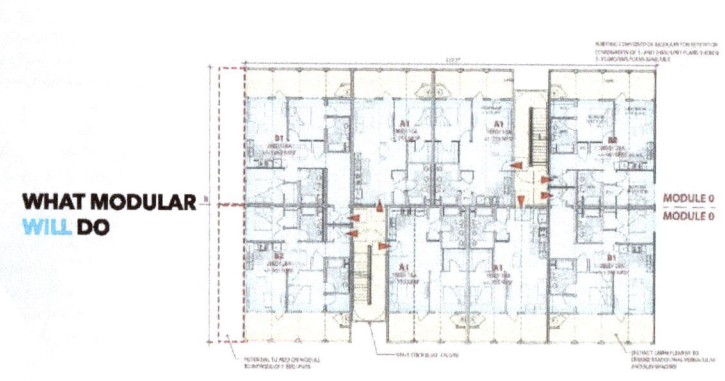

WHAT MODULAR WILL DO

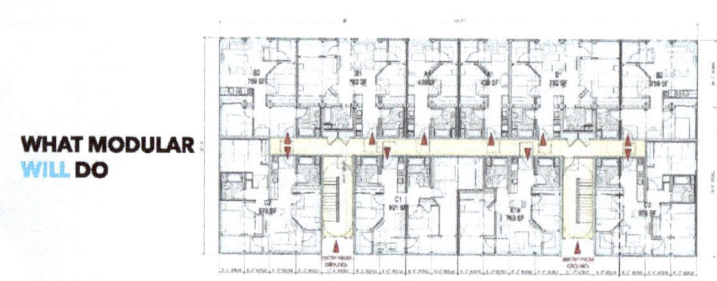

PROFIT BY DESIGN

S1
+/-320 SF

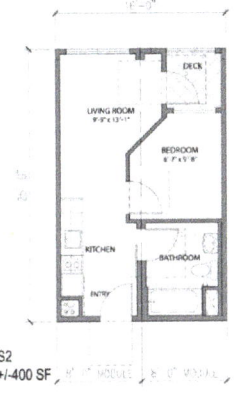

S2
+/-400 SF

WHAT MODULAR WILL DO

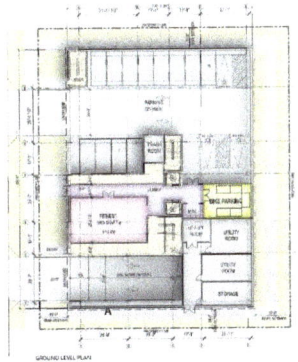

GROUND LEVEL PLAN

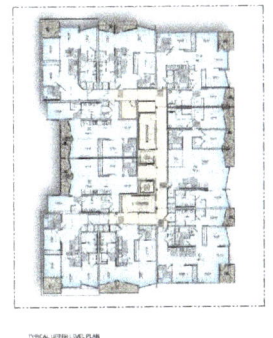

TYPICAL UPPER LEVEL PLAN

PROFIT BY DESIGN

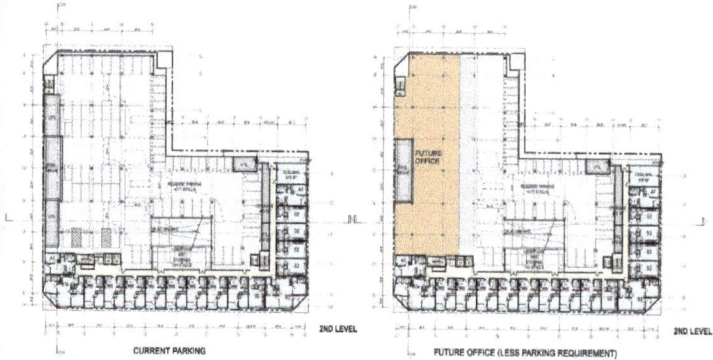

PROFIT BY DESIGN
Back to Basics

What is it that architects and engineers do? Who needs them? When are they useful and for what period of time? How do they interface with the construction process? Why are design professionals necessary players in today's society? These basic questions can be asked of any set of professionals in a service oriented economy. But these questions are most relevant as they relate to design professionals because so few design professionals readily have the answers.

If a design student is nearing the completion of his or her formal university training and heading for the threshold of this profession, their future is filled with both optimism and apprehension. The best equipped, burgeoning young professionals, with high grades and a creative portfolio of design studio work, may be shocked to learn that the future will revolve around performing services for someone else (either an employer or a client or both). This realization is often difficult to comprehend and accept. The notion that architects and engineers "serve" (not just create) can be confusing at first. It takes time to witness the many variations of "service" to clients and even longer to recognize the need for "service" to the profession.

What architects and engineers do is perform work for a fee. This is not unlike the legal or medical professions. It is also akin to the accounting and psychiatric professions. Professional A/E services are many and varied, often involving other professionals, specialists, consultants and experts from allied fields. Architectural education provides a good platform for career pursuits in a wide range of artistic and environmental sciences. Architects and engineers are supposed to be well equipped to organize and manage the professional design services delivery process.

Services provided by architects and engineers are based in analytical skills and expressed through the creative application of art, science, physics and reason. When a client purchases services from design professionals, they are often unable to interpret the quality and value of such purchases.

PROFIT BY DESIGN

This fact increases the mystique surrounding architects and engineers. Often, this fact belies an attitude of suspicion and apprehension on the part of the client. Compared with the services of a doctor or lawyer, design professionals perform a wide range of relatively passive skills. When the need arises for a doctor, lawyer or accountant, the resulting services performed by them seems more tangible and finite, with measurable result. Design services appear far less tangible. Benefits of good design may take years to manifest and recognize.

The need for architectural and engineering services can be seen throughout the existing built environment. The enormous stock of obsolete buildings, the shortage of adequate housing throughout the world, the continuing decay of roads, bridges, dams, utility infrastructure, unsafe schools and public places in both urban and rural settings are but a few real examples. The wide range of services required to improve and/or replace the built environment with more modern infrastructure and facilities represents an opportunity for the next generation of design professionals. This range of services and the underlying skill sets needed to perform such services are ever-expanding, merging and evolving. The need to define, clarify and explain the services available from and through the A/E profession is a serious challenge for successful practitioners.

The idea that architects and engineers are taught a specific set of basic services in professional schools is an attempt to establish parameters of understanding that allow design professionals to communicate first with one another, secondarily with consultants, and lastly with clients. For example, architects today generally know what "programming" is and how it applies to most projects. Clients however, may lack appreciation for programming skills and be confused about the relevance of this phase in the design process. So, in addition to defining the services necessary to successfully execute the work, the design professional must be capable of communicating the need for such services to the less aware client. Clarity of communication is key. In a business sense, design professionals face the challenge of overcoming the client's lack of understanding of the design process. Architects and engineers must be prepared to teach their clients in terms they can understand.

Basic design services are repeatedly defined for architects and engineers in a variety of resource materials. Professional societies have invested millions of dollars in practice aids and handbooks to provide A/E practitioners with language for use in presentations, negotiations and contracts. Projects "from hell" result when the client and design professional fail to adequately discuss and digest the definition of services to be provided, which may differ widely from project to project. Clear communication is essential and no project can be successful if the client (the buyer) lacks an appreciation of what the A/E (the seller) is selling. The "buyer beware" attitude taught universally in a capitalist society applies to architectural services as well. Design professionals have a duty to clearly explain the relevance of and the need for the services they provide.

In this text, basic services are redefined in the simplest of terms, in order to provide a baseline for communicating with clients. The definition of "basic services" also allows for the isolation of "supplemental services" and their definition. Both sets of services must be understood by architects, engineers, consultants and, most importantly, clients.

One of the AIA's most useful publications was written and published in 1978, entitled "Client's Guide to Architectural Services." Originally produced by the Boston Society of Architects, this early manual offered guidance to clients interested in retaining professional architects and engineers. In this document, an effort was made to simplify descriptions of architectural services and to organize those services in ways that could be understood by clients.

Services required for specific projects form combinations as varied as projects themselves. The following list of design phases organizes basic design services in several distinct categories.

<u>Pre-Design Phase</u> includes those services necessary to establish the programmatic, financial, and time constraints and requirements prior to beginning design: project administration; disciplines coordination; document checking; agency consulting; reviews; approval; owner-supplied data coordination; programming; space schematics; flow diagrams; existing

facilities surveys; marketing studies; economic feasibility studies; project financing; project development scheduling; project budgeting; and presentations.

Site Analysis Phase includes those services necessary to establish site-related constraints, requirements, and planning for the project. Some are provided during pre-design activities and some during project design: project administration; disciplines coordination, document checking; agency consulting, review, approval; owner-supplied data coordination; site analysis and selection; site development planning; detailed site utilization studies; on-site utility studies; off-site utility studies; environmental studies and reports; zoning processing assistance.

Schematic Design Phase includes those services necessary to prepare schematic design studies consisting of drawings and other documents illustrating the scope and relationship of project components for approval by the owner. Designs are normally conceptual in character: project administration; disciplines coordination; document checking; agency consulting, review, approval; owner-supplied data coordination; architectural design, documentation; structural design, documentation; mechanical design, documentation; electrical design, documentation; civil design, documentation; landscape design, documentation; interior design, documentation; materials research, specifications; project development scheduling; statement of probable construction cost; presentations.

Design Development Phase includes those services necessary to prepare, from the approved schematic design studies, documents which fix and describe the size and character of the entire project for the owner's approval: project administration; disciplines coordination, review, approval; owner-supplied data coordination; architectural design, documentation; structural design, documentations; mechanical design, documentation; landscape design, documentation; interior design, documentation; material research, specifications; project development scheduling; statement of probable construction cost; presentations.

Construction Documents Phase includes services necessary to prepare, from the approved design development, documents, drawings, specifications, and other documents setting forth in detail the requirements for construction of the entire project for approval by the owner: project administration; disciplines coordination, document checking; agency consulting, review, approval; owner-supplied data coordination; architectural design, documentation; structural design, documentation; mechanical design, documentation; electrical design, documentation; civil design, documentation; landscape design, documentation; interior design, documentation; material research, specifications; special bidding documents; scheduling; statement of probable construction cost; presentations.

Bidding or Negotiating Phase includes those services necessary to assist the owner in obtaining bids or negotiated proposals and in awarding and preparing construction contracts. In the case of phased construction, the owner may authorize bidding and negotiation on portions of the work prior to completion of the construction documents and prior to completion of the construction documents phase statement of probable construction cost: project administration; disciplines coordination, document checking; agency consulting, review, approval; owner-supplied data coordination; bidding materials; addenda; bidding, negotiations; analysis of alternatives, substitutions; special bidding services; bid evaluations; construction contract agreements.

Construction Contract Administration Phase includes those services during the administration of the construction contract by the architect as set forth in AIA Document B141, Standard Form of Agreement Between Owner and Architect: project administration; disciplines coordination, document checking; agency consulting, review, approval; owner-supplied data coordination; office construction administration; construction field observation; project representation; inspection coordination; supplemental documents; quotations requests; change orders; project schedule monitoring; construction cost accounting; and project closeout.

Post-Construction Phase involves those services by the architect and other professionals intended to facilitate utilization of the project: project administration; disciplines coordination, document checking; agency consulting, review, approval; owner-supplied data coordination; maintenance and operations programming; start-up assistance; record drawings; warrant review; post-construction evaluation.

The foregoing are considered "basic services," distinct from "supplemental services." In an overly simplified way, supplemental services can be described as everything necessary to accomplish or enhance a project, not already described in basic services. According to the early definition derived by the Boston Society of Architects, supplemental services are those not readily anticipated at the project's outset.

<u>Supplemental Services</u> are those services for which a need cannot be predetermined nor scope determined and which do not easily fall into one of the other eight phases or which span several phases such as: special studies; renderings; model construction; life-cycle cost analysis; quantity surveys; detailed construction cost estimates; energy studies; environmental monitoring; tenant-related services; graphics design; fine arts and crafts services; special furnishings design; non-building equipment selection; project promotion, public relations; leasing brochures; expert witness; computer applications; materials and systems testing; demolition services; mock-up services; still photography; motion pictures and videotape; coordination with non-design professionals; special disciplines consultation; and special building type consultation.

Detailed descriptions have been developed for each of the services listed here and may be found in AIA document B162 "Scope of Designated Services."

<u>Specialized Services</u>. While more design firms are providing a comprehensive range of services, many firms have also specialized in particular building types. The concept of a comprehensive range of services includes services to an individual project that requires specialists in various aspects of building design and construction. Some firms concentrate on selected types of work, others maintain in house specialized groups and many supplement their marketing and project type

potential by engaging or associating with firms known for the particular expertise desired.

<u>Comprehensive Services</u>. Architects currently offer services expanded beyond those traditionally required for the design of simple buildings. This expansion has been in response to new demands on owners, operators, and users of buildings, and of the public agencies regulating environmental design and construction processes, as well as the increasing complexities of the built environment.

As the reader continues to explore this text, it is important to grasp the idea that architects and engineers are "selling" professional time. With each occurrence of a "sale" of A/E services should come the necessary "profit" made possible by that sale. The commodity aspect of professional design services is based in time. Investing professional design time in a client's project must yield an acceptable design solution (in response to the program), but profit must be earned with each and every hour dedicated to the job. The total compensation for design services must be derived from a requirement to be reimbursed by the client for all costs and expenses associated with delivering the services, with adequate profit factored into the cost computation.

Many firms describe their services as "value-based" or claim to provide clients with "value added" over the duration of the project. Such pronouncements have little impact on profit and are usually perceived as marketing slogans or as an effort to elevate the qualitative side of the business above the quantitative thirst for cash. The definition of "value added" rarely contains a realistic description of a new services delivery method. The least common denominator among all successful A/E firms is the derivation of profit from a carefully crafted business approach. The recognition that professional design time among a certain set of employees is finite, valuable, allocatable and manageable is requisite to understanding the commodity nature of A/E business.

PROFIT BY DESIGN

PROFIT BY DESIGN
The Profit Paradigm

In recent years, many firm principals doubled as magicians, managing their firms in such a way that they made bonuses disappear. Some blamed it on the recession we now face; others held September 11, 2001 responsible for the firm's poor performance. Even historically strong firms found themselves asking, "Is it possible to manage A/E projects successfully (and maintain profitability) during a global recession? How can we produce creative, dynamic, and inspirational architecture with both eyes on the 'bottom line'? In an A/E practice, what should be the rules for navigating through uncharted economic waters?" Let's look at the facts:

Fact: Many architects and engineers are poor business managers.

Fact: Managing a successful A/E practice is much more complicated than managing a pure "A" (Architecture) practice, mostly due to the multi-discipline nature of the practice.

Fact: The creative, artistic, quality driven practice of architecture, with emphasis on client satisfaction and exploring many functional options, is expensive. Choices and the complexity of thought comprising 'flexible design alternatives' are VERY expensive.

Fact: The business of providing design services to the public (or to specific client types) only makes sense if the level of compensation (fee) is sufficient to cover ALL costs and yield more "profit" than the partners could earn by investing their money in a conventional CD, Treasury or Municipal Bond.

Fact: The business side of providing A/E services is not well understood by practitioners or even taught in schools of architecture, engineering or schools of business.

Fact: The tools for delivering quality design services from Pre-Design through Post-Occupancy are different from the tools needed (and used) to run a profitable business.

PROFIT BY DESIGN

In the early 1970s, the American Institute of Architects embarked on an effort known as Cost-Based Compensation Guidelines. After dozens of committee meetings and the usual venting of frustrations, an interesting set of tools were evolved which included the architect's "Phase/Service Matrix" and related A/E specific cost accounting methodologies.

These tools were generally designed to help the "average" non-business oriented architect cope with the trauma of delivering services and getting paid for the time spent solving physical and environmental problems. The matrix was a useful, visual, organizational tool. It helped architects categorize service types and quantify administrative support time. The matrix was an integral part of what became known as Compensation Guidelines for Architectural and Engineering Services. As with most good ideas, the Guidelines were ignored for many years.

Later, the AIA Contract Documents were modified to embrace many of the ideas embedded in the Compensation Guidelines. Still later, organizations like Harper-Schuman (now Deltek) caught on and revised their cost-accounting procedures to offer more specific, automated accounting assistance, tailored to A/E practice. Then, CNA/Schinnerer and DPIC began offering business-oriented advice and courses for architects and engineers, largely aimed at risk avoidance, but based in the historical evidence that architects are not always "good business people."

If it is true that architects and engineers are generally good problem solvers, but poor business people, how do good firms survive recessions? How do they survive canceled projects? Severe swings in market share? Mergers? Acquisitions? Ownership Transition? Moreover, how do good firms remain in business, produce quality work, earn good fees, generate profits for shareholders, and stay on the cutting edge of design and technology? Answer: They accept certain fundamental, empirical, tangible, and measurable precepts.

To have a chance at being profitable, an A/E firm must:

- have a business plan that is based on generating a certain minimum profit;

- take care to accept only projects of a certain minimum potential profitability;
- continually balance backlog with projected staffing;
- maintain high utilization of all billable staff;
- achieve a prescribed minimum multiplier for every hour devoted to a job;
- control overhead and operational expenses;
- minimize the investment necessary to secure future work;
- collect the fees that are earned in a timely manner;
- be vigilant in the allocation of manpower and consciously account for support staff time as it is applied to each project;
- recognize ALL costs associated with producing the work, including reproduction costs and other reimbursable expenses;
- produce a design product superior to that of competing A/E businesses.

What a novel idea! Produce innovative, lasting, notable architecture and engineering solutions while remaining profitable and "in business" long enough to accept the AIA 25 year award. How often does this happen? When does an A/E practice merit the Firm of the Year Award for "good business practices and profitability?"

As each New Year gets underway, many firms are still closing the books on the previous year and realizing that earnings did not meet expectations. So, what needs to change in future years? What should the New Year's resolution be for an A/E firm that began last year with high hopes and good profit expectations, but floundered somewhere along the way? After all, they say that "insanity is the practice of doing the same thing, time after time, expecting a different result."

When we dissect the way most firms practice, it is likely that poor management and unrecognized opportunities lay at the root of diminished profits. It is probable that the following items occurred (in total or in part):

- The firm didn't have a business plan prescribing both

revenue and profit targets.
- Upper management relied upon the judgment of project managers who were once taught to minimize labor devoted to their projects (this is not a good practice).
- Project starts were delayed by clients or through protracted contract negotiations.
- Too many idle staff were retained in anticipation of new work on the horizon.
- Insufficient attention was devoted to controlling overhead and production expenses.
- Projects were cancelled with little notice…and the total cost of the effort up to the point of cancellation was not recovered.
- Consultant costs got 'out of hand' and invoices from consultants lagged substantially behind project closeout.
- Internal cost-accounting systems were slow to indicate that projects were losing money.
- Short-cuts may have been taken to minimize design and CD efforts, believing that 'problems can be solved in the field'… to the detriment of both quality and time.
- The idea that "profit" is an hourly and daily occurrence (not just at the end of the project) was ignored.
- Little or no effort was directed toward shifting true project costs (including clerical time and reproduction) onto the projects. Overhead was "way too high."
- The firm agreed to perform services and accepted projects for compensation far short of that actually needed to accomplish the job(s).
- Collection efforts were too slow, and the firm borrowed too much money to float the client's finances throughout the project.

More attention needs to be paid to insuring profitability and "planning for profits." Profits are not accidental by-products of a good client-architect relationship. Profit should be considered "the reason" we are in business. In a recession especially, more structured project and office management is needed, with much greater discipline. A measure of success much different from design awards and name recognition needs to be embraced by A/E firms. For the past several years the slogan has been "the work is out there." Profitable work has been harder to identify

PROFIT BY DESIGN

and many times harder to deliver. As a recession deepens and begins to impact projects in design (which may be cancelled), assuring "profit" is tantamount to assuring survival.

A "fully integrated" A/E practice can be profitable while producing notable, quality work. One key to this in a fully integrated A/E practice is the conscious, sometimes relentless, inclusion of engineering disciplines up front, in the early (schematic) stages of design. In this way, engineering ideas are integrated early into the architectural thought process, thus framing or even eliminating certain design alternatives that may not make sense in engineering terms. So, less time is spent in the iterative, trial and error feedback loop. And, less time is spent frustrating the client with multiple options, some of which just won't work.

In the classic A/E approach to a large design project, 60% of the fee can be spent achieving a satisfactory, client-endorsed 35% submission. This is often the case in government work. Then, with only 40% of the fee remaining, the M/E/P engineering effort is initiated in tandem with design development and construction document phases. Projects are far more likely to "go south" in the Construction Documents and Specification phases – with little or no fee left to correct problems, perform adequate Quality Assurance, or assure adequate Construction Administration.

One of the most uncomfortable aspects of the usual "design it first – then, engineer it" model is that the customary engineering response to a schematic architectural solution at the "hand-off" becomes routine (stagnant)… the engineer simply determines…capacity (load), delivery system (piping & duct distribution), and controls (location of thermostat). It is no wonder that technology stagnates and every new building relies on the same old basic systems…Variable Air Volume or some derivation thereof as the comfort delivery method of choice.

PROFIT BY DESIGN

Evolving design theory and the innovative application of new technology can best merge at the front end of the design process. The truly "integrated" firm would approach every major project in this manner and subscribe to a set of "design guidelines" at the initial kick-off meeting to delineate the limits of schematic design exploration. Including engineering disciplines up front and use of design guidelines to provoke early decisions on materials, systems and cost parameters can be remarkably successful. This is a sure way to maintain control over project costs, assure the best thinking up front, and save schematic design time.

One notable impact of the Cost Based Compensation Guidelines of the early 1970s was that architects and designers were suddenly able to recover the cost of clerical time on most projects (where allowable). According to a Case & Co. survey (as far back as 1976), just a subtle change like including administrative and clerical time in fee proposals, negotiations and contract clauses caused profitability to climb from 11% to 16% on most jobs because overhead had been reduced and billable project hours adjusted to reflect the "true cost" of labor needed to perform the work. Imagine that…profits increasing by 45%, simply by recovering clerical/administrative time on a project!

Similarly, the notion that reproduction costs can be charged off to the project (and borne by the client) is not a recent revelation…but (largely due to tracking issues) one which has been unstructured or avoided. The recent trend toward establishing FMs (Facility Management Service Centers) in larger A/E offices is indicative of this effort to recover costs. With reproduction on most jobs averaging 5-8% of all project costs…. the planned recovery of these costs can significantly improve profits. Why should reproduction of drawings and specs be an overhead cost? Bottom line, they shouldn't. Why should we give away money to help a client visualize our design solutions? Even if reproduction costs (including internal check-sets) were recovered on a direct cost basis (with no mark-up) firm profitability goes up by enormous margins. If the average A/E job produces only 6-7% profit on net revenues, shifting that 5-8% reproduction cost from overhead (cost) to reimbursable (revenue earning) can improve profits by 80%

or more. Now, if we carry this strategy to all projects, we have nearly doubled our profits for the coming year and found a way to better protect future staff bonuses…just by using common business sense. It's crazy to expect that a firm can achieve higher profits this year by doing the same things and practicing the same way as in years past. In the year ahead, stop and look back at least year's earnings and costs. Then, do things differently.

This book is about changing the way we conduct ourselves as business entrepreneurs and profit seekers.

PROFIT BY DESIGN

PHASE/SERVICE MATRIX

PHASE 1: PREDESIGN SERVICES
- ☐ Project Administration
- ☐ Disciplines Coordination/Document Checking
- ☐ Agency Consulting/Review/Approval
- ☐ Owner-supplied Data Coordination
- ☐ Programming
- ☐ Space Schematics/Flow Diagrams
- ☐ Existing Facilities Surveys
- ☐ Marketing Studies
- ☐ Economic Feasibility Studies
- ☐ Project Financing
- ☐ Project Development Scheduling
- ☐ Project Budgeting
- ☐ Presentations

PHASE 2: SITE ANALYSIS SERVICES
- ☐ Project Administration
- ☐ Disciplines Coordination/Document Checking
- ☐ Agency Consulting/Review/Approval
- ☐ Owner-supplied Data Coordination
- ☐ Site Analysis and Selection
- ☐ Site Development Planning
- ☐ Detailed Site Utilization Studies
- ☐ On-site Utility Schedule
- ☐ Off-site Utility Schedule
- ☐ Environmental Studies and Reports
- ☐ Zoning Processing Assistance
- ☐ Project Development Scheduling
- ☐ Project Budgeting
- ☐ Presentations

PHASE 3: SCHEMATIC DESIGN SERVICES
- ☐ Project Administration
- ☐ Disciplines Coordination/Document Checking
- ☐ Agency Consulting/Review/Approval
- ☐ Owner-supplied Data Coordination
- ☐ Architectural Design/Documentation
- ☐ Structural Design/Documentation
- ☐ Mechanical Design/Documentation
- ☐ Electrical Design/Documentation
- ☐ Civil Design/Documentation
- ☐ Landscape Design/Documentation
- ☐ Interior Design/Documentation
- ☐ Materials Research/Specifications
- ☐ Project Development Scheduling
- ☐ Statement of Probable Construction Cost
- ☐ Presentations

PHASE 4: DESIGN DEVELOPMENT SERVICES
- ☐ Project Administration
- ☐ Disciplines Coordination/Document Checking
- ☐ Agency Consulting/Review/Approval
- ☐ Owner-supplied Data Coordination
- ☐ Architectural Design/Documentation
- ☐ Structural Design/Documentation
- ☐ Mechanical Design/Documentation
- ☐ Electrical Design/Documentation
- ☐ Civil Design/Documentation
- ☐ Landscape Design/Documentation
- ☐ Interior Design/Documentation
- ☐ Materials Research/Specifications
- ☐ Project Development Scheduling
- ☐ Statement of Probable Construction Cost
- ☐ Presentations

PHASE 5: CONSTRUCTION DOCUMENTS SERVICES
- ☐ Project Administration
- ☐ Disciplines Coordination/Document Checking
- ☐ Agency Consulting/Review/Approval
- ☐ Owner-supplied Data Coordination
- ☐ Architectural Design/Documentation
- ☐ Structural Design/Documentation
- ☐ Mechanical Design/Documentation
- ☐ Electrical Design/Documentation
- ☐ Civil Design/Documentation
- ☐ Landscape Design/Documentation
- ☐ Interior Design/Documentation
- ☐ Materials Research/Specifications
- ☐ Special Bidding Documents/Scheduling
- ☐ Statement of Probable Construction Cost
- ☐ Presentations

PHASE 6: BIDDING OR NEGOTIATIONS SERVICES
- ☐ Project Administration
- ☐ Disciplines Coordination/Document Checking
- ☐ Agency Consulting/Review/Approval
- ☐ Owner-supplied Data Coordination
- ☐ Building Materials
- ☐ Addenda
- ☐ Bidding/Negotiations
- ☐ Analysis of Alternates/Substitutions
- ☐ Special Bidding Services
- ☐ Bid Evaluation
- ☐ Construction Contract Agreements

PHASE 7: CONSTRUCTION CONTRACT ADMINISTRATION SERVICES
- ☐ Project Administration
- ☐ Disciplines Coordination/Document Checking
- ☐ Agency Consulting/Review/Approval
- ☐ Owner-supplied Data Coordination
- ☐ Office Construction Administration
- ☐ Construction Field Observation
- ☐ Project Representation
- ☐ Inspection Coordination
- ☐ Supplemental Documents
- ☐ Quotation Requests/Change Orders
- ☐ Project Schedule Monitoring
- ☐ Construction Cost Accounting
- ☐ Project Closeout

PHASE 8: POST CONSTRUCTION SERVICES
- ☐ Project Administration
- ☐ Disciplines Coordination/Document Checking
- ☐ Agency Consulting/Review/Approval
- ☐ Owner-supplied Data Coordination
- ☐ Maintenance and Operational Programming
- ☐ Start-up Assistance
- ☐ Record Drawings
- ☐ Warranty Review
- ☐ Postconstruction Evaluation

PHASE 9a: SUPPLEMENTAL SERVICES
- ☐ Special Studies
- ☐ Renderings
- ☐ Model Construction
- ☐ Life Cycle Cost Analysis
- ☐ Value Analysis
- ☐ Quantity Surveys
- ☐ Detailed Construction Cost Estimate
- ☐ Energy Studies
- ☐ Environmental Monitoring
- ☐ Tenant-related Services
- ☐ Graphic Design
- ☐ Fine Arts and Crafts Services
- ☐ Special Furnishings Design
- ☐ Non-Building Equipment Selection
- ☐ Project Promotion/Public Relations

PHASE 9b: (CONT'D) SUPPLEMENTAL SERVICES
- ☐ Leasing Brochures
- ☐ Expert Witness
- ☐ Computer Applications
- ☐ Materials and Systems Testing
- ☐ Demolition Services
- ☐ Mock-up Services
- ☐ Still Photography
- ☐ Motion Pictures and Videotape
- ☐ Materials and Systems Testing
- ☐ Special Disciplines Consultation
- ☐ Special Building Type Consultation

The Profit Paradigm   Copyright 2023, Steven L. Beigel, AIA

PROFIT BY DESIGN
Attitude about Profit

The idea that profit is earned with each hour invested in a project is crucial. Profit is not a once per month figure at the bottom of a balance sheet, nor is it the amount of money residing in the bank account after all the bills are paid. Profit is why we are in business. It must be planned for, earned, protected, reported, and ultimately distributed to partners, shareholders, and employees. For certain, profits do not happen by accident. They are a necessary and visible part of every negotiation, and the best negotiators are able to achieve greater profits through their awareness of profit goals.

Architects and engineers need to focus on profit as one very important criterion in that set of elements that involves "business" apart from the programmatic considerations of "the project." The same level of care that they apply to understanding and interpreting client needs must be devoted to the financial and business aspects of the project, beginning with the negotiation, but extending on through contract execution, direction to the business office, project management and data control.

Attitude about profit should be part of the office or corporate culture. It is not enough for one senior person in the firm to become the "watch-dog" of profitability. Leadership is needed to teach and instill a sense of financial responsibility throughout the firm and the attitude concerning profit in the front office should pervade every project team, department, discipline and support function. Imagine the frustration if the CEO of the mid-size A/E firm was well versed in financial management, understood profitability and how to generate larger and larger profits each year, and no one else in the firm cared. Ignoring the financial vitality of an office is fatal – and many young, newly established firms fade quickly due to poor business decisions and a lack of discipline about money.

Developing and embracing a proper attitude about making money requires several, very simple steps:

PROFIT BY DESIGN

1. Recognition that profit must be generated on an hourly and daily basis – not just at the end of a job.
2. Realization that profits must be planned for, and care must be taken to carry out the plan.
3. Acceptance of the fact that banks and investors in an A/E business must be able to see consistent generation of profits from month to month, quarter to quarter, and year to year.
4. Treatment of profit in unselfish terms, that is – as a necessary part of running a business – not as a "reward" for work well done. Profits are derived from work done, regardless of quality or success of the design solution.
5. Profits should be viewed as a cost for preparing the work product. In many other businesses owners make pricing decisions and set values on merchandise based on the cost of goods and services, plus some minimum, fixed profit they intend to charge for those goods and services. In an A/E practice, the same logic should be applied. The profit figure can be considered a fixed percentage of every working hour – and a cost that the firm is charging the client/customer for purchasing services from the firm. Some firms consider this a premium, but successful, well run firms relentlessly set profit targets for each project, each office, each calendar month, and each quarter and fiscal year.
6. Communication of profit goals throughout the staff and periodic discussions about the rationale or make-up of profit targets should be freely shared. If the staff understands the logic behind profitability goals, and they repeatedly hear senior management attention being given to "status" of their projects as it relates to profit, they will tend to business with an understanding that their work must be profitable. They will be more responsible with project costs, hourly budgets, and keep an eye on the bottom line.
7. Adopting a financial reporting system that isolates profit and displays the profitability of the work on a weekly or monthly basis is key. Project managers will insist on having good project data, but they are usually concerned about hourly budgets, phases of the work, consultant costs, or disciplines engaging at the proper

PROFIT BY DESIGN

interval. Revealing profits in the form of profits earned to date is extremely useful to a project manager – and there is no good reason to conceal profit data from team leaders.

Attitude about profit should also be shared with project team members outside of the firm. Consultants should know, on a limited basis, the overall firm attitude about generating profit on the project. They should know at the outset if a decision has been made by the principal A/E firm to undertake the project at a reduced profit. Conversely, the prime A/E firm should make it clear to consultants that the anticipated profit performance of a particular job is predicated on accomplishing the work on a specific time table, with only one or two iterations of revisions, and with a billing cycle that might be peculiar or out of sync with the consultants' normal billing cycle. Specific details about the percentage of profit expected from the project should not be disclosed to consultants – but the attitude about how profits will be generated and what adjustments in work flow may be required to achieve the profit target is an essential discussion at two stages – before consultant contracts are signed, and – at the project kick-off meeting (with consultants in attendance).

Architects and engineers need to overcome the notion (stigma) that profit is a nasty word. Clients expect that an A/E firm will perform work and make a profit. Profit can be talked about openly (with clients and staff) and with the same emphasis as

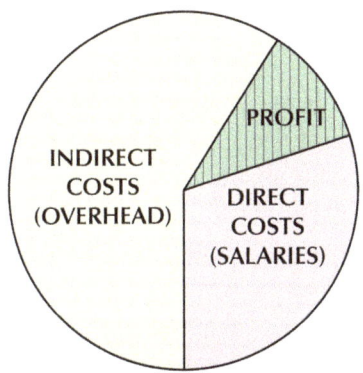

Approximate Relationship Of Costs (Typical)

direct costs, overhead, consultant fees, reimbursable expenses, and retainers. Profit should become as much an everyday term in an A/E office, and among the A/E team, as "design" or "square feet" or "project budget" or "code requirement."

Reporting profit data to the staff is an important aspect of instilling and maintaining an attitude about profit. When profit goals are set for an entire office, they should not be changed or revised as the year unfolds. Periodic reporting in a staff meeting or with a select group (such as department heads) will help insure that profit concerns are reinforced throughout the office. Providing good data (not "guess-work") about the relative performance of the office, firm or project (in comparison to profit goals) is beneficial toward achieving financial goals. Set the profitability goals, understand the goals, provide good actual performance data for comparison to the goals, then communicate, discuss, debate, and (if necessary) adjust the project management methodology to better meet profit goals.

An unhealthy attitude about profit stems from being secretive and/or mysterious about finances. Far worse than not having an attitude about making money (at all), is having a bad attitude rooted in suspicion that "the partners are skimming the profits" or "they're not telling us the whole story", or "we must be making money, we're still in business." Suspicion and divisiveness can kill a firm and cause clients to seek services elsewhere. If staff feels used and out of the loop – they will migrate to another firm where their role in the financial vitality of projects is more highly revered.

Attitudes about profit can and do vary across the A/E profession and each firm has a unique personality as it relates to profit. Some firms are evangelical about making money and the notion that profit is all important pervades every aspect of business. In such firms, profits are carefully planned and achieved, based upon firm revenue projections and manpower allocation, but added to the mix are efforts to achieve greater profits on such things as consultant services (the mark-up) and reproduction expenses (the handling or management fee). Sophisticated thinking goes into some profit planning schemes, where many project managers deliberately overestimate and overbook consultant fees, intending to pay them less than

PROFIT BY DESIGN

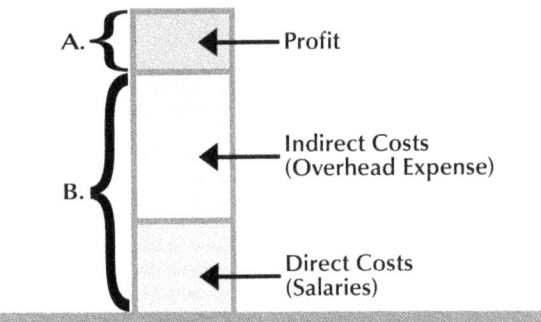

Basic Elements of Billable Time
A = Profit (The reason an A/E is in business)
B = The cost of earning profit

appears in the project budget, so that at the conclusion of the project a "fund" comprised of unrecognized and unspent consultant fees drops to the bottom line in the form of profit.

When senior management has crafted a comfortable attitude about profit, it must be thoughtfully and clearly communicated to all staff. It is particularly important that project principals, project managers and key members of each project team be aware of this attitude, much in the form of a mantra, such that the emphasis on profitability is consistently brought to all phases of the design process. As this is done, an awareness of project budgets and concern for the project making money on each phase will result. Project teams will become much more alert to deviations from the project work plan, scope creep, and manpower allocations as they relate to the bottom line profitability of their project. This heightened concern for a project staying on course on the part of the entire project team is beneficial in every regard. When the team demonstrates responsible project management and concern for the overall financial performance of their projects, in all phases of design, construction documents, bidding and construction administration, the entire office will enjoy the success of projects well planned, well executed, and profits being realized in a timely way. Very tangible benefits will be derived from closely scrutinizing project scope and identifying of "extras" for which additional fees may be charged.

Extreme attention to profit and profitability will include

PROFIT BY DESIGN

dissecting the many aspects and expense categories of a job such as direct labor, overhead, consultant costs, reimbursable expenses, reproduction costs, meeting time, research and development, and then devising a profit goal and profit scheme for each category of expense. This can be taken to an unproductive extreme where a point of diminishing returns is reached as overhead and direct labor budgets are impacted to the detriment of the schedule and quality of the work. Nevertheless, the time, attention and concern for generating profits from all aspects of the business is healthy and should be encouraged.

Attitude about profit can be good or bad or many things in

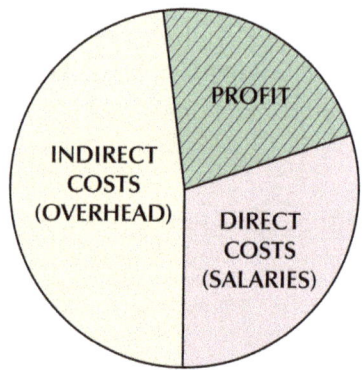

**Enhanced Profit
(by controlling direct & indirect costs)**

between. Profit must be considered a necessary good, not a necessary evil. Profit is the lifeblood of a successful A/E practice. An attitude about profit should be clear, concise, well recognized by partners and staff, discussed openly, and shared (at least in limited ways) with consultants, suppliers, vendors and shareholders.

PROFIT BY DESIGN
Earning Revenue

In professional services delivery firms there are several commonly used methods for "earning revenue." In delivery of architectural and engineering services, some firms consider revenue earned when the invoice for services rendered is issued to a client. Other firms consider the fees earned when the client pays the invoice and the money is deposited into the A/E's bank account. Still other firms consider fees earned when a particular phase of design is reached or a project milestone is achieved. Whichever method prevails in a particular firm's accounting culture, it is important to understand the distinction between "earning revenue" and "recognizing revenue."

To help make this distinction clear, it is necessary to introduce the concept of accrual accounting and reporting, which is the predominant method for preparing financial statements and reporting account details. There is a difference, in accounting terms, between actually having the "cash" on deposit resulting from services rendered and posting the earnings into the accounting system without the cash being in the possession and control of the firm. Data needed for financial reporting and accounting is separate from the act of receiving cash. Similarly, the fact of incurring an expense is separate from the act of paying cash to satisfy a debt represented by that expense. There is a difference between having cash and having wealth.

Simply stated, revenue is recognized when sales are consummated or services provided that create an obligation on the part of the client to make payment. Accrual accounting attempts to match expenses with the earning of revenues generated regardless of when the cash is actually received from a client or paid to a supplier/vendor. Understanding this concept merely requires that senior management in an A/E practice concern themselves with investing staff hours toward projects in order to earn revenue, without regard to how much money is in the bank account. The act of issuing invoices and collecting fees (debts) are separate problems. Accounting for labor hours, expense and earned revenue must be totally isolated from accounting of cash on hand or in bank accounts.

PROFIT BY DESIGN

In the performing and delivering of A/E services, there are many schools of thought and guidelines that attempt to define when an "obligation to pay" is created on the part of a client. Depending on the contract which outlines the basic scope of services, schedule of delivery, budget and other terms, different types of transactions (different contracts) may set different criteria for obligating a client to pay for services.

In the absence of specific contract language clearly setting forth a definition of earnings and obligations (different from an agreement to pay or payment schedule), it is desirable on the part of the A/E to earn the revenue at the earliest possible moment in the design process. The earlier revenue is earned, the sooner it will be billed and the faster clients will pay the invoice. However, in strict conformance with accrual accounting standards, the obligation for a client to pay for design time should occur immediately after the instrument of contract is signed and time is posted to the project account. The usual vehicle for tracking these labor expenses is the time card. Time cards (or time sheets) are the foundation of a firm's financial accounting system.

Several important things occur when a staff member posts time to a project on a weekly time sheet: 1) the firm has incurred an obligation to pay for that staff member's time, 2) the project account is showing budgeted time being consumed toward the execution/completion of the agreed upon scope of services, 3) it is likely that other incidental and reproduction expenses (out of pocket) are being posted to the project account, 4) records of unbilled, work-in-process are being created for the project in the accounting system, 5) that portion of the firm's overhead (including rent, utilities, payroll burden, taxes, insurance, business development, management, etc.) is being taxed to support the particular project underway. If the project were to suddenly terminate or be cancelled, the A/E firm would have incurred direct payroll, overhead and out of pocket expense to the benefit of the client. Therefore, the obligation to pay for the A/E services occurs well before an invoice is issued, at the instant that a record of the firm's work effort or expense is established. This is key to the successful application of accrual accounting in an A/E services delivery environment. Record keeping and a paper trail must be visible and well documented.

Certain projects are undertaken with a prescribed payment schedule in the compensation portion of the Owner/Architect contract. It is vital to recognize that, despite the agreed upon payment schedule, an obligation to pay is still created when the A/E begins work and applies time/effort to the project. In other words, if the project is cancelled in advance of reaching that first specified milestone (or interval) for billing and payment, the client still owes the A/E compensation for work performed prior to and up to the moment of cancellation. Other clauses within most Owner/Architect agreements address conditions of termination and require that all time and expense invested by the A/E (on the clients' behalf) be adequately compensated as a condition of termination. In fact, most agreements consider that payroll periods often span a two-week time interval and allow for 2 weeks notice prior to contract termination to allow open time sheets to be completed and posted along with any residual out-of-pocket expenses.

So, the revenue on a project is earned when the staff member fills out the time card and that time card is entered into the firm's payroll accounting system. But, sometimes this process is time-consuming by and of itself. It can take 3-10 working days for a busy central accounting office to post time from time cards received for the most recently closed payroll period. The larger the firm, the more lag time may exist between time card collection and posting.

Revenue is recognized when time and expense is actually recorded in the accounting system as having been allocated to a project. When professional time and related costs are reconciled to a particular job, the accounting system recognizes that certain revenues have been earned from that project's owner/client.

In government contracts, where very vigorous procedures have evolved for contract termination (with or without cause), the mere act of filling out the time card by the staff member is considered a record of the expense incurred. In other words, at the end of an 8-hour work day, whenever the staff member fills in the weekly time sheet for a particular day, the obligation for the client to pay for that time is created, whether or not the time is yet entered into the accounting system. This is an important concept which underscores the importance of daily time recordation. Many firms insist that time be recorded at more than one interval in a normal work day.

There are hundreds of examples to point to where federal government projects are cancelled, due to budgetary and/or political constraints, and the A/E is notified to stop work. In the most serious of such cases, the government actually sends representatives to the A/E office to enforce the "stop work order" and collect copies of time sheets right off the desks of employees who are working on the particular job.

This right to stop work and collect time sheets is stipulated in all federal service contracts. In the event that this occurs, only those staff hours recorded up to the moment time sheets are collected comprise the government's obligation to pay. Therefore, large A/E firms that service federal agencies and depend upon some portion of their business coming from federal contracts are disciplined in the practice of having employees complete time records on a daily basis. Thus, the obligation to pay is recorded daily on the time sheets – even though not yet entered into the firm's payroll accounting system. Recent improvements in automated time management and integrated time keeper programs make it possible (but not yet widely practiced) for daily time records to be posted directly from a staff member's terminal to the primary payroll/accounting system.

Understanding the relationship between earning revenue and profitability is critical to maximizing revenue and, therefore, profits. The earlier that revenue is earned in the course of performing work for a client, the sooner that all income producing aspects of the firm's revenue stream benefit. Stated another way, the earlier revenue is earned on a project, the sooner the firm's direct salary expense, overhead expense, and profit can be recognized. Remember, revenue is earned when time is posted . . . and revenue includes the full multiplier established for that job at the outset of the contract, as represented in the work plan and booking instructions sent forward to accounting by the project manager.

Bankers and external auditors (both sets of professionals intimately familiar with accrual accounting) are most interested in accounts receivable and cash flow as indicators of the viability and vitality of an A/E business. Records of accounts receivable include both billed earnings (the aggregate amount of money for which invoices have been issued) and unbilled earnings (everything else that is reflected in the time sheets, accounting records, work-in-progress and project status reports) representing revenues earned, but not yet billed. Bankers and creditors are interested in the "big picture" which includes how much money the firm is earning and, secondarily, how long it takes to actually collect the money.

Audits generally show that an A/E firm earns revenue at a reasonably constant rate (provided the staffing level is steady, backlog exists to sustain the staff, and the accounting system is functioning properly). Receiving payment for services rendered is somewhat more variable as clients process invoices for payment at peculiar times or at intervals not within the A/E's control. Collecting fees (based upon an invoice issued by the A/E) can take weeks or months depending upon the client, the project, the availability of funds, qualitative concerns about the work, the general state of the economy, and a host of other variables well beyond the A/E's sphere of influence. Patterns develop over time and such payment patterns are identified by accountants and auditors as part of the process of determining the creditworthiness of a firm. If history demonstrates that the A/E office normally collects 80% of its accounts receivable within 90 days of issuing bills, then it is a good bet that this trend will continue into the future. Banks and creditors will scrutinize the earned revenue figures contained on the books (billed and unbilled) and determine a baseline comfort level with the firm in order to justify a "line-of-credit" (LOC) to assist the firm in meeting its payroll and expense obligations while waiting for funds to be received from clients.

Therefore, the earlier earned revenue is recorded through time sheets being entered into the system, the more viable the business will appear. Consistent posting of billable hours, at multipliers that meet or exceed the expected earning rates of projects, the higher earnings, profits and the credit rating will be for the particular A/E firm.

Conversely, allowing unbilled time to accumulate in the form of work-in-progress (WIP) is detrimental to a firm's financial standing. Large monthly WIP can indicate poor management and/or a disorganized central accounting function. When earned revenue is recorded from time cards, it should be entered into the accounting system (recognized) and billed as quickly as possible. Many firms produce client invoices every two weeks, consistent with payroll and expense accounting.

In an accrual accounting environment, consistency is a key word. Accrual accounting does not respond to anomalies, such as large checks arriving at the same time, being deposited into the firm's checking account. Again, when and how the money is received is not relevant to accrual based accounting. Earning the revenue is paramount. Recognizing the revenue on the books, as it is earned in some prescribed formulaic way, is the essence of the accrual method.

The problem with cash accounting is that revenue may be earned and cash payments made for all expenses needed to generate that revenue well before the revenue is received in cash. In a professional service business, not recognizing revenue when it is earned distorts the true operating performance of the company. In a cash based system, expense could easily be distorted by the timing of cash payments for products purchased and/or services received. Many A/E firms fall prey to thinking they have more money than they actually have, by simply delaying the payment of bills. Firms often allow their temporary bank balance to influence decision-making. Cash accounting is not indicative of the true financial position of the enterprise.

Accrual accounting focuses on the economic substance of the event instead of just the movement of cash in and out of a bank account. It recognizes that revenue is earned long before the cash is received and that revenue is meaningful (as the life blood of the firm) when it is earned, not when cash is received. Accrual accounting also recognizes that expenses are incurred and recorded on the books as obligations at the time supplies and materials are shipped to or consumed by the A/E firm. The obligation to pay for something becomes recorded and real as soon as the benefit of services is received by the A/E, whether or not cash payment is made at the time.

When earning revenue and providing professional A/E services within the context of an accrual accounting system, purchases generally become expenses at the exact moment the materials are used or consumed in the process of generating revenue. This matching of expenses with the revenue they generate (including direct, indirect, overhead and profit) is the fundamental principle of accrual accounting.

Within the framework of accrual accounting, periodic recognition of earned revenue and expenses must be allocated to the same time periods. That is, expenses allocated to generate revenue in a particular period, must be accounted for in that same period. This concept is referred to as the matching of revenues and expenses and relates directly to the use of staff time, property, plant and equipment (including debt service, if any, on fixed assets) necessary to earn the revenue.

The most successful and well managed A/E firms strive to earn and recognize revenue as early as possible and bill those earnings quickly. Financial vitality of an A/E practice is measured by earnings and accounts receivable, not by cash in the bank. As the economy cycles in and out of recession, demand for cash changes. During bad economic times, having cash is of greater value. Accounts receivable are still the most significant measure of the firm's worth. Provided that a firm's receivables are good and can be collected within a reasonably predictable time, the firm will remain a viable enterprise.

PROFIT BY DESIGN
Macro-Management

In any A/E office, the three largest categories of expense are: 1) salaries (direct costs) for personnel; 2) rent (including utilities and maintenance), and; 3) reproduction services (including supplies and equipment). Farther down the list are items such as rental of computer equipment and software, furniture, drafting boards, and the myriad of miscellaneous graphic arts and model making tools. It should be obvious then that these three largest consumers of corporate resources are the areas where most attention must be directed to assure efficiency and balance.

The value of staff is often difficult to determine. It depends on the type of firm, the firm's view of education versus practical experience, the nature of the practice (A/E versus pure A) and the specialty (if any) developed by the firm or office. For example, a large A/E office may value highly an employee who is trained in both architecture and engineering over someone trained in a single discipline. The small interior design firm may regard the practical experience of an employee who once worked for a commercial real estate company more highly than a licensed design professional. An engineering firm may place more value on an unlicensed mechanical engineer with 30 years experience in trouble shooting boilers and chillers over the licensed engineer with only 2 or 3 projects to his/her credit. Whatever the case, the rate of compensation and the value of these staff to the respective firm must be viewed in the context of the amount of profit they can generate for the firm or office. In staffing decisions a question to ask is "Can we make money with this person?" by effectively selling the staff member's time.

Initially, this assessment is done at a macro level by using average hourly rates for all staff (combined) and then applying the appropriate multiplier (including overhead and profit) to establish a projected average hourly billing rate. On a macro scale, this is the overall important first step in determining how the firm must perform and the likelihood of attaining speculative profit goals. Care must be taken to discount the anticipated number of hours a staff member might not be billable in any given year. This utilization factor should be applied to all technical project staff for the initial macro level assessment.

For example, if an office of 62 people has 40 technical staff who normally work on projects and the remaining 22 are considered "overhead, marketing, senior management, and/or support staff," then the compensation and billing for this office is going to depend on the 40, not the 22. If the average hourly rate of compensation (hourly wage) for the 40 billable staff is $50 per hour and the overhead rate for the firm is 150% (excluding profit), and the office has a profitability target of 15%, then the initial estimate of an average billable hourly rate is:

$50.00 (average direct hourly payroll)
x 2.50 (combined direct and overhead costs)
$125.00 (basic hourly rate, absent profit)
x 1.15 (factor for profit @ 15%)
$143.25 average billable hourly rate.

The initial target rate for all billing is thus $143.25 per labor hour devoted to the project. However, closer analysis is necessary to be certain the overhead rate is correct and that staff utilization has been factored into the equation.

For example, if the 40 staff are being compensated on the basis of a standard 40 hour work week, then 2080 hours is a standard working year for a lone employee. It is incorrect to assume that each of the 40 staff will work on projects for 2080 hours – a solid year. Reductions in the billable hours should be obvious, beginning with holidays, vacations, sick leave, personal leave, and basic U.S. Labor Department requirements. In most companies that comply with all U.S. labor laws, the impact of "time-off" for various items will average around 17%. That is to say that a single staff member only has 83% of those potential 2080 annual hours that may be applied to projects as "billable" time. So, only 1726 billable hours (on average) can be expected from a full time technical staff member in this scenario.

PROFIT BY DESIGN

Then, it is necessary to scrutinize the reality of a working day within the office. This reality check, still in the macro sense, reveals that on any given working day, the average technical staff member is spending approximately 2 hours per day on coffee breaks, internal non-project related communication, general research (not project specific), phone calls to family and friends, responding to management related e-mail, and filling out time records (automated or by hand). This is astonishing, but very close to the truth in most large A/E offices. Only 75% of the normal 8 hour working day (6 hours) is actually spent "working" on a project. This too must be factored into the office utilization formula. If another 25% of the 1726 hours is unproductive time (non-billable), the average billable time (annualized hours) for a technical (billable) staff member drops to 1294 out of a standard 2080 hour year. This remarkable fact can ruin an A/E office within the first year, if consideration is not given to adjusting the necessary average billing rate upward to compensate for unproductive time.

Back to our original example where we assumed all 2080 hours per technical staff member were being billed. Still at a macro level, with only 1294 likely hours (on average) being billable by each of our 40 technical staff members, the following considerations are essential:

- That margin of unproductive time (2080 – 1294 = 786 hours) is still being paid for by the office in the form of direct salary. Therefore, this cost is the same type of personnel expense as those 22 other overhead personnel who don't generate revenue at all. If the office is already paying for 2080 x 22 = 45,160 overhead staff hours (as part of our original 150% overhead estimate), the reality of this scenario is that the firm is really paying for 31,440 more unproductive hours (786 x 40 staff) than the 22 people combined. This total of 76,600 person-hours (non-billable time) carriers a very high direct cost to the firm, but an even higher cost to the firm when we consider that no revenue is being generated to compensate the office for this extra time.

- The impact of this realization can be dramatic on any office, regardless of size. If our original overhead rate of 150% is wrong, (by a considerable margin), the result can be no profit t all and the inability to cover the office overhead expense through application of the original average hourly billing rate. If our original projection of non-billable direct staff cost was off by a factor of 66%, this will have a major impact on the overhead rate and our required average billable hourly rates. In short, the overhead rate must be accurate. Utilization of technical staff must be scrutinized. Even the slightest miscalculation can result in dramatic cost savings or enormous cost overruns. With relatively small planned profit margins (15% plus or minus) anticipated in an A/E practice, a slight mistake can mean the difference between some profit and no profit at all.

If, as in the example, the "indirect labor" (that non-billable, overhead staff cost) made up 50% of the total overhead rate, this portion of the original formula was wrong by a factor of 66%. Therefore, instead of a 150% assumed overhead rate, the correct figure is more accurately represented by 200% overhead (75 x .66 + 150). At our average direct payroll cost of $50 per hour, we must charge $150 per hour to cover our direct plus indirect costs (our break-even rate) and $172.50 per hour to generate the expected 15% average hourly profit ($150 x 1.15).

$50.00 (average direct hourly payroll)
x 3.00 (combined direct and overhead costs)
$150.00 (basic hourly rate, absent profit)
x 1.15 (factor for profit @ 15%)
$172.50 average billable hourly rate.

The difference between these two calculations ($143.25 versus $172.50) could be the difference between life and death to an A/E office.

At 15% planned profit ($22.50 per hour for each hour billed at the calculated average rate of $172.50), the firm can reasonably expect to earn (51,764 billable hours x 22.50 = $1,165,000) well over $1 million gross (pre-tax) profit in a normal year. If the correct rate is not determined and the original incorrect overhead rate (stemming from higher than realistic estimated utilization) is applied, then the firm will not earn any profit at all – and will lose approximately $350,000 over the course of the year. For small and mid-size firms, losses of this magnitude are fatal.

The $22.50 per hour profit figure in our example is gross, pre-tax profit. In order to realize this profit, total revenues for the firm in this example must be $8,929,290.00.

The unfortunate set of decisions which precipitate from a macro-level analysis of this type are important and urgent. If the $172.50 average hourly billing rate (for all billable technical staff) is too high when compared with other firm's billable rates in the area, then the firms' overhead rate is too high and/or direct salaries may also be too high. If the firm cannot compete effectively in the marketplace (be cost competitive), cover its expenses, and generate the desired profit, the business plan is flawed – and something must change.

Cutting overhead is the usual response in a scenario where, after some analysis, senior management recognize that the firm is floundering, or worse, on the verge of bankruptcy. If the signals are recognized early enough, and the elements of direct costs, indirect costs and overhead are well understood – cutting overhead staff does not need to be the only solution.

Reflecting back on the example given, a mere shift of indirect (overhead) hours back into the billable category has a resultant positive effect on overhead (overhead is reduced) while billable hours go up. If the work (contracts and backlog) exists to support the additional effort – (if the available work can absorb the additional staff hours) – and the work can be executed efficiently, the average hourly billable rate can be adjusted downward, to a more competitive plateau, while at the same time maintaining the earned revenue and profitability targets. Simply put, if you are covering all your costs and generating requisite profit margins, even though it requires a greater number of billable hours to create that profit, the office profitability goal can be achieved.

This macro-level look at what comprises an average billable hourly rate is only useful for establishing annual budgets and large scale project budgeting at best. To get serious about

PROFIT BY DESIGN

understanding office overhead and causing efficient use of both direct and indirect staff time (the largest expenses A/E firms have), more effort is needed to investigate and reduce overhead – and inspire billable staff to increase utilization (work more billable hours) thus improving the billings, increasing accounts receivable and reducing indirect costs. If staff members are able and willing to work more hours, beyond the normal 2080 per year, then higher profits can be realized. This is particularly true when additional staff compensation is held to a minimum.

When utilization is low and profitability targets seem beyond reach, the release of full time employees is always an option. This is a difficult decision for any manager. When circumstances dictate a reduction in force, then it must be carried out dispassionately and promptly, in the interest of the financial well being of the firm. However, there are other options, many of them infinitely more desirable and humane than releasing capable staff members. The stability of an office, again in a macro-sense, can be viewed as a signal (internally and externally) that the office is well managed and meeting its revenue and profitability objectives. Proper fiscal planning and the application of Macro-management devices such as this help avoid traumatic shifts in office staffing and project assignments.

When applying a Macro-management strategy, remember to carefully assess the office or firm overhead rate and fully understand the elements of office overhead. Use Macro-management to help establish a business plan and set realistic profitability goals. Be reasonable in the expectation of staff efforts and the numbers of staff hours that can be devoted to billable projects. This macro level assessment of an office's or firm's earnings capability may be used on specific projects to determine the likelihood of financial gains attributable to hose projects. The macro level assessment can become more detailed and more accurate using actual staff labor rates (in all staffing categories) rather than direct payroll averages.

PROFIT BY DESIGN
The Relevance of Financial Statements

To many A/E firm managers, financial statements may be little more than a set of evil, computer-generated reporting documents. After all, designing cities, buildings, roads, bridges and other structures (and getting paid reasonable fees for such services) is far more interesting, stimulating and rewarding than pouring over computer print-outs loaded with figures, percentages and expense categories. However, financial statements are the true indicator of the economic well-being of the firm.

What is a financial statement? The term financial statement means, in its simplest form, the balance sheet, income statement, statement of cash flows, and possibly statement of changes in owners' equity (and/or shareholders' equity) which together constitute a fair presentation of the company's financial condition at the end of an accounting period. This definition may be broadly construed to apply to all financial statements associated with any business. The important things are: a) to have them, and b) understand how they should be used.

Many financial institutions, investors and lenders will place higher value on management than financial statements. Yet, financial statements are the most empirical measure of management's success, strengths and/or weaknesses. While it has been said that "It's Management that Counts!" . . . objective data about the firm's management history and performance of senior managers is reflected in the balance sheet.

Different management teams may pursue different aspects of the firm's business plan with greater zeal, and different results can be expected in the financial statement that represents each type of effort. Therefore, financial statements are similar to report cards that evidence the relative success of a particular business tactic, or management approach. Financial statements may also be used to compare the relative success of one firm with another, to determine financial strength, business viability and credit worthiness. In an A/E enterprise, with very few fixed assets and no inventory, the accounting of time becomes the relevant indicator.

Financial statements contain both strictly historical data and estimates about the future and are used to assess both current and future business conditions. They are limited by their inability to accurately forecast future events and they are open to interpretation on any point that requires speculation about current or future trends. The more variables which may impact the business in the future, the less reliable the financial statement as a forecasting tool. In the context of an architectural and engineering business, the goal is to minimize the number of variables and develop both reporting and forecasting models based on accurate historical data. To the extent that historical data has been used from prior years to reasonably predict future performance, it may continue to be used with a degree of reliability. At best, a set of financial statements contains accurate, historical data about cash, accounts receivable, liabilities, assets, revenue recognition, total revenues, backlog and profit. These are all elements of the firm's performance viewed by looking back on an isolated (well defined) period of time. The utility of these facts and their relationship to future events must be approached carefully as certain interpretations will be more indicative and reliable than others.

In the A/E design business, most assets are the people who are employed by the firm. These "walking assets" are often difficult to quantify other than on a strictly empirical basis by using billable hours as the expression of their value to the organization. Equipment, furniture, drafting supplies, etc. all have useful lives from which future value can be estimated. Intellectual capabilities and talent in a service oriented business are intangibles that make prediction of future events and worth extremely difficult. Inventory can be measured. Talent can be only estimated by some specific knowledge of past performance extrapolated forward to a set of future assumptions about project types and personnel availability. Even then, the judgment of senior management regarding the likely performance of staff and the relative ease of executing the work play a major part in the assessment. Staff can walk out the door at any point, placing the viability of the firm's business plan, its financial outlook, and client relationships in jeopardy.

One serious flaw with financial statements, is that non-monetary assets (such as personnel) are carried on the books at their historical costs, adjusted for depreciation and other diminution of value to reflect economic loss. Realistic losses in economic value occur incrementally and at varying rates (depending upon the asset in question) substantially prior to their actual recognition by accountants during the preparation of financial statements. In theory, personnel assets should increase in value based upon growth in experience levels and rates of compensation. Predicting what new experiences will be gained by staff, and assigning value to such anticipated learning opportunities is difficult and requires both conjecture and sophisticated planning. Because personnel costs are usually carried on the books at current rates (which result from experiences gained in prior years and compensation levels set in the last raise cycle) predicting the replacement cost of walking assets is nearly impossible.

Statements of asset value at historical costs may be an understatement of the real asset value at replacement cost or current market value. When people are the largest portion of the asset base (as in the case of an A/E enterprise), this becomes complicated. A statement of "current value" would, therefore, need to be adjusted to offset things such as depreciation and hidden costs (professional search fees and/or incentive packages) if more accurate information of a firm's current worth is needed. The present economic value of all assets (including walking assets) should be of far greater interest to users of financial statements than historical data (cost-based figures) because it more precisely reflects what the firm is worth. The distinction here is setting an appropriate value on present worth which may (and probably does) differ from that which is indicated by purely historical data.

In an A/E business venture, sales and the performance of work are presumed to be final and recorded on the books under the presumption that there will be no unusual returns or re-work, based upon defective plans or misinterpretation of a client's program. This presumption that fees charged for time spent on a particular project is generally good, but some provision may be needed for deficient work, re-work, corrective work and bad debts (the client's failure or refusal to pay for the work). The magnitude of such a provision may be variable, clearly the product of management's estimate of the risk of such an event, and is provided for on the financial statement through creation of reserves, contingencies, discounts or write downs, (described in other portions of this text). In an A/E business, showing entries in the financial statement for anticipated losses as a debit against earned revenues (specifically as an offset of profit) should be routine and expected. Discount factors and/or write downs in an A/E business can be a substantial part of the profit earned in a particular cycle.

For comparison purposes, banks and other financial institutions are required to establish future losses on loans currently outstanding. This is commonly referred to as "loan loss ratio." Even though banks have no way of actually knowing which loans will go bad (or produce losses) they will set a certain percentage of expected revenue as their "loans loss reserve" in anticipation of some future economic event where the economic environment may become considerably worse than that which has immediately preceded it. In the architectural and engineering services business, setting aside a certain fund as a reserve (to be held for a specified period of time for the concern for potential rework or corrections has been eliminated) is a wise practice. Such an entry should be reflected on the financial statement (monthly, quarterly and annually) as a reduction in current asset value of the firm.

Many A/E firms meet with misfortune early in corporate life. Small firms are born every day and struggle through the early years without much in the way of assets, capital and credit. If a young company meets with a sudden catastrophe, a lender or shareholder expects to recover a loan or investment through reported current asset values. Unfortunately, many times, these reported asset values are not worth anything near the value assigned in the financial statements. Herein lies the dilemma. Fairly and accurately stating the value of the assets within the firm requires balance and consideration for the broad uses and potential applications of the data contained in the financial statement. If a rapid sale of assets (liquidation) becomes necessary, value realized will likely be far below the stated value of assets on the books. This is typically the case in bankruptcies, mergers and acquisitions. If the A/E company's inventory (including walking assets) were really worth what was claimed, it would be liquidating or selling at its cost plus some profit as reflected on the latest financial statement.

Design firms cannot ignore the fact that their asset base is substantially made up of labor. As such, most design firm assets could simply walk out of the door, leaving the time value of the company severely diminished. The real value of other fixed assets, including furniture, equipment and cash on hand usually will be discounted during a "fire sale" scenario. If a design firm is a healthy going concern, it isn't worried about disposal of assets and reduced asset value when confronted with termination of operations or selling of assets. With such minor fixed and real assets in an A/E business, most of these asset values can, and will be, thrown out the window in the event of a liquidation.

In times of crisis (like a liquidation or bankruptcy of the firm), financial statements should be the most valuable. Investors and bankers will look to the most recent financial statement and assets summary (part of the financial statement) for security, believing that fixed assets are at least usable by or sell-able to some other healthy going concern. This is only the case when the fixed assets in question are new and still have value in the larger competitive marketplace. Outdated technology, older computers, obsolete software, customized equipment and/or used drafting and business furniture have little or no value. Often, A/E firms get into trouble precisely because the assets they have invested in no longer meet the needs of their markets. Even aged accounts receivable (usually a good asset in a professional services company) may become vastly more difficult to collect when the client or customer becomes aware that the firm is in trouble and doesn't expect to get any more service or attention from the A/E.

These limitations of financial statements are often offset by the fact that firms and their accountants continually review and evaluate financial data and assumptions on which asset value is based. Revisions, when necessary, should be made without hesitation if errors in judgment are discovered regarding estimates, assumptions, and unforeseen events. Adjustments to financial statements are expected and become necessary from time to time. Adjustments should be modest, when they occur. Extreme fluctuations in any category on a financial statement are a cause for concern, demanding deeper investigation, and further scrutiny. Similarly, frequent corrections or adjustments (even in modest proportions) will diminish confidence in the financial statements.

In today's corporate environment, reliability of financial data is being challenged as never before. Creative accounting techniques and skillful manipulation of earnings to satisfy corporate aspirations can lead to distrust and lack of confidence in a firm's financial disclosures. Senior management within an A/E firm should learn the importance of accurate financial reporting. Understanding the basic elements of a financial statement and testing the accuracy of the data can help inspire confidence. Lessons learned from Enron, WorldCom, Tyco, Global Crossing, and others teach us that financial disclosures can be artfully manipulated and extremely dangerous.

On the positive side, banks, investors and shareholders will study financial statements and make decisions about future investment and credit-worthiness based upon the data presented, complete with relevant assumptions and speculation about the future. In an A/E context, banks will place the highest value on accounts receivable and make credit decisions based upon the likelihood that some portion of billed fees due to the firm will be collected within a reasonably short amount of time. The fixed assets owned by the firm will have very little or no value to the lender, even though the lender will insist on assignment of these assets as partial security for a line of credit.

Accounts receivable (AR) represent a collectible debt to the firm, (usually in the form of cash) which can be converted to cash in the bank with minimal effort and on a reasonably predictable schedule. If, for example, the track record of the firm or office demonstrates that 80% of all accounts receivable are usually collected within 90 days of billing (a fairly normal cycle), then the bank will consider loaning some portion (occasionally a large portion) of the fees represented by 80% of all accounts receivable, to help the firm have access to cash. Thus, the A/E firm can meet payroll and other expense obligations while collections are taking place. Establishing a track record, based on financial statements, ARs and collections can influence a firm's creditworthiness.

Financial statements are highly useful instruments of analysis and decision making for profitability. Despite their many intrinsic limitations, financial statements are vital to the health of an ongoing enterprise and the single most valuable document to lenders, investors and shareholders.

Financial reporting is not an exciting aspect of an A/E business. Preparation of financial statements may be challenged, scrutinized and/or adjusted based upon new information. In an A/E business, financial statements should emphasize accounts receivable over personnel and fixed assets. Receivables are predictable. Personnel assets are less tangible and difficult to value. The financial statement should be simple, concise and updated frequently.

Financial statements offer the user the clearest practical picture of what a firm has accomplished and where it stands (financially and as an on going business concern) as of the reporting date. Such information, though limited, is far better than following hunches and over-zealous press releases from the marketing staff as a guide to informed business decisions. Financial statements should present factual information, absent exhilarating comments and opinions about the future. However, it is common practice to qualify a financial statement with the "preparers' view" of the data and the relative weight assigned to each major category of information. If unusual circumstances exist, or the preparer is aware of an event that may impact the financial condition of the firm in the near term, these impending circumstances should be disclosed and discussed.

When preparing a financial statement, facts are required. Variables and assumptions about work load, staffing and expenses must be held to a minimum. Financial statements may be used to indicate the relative strength of an investment on one hand, and/or the need for stronger management or a cash infusion on the other. Whatever the intended purpose of a financial statement, it must be accurate and reliable.

PROFIT BY DESIGN
The Overhead Rate

Overhead consists of those cost items which are not directly assignable to a particular project because they are either common to all or it is too difficult or expensive to allocate them indirectly. For consulting engineers, architects, and other design professionals or consultants, cost accounting involves tracking both direct costs and indirect costs. Direct costs are represented by 1) direct labor costs which constitute the remuneration paid to employees working on projects for clients and 2) other direct costs (ODC's) which are services, materials and expenses specifically required for a client's project. Indirect costs likewise are comprised of two principal categories: 1) indirect payroll-connected costs such as vacation pay and social security taxes and 2) general and administrative (G&A) costs, which are the myriad of cost accounts needed to maintain a business, including direct payroll costs for professional and support staff when they are not charging time directly to projects.

The various accounts which constitute indirect costs are accumulated to determine the firm's total overhead, which in turn is expressed as the overhead rate, the ratio of indirect costs to direct labor costs. The numerical value of a firm's overhead rate, generally varying between 0.9 and 2.0, is viewed as an outward projection of the firm's management capability and its relative costs to perform projects. The overhead rate is sometimes used by clients as one factor in deciding whether to engage a firm.

The overhead rate also is used to estimate overhead expenses for project proposals through its inclusion in the firm's multiplier, which is an extension of the overhead rate to include profit. The overhead rate and multiplier are explicitly included in two standard types of contracts utilizing the form of 1) Salary Cost Times a Multiplier plus Direct Non-Salary Expense and 2) Cost Plus a Fixed Fee. They are implicitly included in calculations to determine the fee for Lump Sum contracts. The overhead rate and multiplier are used to allocate overhead expenses to current projects for billing purposes, and they can provide a convenient management control tool to evaluate the performance relationship between direct labor and indirect costs.

Despite the outwardly immutable nature of a firm's overhead rate, considerable variation is possible in terms of 1) the theoretical classification of direct and indirect accounts; 2) efforts to identify and charge indirect costs to direct accounts; 3) actual overhead cuts; and 4) the denominator of the ratio, the volume of direct labor that the firm's marketing efforts can produce.

How is the Overhead Rate Computed?

The overhead rate is universally accepted as the ratio of total indirect costs to direct labor costs for the accounting period, usually the fiscal year. It is calculated in the following manner by example:

GIVEN:

Direct labor costs = $1,000,000
Indirect Payroll-related costs = $250,000
G & A costs = $1,250,000 Total Indirect Cost = $1,500,000

THEN:

Indirect Payroll-Related
Overhead Rate = 250,000/1,000,000   =   0.25

G & A Overhead Rate = 1,250,000/1,000,000 =   1.25

Total Overhead Rate = 1,500,000/1,000,000 =   1.50

The indirect payroll overhead rate and the G&A rate are presented separately for federal government work, but the total rate is used elsewhere more frequently.

A tabulation of typical indirect cost accounts is presented in Table 1. The accounts are divided into indirect payroll-connected costs and the more numerous General and Administration (G&A) costs, with the largest single item generally being payroll for indirect time. Historical data collected since 1979 shows that indirect labor accounted for a mean of 40.7% out of the overhead rate of 148.2%, as shown in Table 2. The large overhead cost for indirect time, besides the obvious cost of purely support personnel, is due to professional and technical staff not charging billable time. This results from their need to accomplish certain overhead functions such as management and proposal preparation as well as a lack of work between projects. Most A/E firms budget to carry these employees over slack times in order to maintain available staff and their skills. It is a cost, but a largely controllable cost, of doing business.

Although the calculation of the overhead rate is straightforward, the inclusion of the various indirect cost accounts and the degree to which firms record and charge G&A costs to their respective projects as direct costs allow for considerable variability in the numerical value of the rate. Currently, there is no universally accepted accounting methodology for determining allowable overhead costs with the federal government, municipal clients, and A/E firms themselves adopting different procedures leading to increased accounting and audit burdens.

The most constructive recommendation that has been made is that the Internal Revenue Services criteria for reasonable corporate income tax deductions (see IRS Code, Sec. 161-192, Sec. 241; 1.241-1) be adopted as the simplest and most equitable solution for determining allowable overhead costs. The National Society of Professional Engineers (NSPE) has published a Financial Management Handbook for Engineering Firms and has developed a Computerized Financial Management System for use by professional services consulting firms in their financial administration and in determining their overhead rate.

Since the early 1980s, many advances have occurred in CFMS accounting for design professionals. As computer software has become more sophisticated and versatile, so too have the number of variables increased that require financial analysis.

The Overhead Rate and the Firm's Multiplier

A/E firms compute their multiplier to determine the ratio of net revenue to direct labor costs, indicating the dollars of revenue generated by each dollar of direct labor. The multiplier is computed in this manner:

<u>Total Revenues – Reimbursable Expenses – Nonsalary Direct Expenses</u>
Direct Labor costs

The multiplier is used mostly to estimate the fee for future work and to establish employee's billable salary rates as shown below:

1) **Direct labor costs x multiplier = Fee**
2) **$20/hr x 3.0 = $60/hr = Employee X's billable salary rate**

The overhead rate and expected pretax profit can be used to calculate the multiplier and are generally more useful for estimating fees:

GIVEN:
Direct labor rate = 1.0 Overhead rate = 1.5
Pretax profit = 20% or 0.20

THUS:
(1.0 + 1.5) = 2.5 (Basic multiplier without profit)

Since profit is computed on direct labor and overhead,

2.5 x 0.20 = 0.5
Multiplier = 2.5 + 0.5 = 3.0

or in a more concise form: **(1.0 + 1.5) x 1.2 = 3.0**

Therefore, the total direct labor cost need only be multiplied by multiplier to determine the fee, and this method of estimating profit provides a convenient means of developing cost estimates based on the current multiplier and expected profit. It is important to note that profit is not an arbitrary figure applied as a percentage, but a target derived from careful consideration of office or firm financial goals.

PROFIT BY DESIGN

TABLE 1
Indirect Cost Accounts
Indirect Payroll-Connected Costs
Vacation Pay
Holiday Pay
Sick Leave
Administrative Leave
Bonuses
Federal Social Security (FICA) Taxes
Federal and State Unemployment Taxes/Insurance
Worker's Compensation Taxes/Insurance
Group Insurance (Health & Life)
Retirement/Pension/Profit Sharing Plans
Entertainment Expenses

General and Administrative Costs	
Payroll for time expended on:	Non-Project Telephone and Telegraph
Administration/Supervision (including secretarial, clerical and accounting)	Membership Dues and Meeting Expenses
Attendance at Workshops and Technical Conferences	Non-Project Auto, Truck and Airplane Operating Expenses
Business Development/ Public Relations	Business Development/ Public Relations
Civic or Professional Activities	Travel & Subsistence
Research and Development	Entertainment
Precontract Activities	Professional Directories/ Advertising
Unassigned/Standby Time (Readiness to serve)	Pre-Contract Activities
Business Taxes (Other than income and payroll taxes)	Travel & Subsistence

PROFIT BY DESIGN

Brochures & Proposals	
Legal and Accounting Services	Administrative Travel and Subsistence
Office Space (Rent, Utilities and Maintenance)	Business Insurance
Professional Liability	
Supplies and Services	Public Liability
Secretarial and Clerical Supplies	General Insurance
Drafting Room Supplies	Other Insurance
Postage and Shipping	(Except payroll-connected)
Non-Project Reproduction, Photography and Printing Computer software licenses	Civic Contributions
Miscellaneous Office Supplies and Services	Research and Development
Office Furniture, Fixtures and Equipment (Rent, Repair and Maintenance)	Professional Registrations and Licenses
Engineering Equipment and Instruments (Rent, Repair and Maintenance)	Library and Reference
	Materials
	Depreciation
	Interest and Bank Charges

TABLE 2	
Key Overhead Items From Historical A/E Firm Data	
(Expressed as Percent of Direct Labor)	
OVERHEAD ITEM	MEAN %
PAYROLL BURDEN	
Mandatory payroll taxes	10.3
Vacation, sick leave, holiday	13.0

Group Insurance	5.7
Annual pension expense	4.5
Bonus, incentive payments, profit sharing	18.2
Total Payroll Burden	50.0
GENERAL & ADMINISTRATIVE	
Indirect labor	40.7
Occupancy cost	10.8
Telephone	3.7
Liability insurance	5.9
Interest	3.2
Bad debt expense	2.9
Total G & A	98.6
Total Overhead	148.2
Unallowable overhead (included in Total Overhead)	10.6
Marketing Expense (included in Total Overhead)	14.0

This information presented in Table 2 was derived from a survey conducted by COFPAES, the Committee on Federal Procurement of Architectural & Engineering Services, and is 20 years old. Not much has changed and more current data is difficult to obtain. Firms are reluctant to report cost and expense related data.

This table gives the mean for all overhead items surveyed. In each case the item is expressed as a percent of direct labor (not direct personnel expense). Not every indirect expense was requested, so the figures will not add up to the total overhead. Note that marketing expense is expressed as a percent of direct labor and not total or net revenues.

PROFIT BY DESIGN

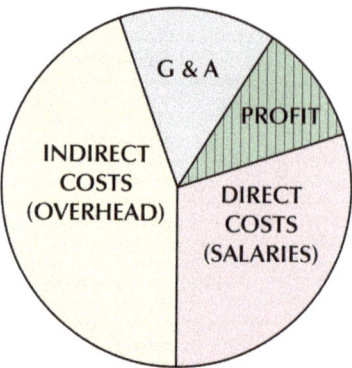

Approximate Relationship Of Costs Showing G&A

Overhead Rate Observations

The decline in financial performance in recent years by A/E firms has been marked by lower pretax profits, higher overhead, and decreased productivity. Cash flow is a main problem, which is heightened by the high interest expense that these firms currently pay for short term borrowing. Other increases in indirect costs which have contributed to higher overhead and to higher overhead rates have included:

- Greater benefits for employees in order to attract and keep qualified staff.
- Increased marketing costs.
- The trend toward office automation including computers, word processing, on-line electronic data exchange and other labor saving devices which increase productivity, lower direct labor costs, and thereby increase the overhead rate even though the clients tend to benefit by improved efficiency and accuracy.

At a time when overhead rates are increasing, many clients (both government and private sector) are becoming more demanding in their contract negotiations for projects, resulting in lower profits. Since a substantial amount of A/E work is done for or funded by the federal government, the peculiarities of the Federal Procurement Regulations (FPR's) have a bearing on a firm's overhead rate and its overall profitability. The principal idiosyncrasy of the FPR's is the unallowable overhead items presented below that are excluded from an A/E firm's overhead rate:

- Advertising Costs[1]
- Interest Expense
- Bad Debt Expense
- Insurance of Principals' Lives
- Contributions and Donations
- Entertainment Expense

[1] Selling costs and proposal costs associated with a firm's marketing and sales promotion are allowable, but advertising costs in support of these business functions are not allowable.

Excluding these accounts has the effect of reducing the effective overhead rate by between 8% and 18% and requiring the firm either to make up the difference out of profit or by passing on these overhead expenses to private sector clients in the form of a "hidden tax." Unfortunately, it is almost universally more expensive in terms of overhead to work for the federal government due largely to the extra administrative burden. The rationale for the unallowable overhead accounts appears to be more rooted in tradition than in accounting theory, but nevertheless, the government usually can be counted on to eventually pay its bills, which makes it an attractive client. On the other hand, and to its credit, the federal government generally is not concerned with the absolute value of the overhead rate for its prime A/E contractors so long as the unallowables are excluded and the overall cost of the A/E services is either reasonable or the lowest cost. Thus, there appears to be a three-point conceptual test for indirect costs to be included in the overhead rate by the federal government:

- Is it reasonable?
- Is it allowable as overhead?
- Have allowables been excluded?

Provided the overhead rate meets these criteria, the federal government accepts it. Although the government is principally concerned with the overall financial capability of its contractors, ironically, A/E firms working exclusively for public agencies are generally less profitable.

There is a perception of frugality and efficiency for A/E firms that have a low overhead rate. Clients, particularly municipal clients, are extremely conscious of a potential consultant's overhead rate and frequently set an upper limit on the multiplier that they will pay in the belief that they will get

less expensive project costs. However, does a lower overhead rate mean lower costs on a particular project? The answer depends on a number of factors, including the firm's salary structure, which employees work on the job, the number of direct hours negotiated, and the accounting procedures used by the firm for allocating direct and indirect costs. It is altogether likely that the overall project cost will be essentially the same or higher regardless of the overhead rate, depending on accounting procedures, all else being equal. Consider the following example of project costs and overhead rates for two hypothetical firms, one of which makes an accounting change by allocating indirect labor to direct labor:

	TABLE 3		
Comparison of Overhead Rate Before and After Accounting Change			
	Before		After
	Company A	Company B	Adjusted
Direct labor	$ 900	$1,000	$1,200
Overhead			
Indirect labor	$ 900	$1,000	$ 800
Other expenses	1,000	1,000	1,000
Total overhead	$1,900	$2,000	$1,800
Total cost	$2,800	$3,000	$3,000
Overhead rate	211%	200%	150%

Company B still has higher total cost after the accounting change than Company A, but Company B now has a substantially lower overhead rate than Company A, without having reduced cost or overhead. It is very likely that Company B would find it much easier to market its services with a lower overhead rate. In fact, many clients may prefer such an indirect cost allocation procedure on the theory that they more closely pay for the specific services that they receive.

There are two fundamental methods of lowering the firm's overhead rate in order to improve its marketability:

1. **Making actual cuts in Overhead**
2. **Allocating a greater portion of indirect costs to direct costs**

An A/E firm may choose to adopt a marketing concept to decide the proper strategy for reducing its overhead rate if it wishes to improve its marketability. First, the firm needs to assess its current market or markets and then to decide whether it wishes to continue as it is or seek another market position. That decision will allow the firm to select an approach to lowering its overhead rate through overhead cuts, indirect cost allocations, or both. For examples of this approach, consider the following situations:

- A firm works mainly as a prime contractor for federal government agencies and it plans to continue in that market. There is no advantage to allocating overhead items to direct expense to lower the overhead rate since the federal government will not dispute the rate so long as it meets the three point test of being reasonable, allocable, and not excluded by the FPR's. On the other hand, the firm may wisely choose to attempt to cut overhead in order to reduce its overall costs to make it more competitive in seeking new government work.

- A second firm places itself largely in the municipal market where it finds its overhead rate a hindrance in working for some local clients. A lower overhead rate would allow it to improve its marketability and at least get through the front door. The firm should consider both the allocation strategy and should also attempt to make actual overhead cuts to gain the greatest advantage.

- A third firm works largely for private industry and has experienced no problems with or questions about its overhead rate, although the total cost is always a concern. This firm may wish to attempt overhead cuts, but likely may choose to do nothing and save the expense of making any changes.

Thus, depending on its market position, there may or may not be any advantage for a firm to attempt to reduce its overhead rate by allocation, although making actual overhead cuts would appear to be universally appropriate so long as the financial benefits outweigh the costs of the cuts. In using the proposed marketing concept strategy for making meaningful reductions in its overhead rate, the firm will likely have little difficulty in estimating the costs to implement the program. However, while the benefits may be largely psychological and hard to quantify, the prospects for improved marketability intuitively can be a very attractive inducement for undertaking the effort.

Opportunities for Overhead Allocations to Projects

Adopting a strategy to allocate a greater portion of indirect expenses to projects can have a favorable impact on the firm's overhead rate, although as previously shown, it does not reduce total project costs. The greatest opportunity is through the allocation of indirect time, which constitutes the largest overhead account for the typical firm. It also has the advantage of adding to the denominator and subtracting from the numerator in the overhead rate, thereby reducing the ratio at a faster pace.

Using both analysis and creativity, a firm might choose to establish a program where certain unique costs are identified and charged to projects as direct costs. Several examples would be direct charges for typing letters, accounting and billing, renegotiations of the contract for a change order, or extra liability insurance required for a project by a client. A reasonable standard for indirect time might be set, such as whenever more than ten minutes is spent on a project, the time is charged to that project. This strategy is also compatible with the idea that difficult clients whose jobs require more traditional indirect services be charged for them. Principals of the firm should charge time to jobs for management, since they typically have the lowest utilization rates and earn the highest salaries.

Principals also should work on projects whenever possible so that they can lend their experience to the effort and at the same time remain involved in the technical aspects of the company's work.

An important feature of cost allocation involves the utilization of internal services provided by the firm. When indirect costs are not allocated, the monetary value of the service is unknown, which can lead to over utilization and lack of control. If unique costs were to be identified and charged to specific jobs, then the allocation system would provide incentive to reduce over consumption and would promote efficiency since project managers would be charged for services on a unit basis.

The chief difficulty with an overhead allocation program is establishing it initially. The reason is that projects are conducted under contracts, which frequently stipulate the number of direct work hours to be charged. Thus, in the initial stage of overhead allocation, there are two areas of concern. The first is for existing contracts which may not have sufficient remaining fee or work hours to absorb the additional charges. The second concern is establishing the proper proportion of what was previously indirect hours and expenses to allocate to the project during proposal preparation and contract negotiation. It likely will take at least one accounting cycle or up to a year to begin to see the results of a lower overhead rate and to gain the experience and data to fine tune the process. However, once the adjustment period is over, the firm should not only have benefited psychologically by its lower overhead rate, but also it may have actually experienced a concomitant reduction in overhead as a result of the incentives provided by the allocation system itself. Nevertheless, management must realize that an overhead allocation strategy cannot be instituted at zero cost. Hence, care should be taken in evaluating the administrative impact of identifying and charging allocable costs so that the perceived benefits do not obscure the implicit costs.

Management Control and the Overhead Rate

The overhead rate is used extensively by A/E firms and their clients as a means of assessing a firm's financial characteristics and for preparing cost estimates for projects. It is used by the firm as a management control indicator, especially when the rate goes up. The reason for its widespread use is that it is easy to calculate and because it presumably connotes vital information about the firm. In actuality though, the overhead rate may provide faulty information to the firm and to clients.

That is not to say, however, that the overhead rate cannot be a useful ratio for management control of overhead. However, overhead is much like the weather in that people are always complaining but do little about it. One of the principal reasons is that managers and project directors, who are in a position to control consumption of overhead services, tend to benefit from the overhead expenditure and may not be motivated in terms of cost reduction.

Therefore, it would seem logical that an A/E firm with an overhead problem or a firm which has decided to make a downward adjustment of its overhead rate through allocations might consider developing an additional evaluation and incentive procedure which would be used to underscore the importance of cost control. The overhead rate could serve as a straightforward management control tool, especially if the rate were calculated on a regular basis, say monthly, for each profit center (or project) in the firm. Management would likely want to calculate the overhead rate for the current period as well as keep a running average of several periods in order to determine trends in the movement of the overhead rate.

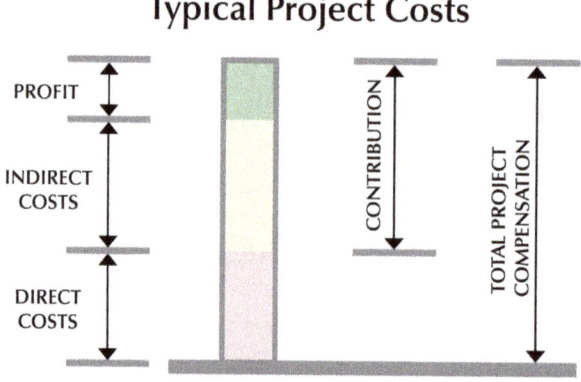

Typical Project Costs

The purpose of this chapter has been to present overhead rate issues facing A/E firms and to suggest various approaches to management control of overhead and the overhead rate. In order to accomplish that purpose, the following key items have been addressed:

- Overhead has been defined in cost accounting terms used by A/E firms. The financial characteristics of A/E firms have been investigated, which has shown that profits have been declining and overhead has been rising. The reasons for this trend include cash flow problems, greater benefit costs for employees, higher marketing and office equipment costs, more restrictive contracts with municipalities and the federal government, and inadequate management control procedures by the firms themselves.

- The method of calculating the overhead rate as well as how it is used by a firm for cost estimates have been presented. The overhead rate is misused by many clients to judge the potential cost of a firm's services, particularly since a lower overhead rate does not necessarily mean lower project costs.

- Two ways have been identified to reduce the overhead rate:

Overhead Allocations, which significantly reduce the overhead rate but do not alter project costs or earnings, and

Overhead Cuts, which reduce the overhead rate less than allocations but which increase profitability or allow for price reductions to be passed on to the client.

- Example calculations in the form of income statements have been presented which demonstrate the effects of overhead allocation and overhead cuts on the overhead rate.

- A theoretical basis for overhead allocations in service industries has been reviewed, and it has been suggested that "unique costs," which would not be incurred without the project, are candidates for being charged directly to the project.

- The economic theory of overhead cost allocations and related organizational behavior has been reviewed to show that:

    - Cost allocations act to reduce the over consumption of overhead services, and

    - Managers should be evaluated and compensated for their efforts to reduce costs in order to overcome the general lack of goal congruence regarding overhead costs..

The conclusions of this historical investigation into the overhead rate issues are that an A/E firm should evaluate its overhead position as well as its overhead rate and use the marketing concept approach to chart its future course of action. For purpose of efficiency, the firm should evaluate and reward its managers on their cost reduction abilities in addition to traditional profitability standards. The overhead rate, calculates at monthly intervals for individual profit centers, can serve as a straight forward management control tool for the firm. To be truly efficient, an A/E firm would be wise to incorporate true overhead cuts and to evaluate its market position to consider whether overhead allocations would improve its marketability through a reduction in its overhead rate.

The calculation of an overhead rate is straight forward and simple. To make significant gains in reducing overhead, analysis of each indirect cost component is necessary.

Certain indirect costs may be reduced or avoided. Other indirect costs may be shifted into direct, project specific cost categories. Periodic evaluation of a firm's overhead rate and the cost elements that comprise all indirect expenses should be performed.

PROFIT BY DESIGN

Basic data and research in this chapter was derived from The Overhead Rate by Jon O. Clarke, published by the National Society of Professional Engineers (May, 1982) referenced in the bibliography.

Utilization

The importance of staff utilization in an A/E firm cannot be overstated. Utilization is the second most important measure of a firm's vitality and ability to succeed. Profit, of course, is the lead indicator. However, a firm cannot profit without constantly monitoring staff utilization data to ensure proper allocation of staff time.

Utilization, as a subject, is addressed tangentially in many management texts and professional periodicals. Within the A/E universe, utilization is poorly understood and seldom emphasized as an important business tool. The AIA HANDBOOK OF PROFESSIONAL PRACTICE (13th Edition) mentions "utilization", but fails to stress its value to a firm's successful business strategy. The AIA HANDBOOK devotes a total of 3 pages out of 988 to this vital aspect of A/E firm management. This indicates a serious lack of attention to one of the most central concepts underlying profitable A/E practices.

In simplest terms, utilization is a ratio derived by comparing Direct Salary Expense with Total Salary Expense. However, many firms view utilization in differing ways, and at least 3 models have evolved to express the relationship between billable expenses and non-billable expenses. These 3 different utilization models are:

A.) Payroll Utilization Ratio =	Direct Salary Expense / Total Salary Expense
B.) Standard Time Utilization =	Direct Project Hours / Total Standard Hours (based upon a standard work week)
C.) Total Time Utilization =	Direct Project Hours / Total Hours Recorded on Time Sheets

PROFIT BY DESIGN

Monitoring utilization is a constant chore for any A/E office or firm. As mundane and statistical as it may seem, the idea of maintaining high staff utilization serves to bolster profits (both potential and actual recognized profits). Small shifts in utilization can have dramatic impacts on profitability. As the amount of personnel time and expense charged to projects decreases, overhead time and expense increases by the same margin. Given a reasonably steady staffing level, swings in utilization to the upside can significantly increase profits.

Conversely, declines in utilization can cause severely diminished profitability and create complicated cash flow problems. Each time staff hours are shifted from billable project work to overhead, billings decrease and overhead costs increase. Reduced revenues from project work at a pre-determined billing rate (usually total average direct cost times a multiplier that includes overhead and profit) shifts revenue away from the income side of the ledger and adds uncompensated costs to the expense side of the ledger in the form increased overhead.

Such a shift in revenue is serious when one weighs the fact that a single 1 hour change in utilization deprives the office of earnings at the established full multiplier rate and adds uncompensated cost to the total indirect expense line at the direct salary expense rate. Therefore, the loss to the firm of a single 1 hour shift in utilization is: Full Billable Hourly Rate + Direct Salary Expense Rate. Lost utilization revenue can be a huge problem for a firm if staff utilization is not managed to some established minimum target.

According to AIA data reported in the *HANDBOOK OF PROFESSIONAL PRACTICE*, architectural firms generally report utilization ratios ranging from 62 to 72 percent. No indication is given as to which method of calculating utilization was applied to generate this data.

However, it should be clear that the ratio of billable project hours to standard hours (based upon a 40 hour or some other standard work week) will result in a much higher utilization rate than will the alternative method.

When total billable project hours are divided by total recorded hours (including overtime hours for those categories of staff normally called overhead or management) the resulting utilization rate declines . . . . unless (of course) all of the additional recorded hours are billable to projects.

One of the truly complicated aspects of managing an A/E practice efficiently is to demand that all staff accurately record both project and overhead time. In this way, the most accurate calculation of time utilization can be derived. However, sometimes the required staff effort on a project vastly exceeds the billing agreement established between the owner and A/E firm principal. When this occurs, there is a tendency for staff to under report direct project hours and shift their time into overhead categories. With proper communication and training, staff can be taught to recognize that this practice results in the same economic deficit as correctly reporting unallowable or "over budget" project hours. When time recorded against project budgets exceeds the established limits, each hour logged above the limit becomes a de facto overhead expense, without generating revenue. Project time logged above budgeted limits and time required for rework or mistakes eats into the planned profitability of the project and reduces the effective multiplier (net) achieved on the job. According to the AIA HANDBOOK, net multiplier is the most common instrument for measuring productivity.

Many firms require that rework and corrective work by a project team be accomplished "off record" or "off line", i.e. not recorded on a time sheet. This is common practice in instances where the rework is clearly attributable to one or two individuals on the project team. However, depending on the rank of the employee and the labor category in which they serve the firm (salaried or hourly) the cost of rework may be required to be absorbed by the firm (in compliance with federal labor laws). In certain cases, rework is performed at overtime rates at even greater expense to the firm. Paying overtime labor rates to perform rework and/or correct mistakes without the ability to bill a client for that work is a strong indicator that a budgetary disaster looms large for the project. Obviously, therefore, overtime should be kept to a minimum.

Payroll Utilization Ratio (PUR) uses direct payroll expense as the basis for comparing staff efficiency and cost. The formula of Direct Salary Expense divided by Total Salary Expense compares the cost of billable project hours to the cost of total compensated staff hours. For example, if in a given week, the total cost of time devoted to billable projects is $65,500 and the total cost of all salary expenses (billable and non-billable) for the same period is $100,000, the ratio of $65,500/$100,000 results in a payroll utilization rate of 65.5%. Increasing payroll utilization with a fixed number of staff and pre-determined salary figures requires increasing the number of billable project hours and reducing the number of non-billable (overhead) hours. Using this measure, changes in payroll utilization indicate fluctuations in staff efforts devoted to billable projects, but also include vacation, sick leave, holidays and personal leave costs as cost elements within the denominator. In simple terms, if this ratio is used as the measure of efficiency for an office, upper limits can be established above which payroll utilization cannot rise, given the predictable fixed costs of vacations, holidays, and leave. As pointed out elsewhere in this text, these costs will vary with each office and A/E firm, and with every reporting period. However (generally speaking), maximum possible utilization calculated using this method will fall in the range of from 87% to 91%.

Many firms choose to address utilization as a ratio of billable hours to total staff hours, or as billable hours to standard hours. This removes the cost of the staff time and any distortions that may result from one category of staff being compensated at a radically different rate than another.

In the case of **Standard Time Utilization** as the preferred method, it is possible to achieve utilization rates of greater than 100%. This can occur when the number of billable project hours in a particular period exceeds the standard hours on which payroll is based. This is made possible by staff members working very hard (many hours) on billable projects and recording all of their billable time. Overhead time or other non-billable time is limited and generally not recorded over and above the 40 hour work week. Therefore, with the upper limit of overhead time fixed and the billable project time limited only by the number of hours in a day times the total number of staff, circumstances and parameters can exist whereby the total number of billable hours exceed the total number of standard hours. For example, if 10 people make up an office and payroll is based upon a 40 hour work week (each staff member) then 400 hours will be the denominator regardless of the total number of hours in the numerator. If billable project time exceeds 400 hours (based upon overtime work or staff spending large quantities of time on project – as in the case of a submission deadline), then utilization of more than 100% will be indicated. If 450 billable hours are recorded on time sheets, then utilization is:

450/400 = 112.5%

Total Time Utilization is another more accurate method of calculating utilization involving the ratio of total billable hours to total hours. This method involves letting the denominator float to reflect the actual number of hours recorded on time sheets for a particular period. Using this method, it is not possible to achieve utilization rates which exceed 100%. In fact, this method more closely resembles the Payroll Utilization Ratio model, absent the real payroll cost data. As a measure of time efficiency and as an indicator of how well the project, office or firm is managing its staff time, this method is very effective. In consideration of our prior example, if the 450 billable hours is compared to actual time spent in all categories of labor (even those exceeding 40 hours per week) with all time accurately recorded on time sheets, then the ratio will be more like 450/550 = 85.7%, under the assumption that 550 is an accurate representation of the total recorded time.

Even though the Total Time Utilization method tracks closely with the Payroll Utilization Ratio, they never actually produce the same utilization percentage due to fluctuations in pay scales and overtime pay rates between categories of labor. For this reason, many A/E firms elect to use the Total Time Utilization method and confine utilization discussions to a comparison of billable time to total time recorded, with all staff encouraged to record all weekly time, (even that beyond 40 hours per week).

Noteworthy is the point that federal A/E contracts are subject to audit at any point in the design process or during the life of

Utilization = Ratio expressing efficiency of labor devoted to earning revenue. Usually expressed as total direct project hours divided by total of all person hours "paid for" within a specific time period. For example:

$$10 \text{ Employees @ } 40/\text{hrs/wk} = (400 \text{ hrs})$$

$$\text{Total Direct Project Hours} = 297 \text{ (Time Sheets)}$$

$$\text{Utilization} = \frac{297}{400} = 74.25\%$$

the contract. In addition, post closing audits and/or defective pricing audits are permitted by federal law on most federal A/E contracts. In the event that an audit reveals more labor hours devoted to a project than the compensation agreed upon divided by the negotiated labor rates and hours, the consequences can be devastating. Federal regulations permit the assessment of back charges and fines if project performance deviates significantly from negotiated labor rates and hours.

If an audit is performed and it is discovered that a firm took more hours to perform the work than were original agreed, the government divides the actual number of labor hours into the total fee paid to the firm and the resulting dividend can be a dramatically reduced average hourly rate. In these circumstances the government may hold the A/E firm to reduced hourly labor rates across all labor categories in future contracts. Therefore, senior management in an A/E office must be aware of the risks associated with requiring staff members to record all labor hours. While this practice helps provide a more accurate picture of staff utilization and personnel management, the data may be construed in other ways (for other purposes) and impact the firm's future business practices.

Another cautionary point that must be made concerns utilization as a measure of project, office or firm performance. Utilization ratios are only valid to the extent that clients actually pay their bills. Not all project time is billable. Non- billable staff hours have the same value as overhead hours devoted to other internal non-billable tasks. If reported utilization is high and billable hours in relation to total hours appears strong, the office or firm is probably performing well financially. If clients fail to pay in a timely manner or if the client contests a portion of the billing, those contested hours become de-facto overhead hours, reducing utilization rates, revenues and profits while increasing overhead expenses.

The most important rule to understand and remember about utilization (no matter which model is used) is that, as personnel time and expense attributable to projects decreases, overhead time and expense increases. When staff time is shifted away from billable project work into overhead assignments (such as research, marketing, management, continuing education, staff meetings, library functions, etc.) reduced project effort, utilization, billings, revenues and profits will result.

The AIA HANDBOOK OF PROFESSIONAL PRACTICE links project utilization with "Quality Management." The Handbook suggests a list of 13 items which might be measured and statistically analyzed in a modern A/E firm. Utilization is at the top of this list.

PROFIT BY DESIGN

Creating Reserves

In many large A/E firms, sophisticated accounting systems have been adopted and modified over time. Such systems become unique to the particular firm. It is common among larger firms to have rigorous procedures in place for booking new work. Sometime these procedures include checklists for client data, billing data, contract ratification, requirements for a written workplan, schedule, list of consultants, estimates of reimbursable expenses, and many other items. The thrust of these pre-booking checklists is to cause the project manager and project principal to verify that the project is viable, the client is serious and capable of paying for the work, consultants are committed and "qued-up" for their role, and that certain minimum revenue and profitability goals can be achieved.

The more sophisticated the accounting system, the more time is required by both project management and accounting personnel to set-up and book the work. Some explanation may be needed from the project manager to the accounting department, so that special conditions of the project (including such items as consultant payment schedules and/or retainers) can be correctly reflected in the instructions that govern how the project is to be managed.

As project budgets are established to support project booking instructions, labor budgets for the project (usually by phase and discipline) are set in place for the duration of the job. So too are budgets for consultant fees and expenses set up in advance. The firm generally relies upon the knowledge and experience of the project manager to set these budgets and send proper instructions/paperwork to the accounting office for entry into the accounting system. In simple terms, the accounting office deducts all estimated fees and expenses for consultants and reproduction (project expenses) and comes to a net revenue figure that represents the portion of the total fee to the earned/retained by the A/E firm. Included in that figure, are all costs for direct labor, indirect labor and expense and profit.

It is important to note (once again) that profit is treated as a cost. When the project gets underway, assuming everything goes according to plan, the work will be performed within the established labor budget, overhead and profit will be earned hourly, daily, weekly and monthly among the way, and consultants will get paid on time and not overrun their budgets. But, this is rarely the case! Very few projects ever progress exactly as planned. Clients change the scope and budgets, review agencies impose new and sometimes contradictory requirements, consultants are delayed in starting their work – a myriad of problems can and do occur to derail the best planned and most carefully managed projects. Deviations in the project workplan must be expected.

The important realization is that when deviations occur to a project management plan, something gives – and revenues (also profits) are not recognized when they were originally planned to be recognized. This is not a desirable situation and only hurts the firm. If projects shift in and out of control, the project manager looks incapable, the office appears poorly managed and the banks that monitor the performance of the firm or office get nervous. Demonstrating proper control over the execution of the work, and having certain safe guards in place, helps restore confidence in the firm and all levels of management.

One such strategy to safeguard against failed work plans and disrupted revenue flow is the creation of reserves. Many firms actively encourage PMs to set aside some portion of the primary firms' project labor budget, in reserve, to offset the prospect of glitches in project management and revenue flow. Some larger firms instill this concept of creating reserves in all project teams, making it a visible and mandatory part of a project management plan. Other firms merely suggest that the PM set aside a small portion of the project budget, just in case something goes wrong. The practice of setting up reserve accounts is commonplace, and it works.

The manifestation of reserves can appear in several ways and in several places within a project accounting system. The most common "reserve account" is one requiring a percentage of the primary A/E firm labor budget to be set aside and not used for labor on the project. The direct impact of this is clear; the A/E firm must apply labor and execute the work (to the same level of quality and with the same degree of thoroughness) with fewer labor hours. If, for example, the firm requires that 20% of the labor budget be set aside in reserve, then the PM must find a way to accomplish the job with the remaining 80% of the total labor budget. As the project progresses, and billings are generated, each labor hour must still cover all direct and indirect costs, and profit, in accordance with the original workplan, (as reflected in the booking documents). The 20% figure remains on the books and in the budget "in reserve" in case something goes wrong and additional labor must be applied. This is considered by some to be a tax, self-imposed by the firm on the project, to provide a form of insurance against project catastrophe.

Obviously, it also challenges the project manager and project team to perform the work in a highly efficient manner to protect (not use) the reserve. If, near the end of the project, it is clear that everything has been managed well and the project is a success without tapping into the labor reserve fund, this amount of money is dropped to the bottom line and recognized as profit for the job, the office and the firm. The impact of successfully applying a reserve strategy and protecting that reserve until project closeout is that greater profits than those originally planned as part of the project billing schedule can be and are achieved. Work is performed efficiently, and resultant profits are much higher than originally planned.

Forcing a project team to establish and protect reserve accounts also heightens attentiveness to project scope and scope creep. If the project team thoroughly understands the original scope, and consciously tries to find the shortest, most efficient course to complete the work, more attention is given to scope deviation and client requested changes. It is much more likely that the project staff will raise a red flag and bring an out of scope service request to the attention of the PM or office manager if the pressures of reserve planning are imposed.

Project reserves need not wait to be recognized until the end of the job. If, for example, a project is being managed and invoiced in phases or on the basis of percent complete, then, at intervals established for each phase, some portion of the reserves may be recognized and dropped to the bottom line in the form of profit. In very large firms with multiple offices and hundreds of projects in production at any given time, having the comfort of reserve accounts is desirable. Some projects may be performing well, and others not so well. The flexibility to recognize reserves (when necessary) to satisfy the monthly profitability goal of an office is extremely beneficial.

When establishing reserve accounts, the accounting department generally insists that a suffix or sub-account (under the project's direct labor budget) be shown on the books with the heading reserve, or labor reserve, or contingency or some other very clear title that expresses the true nature of the account. In this way the amount in reserve can be checked month to month as project progress reports are issued. If it becomes necessary to adjust the labor budget and reallocate funds from reserves back into the project labor budget, this can be done easily and clearly tracked.

In larger and more sophisticated project accounting systems, reserve accounts are assigned the same suffix or sub-account set of codes on every project. Then, at the press of a button, a report can be generated to show all reserve budgets, and the funds remaining in contingency accounts office-wide or firm-wide. This becomes a strong and important management tool.

The experienced and astute project manager who is familiar with reserve accounts and contingent budgeting strategies will employ multiple reserve accounts on a single large job. He/she may set aside the 20% reserve from the labor budget (as discussed above), and he/she may "overbook" one or more consultant accounts thus budgeting higher dollar figures than consultants expect in each consultant account. These consultant contingencies may or may not be coded to show up in the reserve account reporting function. In other words, only the project manager may know that these additional contingencies exist in the project budget. Similarly, reserve accounts can be established for project expense categories, such as reproduction, supplies, photography, and a host of other project related cost categories. These "phantom reserves" can sit on the books for the duration of the project and be unused. At project closeout, all unused budget categories are closed and previously unrecognized revenue is taken in the form of profit. Protecting

PROFIT BY DESIGN

profits and recognizing profits at the right time is a skill that few architects and engineers have developed. Those who know and use these techniques are employed with some of the largest and most successful (and most profitable) A/E firms in the world. Learning these skills and budgeting projects with a specific profit strategy in mind makes a PM a very valuable asset to the firm.

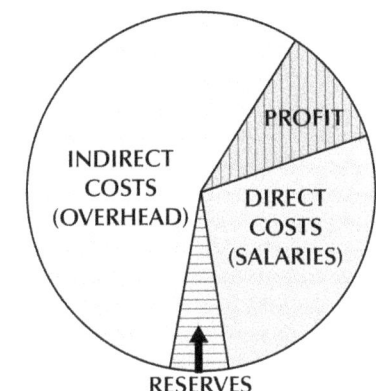

Budgeting Reserves from Direct and Indirect Costs

Creating reserve accounts is contingent upon the project design budget being sufficiently large to support these contingencies and booking strategies. The smaller the project and lower the fee, the less likely it is for reserve planning to be successful. At some point, the PM can't produce the work for less cost than that which is negotiated in the fee. Sometimes, it is frustrating to establish a 10% or 20% reserve on a small project, only to reallocate the entire reserve the following month, because more labor hours are needed. Sound judgment and logic must play a role in the creation of reserve bookings. It may not be worth the effort on smaller, less profitable projects.

There are certain inherent dangers in applying reserve budgets to projects in an organized way. One of the greatest temptations of corporate management is to pre-maturely recognize reserves as "cash on hand" or "excess profit" before the work has been completed. The pressure is always there at the top for the Board of Directors to report "good news" to employees, shareholders, bankers, and accountants, if the reserves appear to be large and recognizable. Self control is often lacking and cash calls sometimes come from the top as office managers and project managers are asked to squeeze all of the reserve accounts out of the system and report all reserves as profit by a prescribed date. There are significant legal ramifications if corporations get so greedy that they begin recognizing profits in advance of earnings.

For example, if a reserve budget shows $100,000 in reserve on a particular project which is also reporting 30% complete (through schematics or DD), then it is proper to recognize 30% of that $100,000 reserve ($30,000) and take this amount in the form of profit to the bottom line – provided that 1.) the project is on track, 2.) the PM is confident that he/she can complete remaining work without needing reserves and 3.) that no claims or other potential problems exist. It would be improper for the corporate decision-makers, the office manager, the PM (or anyone else) to recognize any reserve amount higher than the 30%, even though the temptation is there to take a larger portion or "take it all" due to some event or external need, such as a shareholders' meeting, or an annual report deadline, or as the basis for a line of credit to support the acquisition of another company. Laws and regulations have been developed, tried and tested, to prevent firms from engaging in fraudulent accounting practices, such as recognizing revenues and profits in advance of earning the fees (doing the work). Recent attention to creative accounting practices in the wake of several Fortune 500 company collapses and other scandals involving manipulation of financial statements has revealed just how serious false reporting of revenue can be. Caution is advised before setting in motion internal accounting policies that encourage manipulation of revenues and profits simply to create the impression of profitability.

Careful budgeting and the creation of a detailed work plan usually leads the project manager to understand how much (if any) reserve can be set aside on the project. Incentives can be applied to the idea of strong project management (using reserves) so that PMs and project team members are rewarded (bonuses, extra vacation, firm-paid education and training opportunities) for setting up proper reserve accounts and managing their work (including that of consultants) in an efficient and responsible way in order to protect the reserves, and achieve greater profits.

By creating reserve accounts as the project is booked, the PM is making conscious decisions about profit. If the PM and other staff members are encouraged to create reserve accounts, the result is very careful analysis of the profit potential of the job at all levels. In addition to earning profit in the normal flow of work (profit from hourly billings), profits from both reserve accounts and consultant accounts can be planned, managed and controlled to maximize profit on the job.

If the practice of establishing reserve accounts is successful, profits can be double or even triple those of a project where no reserve fund was created. A project that is booked into the accounting system with a planned 15% profit and reserve accounts as described herein, has the potential to realize much higher profits. Large, complex, multi-year projects can achieve profits of 15%, 20%, 22% or higher, if properly budgeted, planned and managed.

PROFIT BY DESIGN
Estimates to Complete (ETCs)

Without overstating the obvious, the Estimate to Complete (ETC) is a detailed assessment by a project manager of the remaining work effort on a project, expressed in staff-hours, and broken down by discipline. It is a vital measure of both performance of the job and staffing required to meet remaining deadlines/milestones. ETCs are developed without regard to the original project budget, such that they reflect a true and realistic view of remaining work to complete all project assignments.

ETCs are prepared monthly, for all projects and involve the project manager's (and sometimes key project staff) critical analysis of the tasks remaining in the work plan. Once compiled, the ETCs are compared with remaining project budgets (also expressed in staff hours) for an indication as the whether each job is over budget, "under budget", or proceeding according to the established "burn rate" set forth in the original work plan. (The burn rate is defined as the rate at which the budgeted staff hours are consumed, project by project.) Monthly ETCs can be (and usually are) the first official indication that a project is in trouble, requiring immediate corrective action. Project managers, in consultation with the office manager and key discipline leaders, should make immediate adjustments in personnel, team composition, schedule, and man-hour allocations when ETCs reveal a problem. Sometimes, it is necessary to rebudget the job and transfer funds from reserves into the labor budgets to augment available hours and work effort.

In certain instances, ETCs will show that the remaining work effort can be completed for far fewer hours than those remaining in the budget. This is welcome news no matter what the project! Completing required work, and producing a satisfactory work product, with less effort than that anticipated usually means higher profits will be realized on that job. If reserves were booked at the outset of the project and ETCs show the work ahead of schedule and/or under the labor effort allocation, then reserves will be protected and the project will be more profitable than originally planned.

PROFIT BY DESIGN

Generally, if ETCs indicate work is being produced as planned or with fewer hours than originally budgeted, the question becomes when to recognize the revenue and the increase in profit. Should the profit be taken at the end of the month, at the end of the phase, or, at the end of the job? The prudent office manager will consult with the PM and, together, they will determine an appropriate time table on which to recognize surplus profits and/or reserves. Of course, it is prudent to wait until the end of the project, as part of the project closeout procedure, after all expenses are posted and consultant invoices are received, before recognizing reserves and excess (surplus) profit.

When ETCs indicate that a project is performing well (as planned) or well ahead of plan, it is a good idea to acknowledge the PM and project team, and to reward outstanding performance. This is usually done with a cash bonus, paid vacation, or some combination of the two.

As a management tool, it is important to use current ETC data and act on that data quickly. The clock is ticking and if a project is in trouble, rapid corrective action needs to occur. Cost overruns resulting from too many direct labor hours devoted to a phase or project can consume budgets, reserves, and cost the firm tens of thousands of dollars "out of pocket" to complete the work. Failure to act on a project in trouble (as represented by an ETC) can mean no profit on the work, or worse, going deep into the hole . . . consuming earned profits from other jobs to offset the loss on one. Profit margins in a well managed A/E firm are routinely small (from 5% to 11% normally) and it can be devastating for just one project to "go south", draining earned profits from other jobs – and causing severe financial damage to the profitability of the entire office or firm.

Constant attention to ETCs by upper management usually results in better performance on all protects, in all phases. Project managers, if inspired by the notion that rewards may be gained from well performing projects, will dissect and manipulate project budgets and manage the work with rigorous attention to detail. Yet, dangers lurk in data that is "just too good to be true," and closer scrutiny of ETCs is required by senior management. Reviewing ETCs with an internal project team is recommended. The entire team should understand remaining work efforts and estimated hours to complete the job.

For example, if an early stage of a large project is complete, and the PM creates an ETC showing that all remaining phases should be completed for approximately half of the budgeted hours remaining, it would be reckless for senior management and/or the PM to begin recognizing surplus profits or rebudgeting the job this early. Murphy's Law impacts many large A/E projects. Despite early indications of strong project performance, good client satisfaction, milestones being reached well ahead of budget, treat the data carefully and allow surplus profits to accumulate on the books for a time. Reviewing ETCs with the project team brings a greater degree of conservative thinking to decisions needed on the project.

The value of the ETC depends upon its accuracy. In a large, multi-disciplined firm, ETCs may be prepared by teams of people, including department heads and/or discipline leaders. In these instances, the PM generally compiles the ETC based upon data submitted by the team or discipline leaders. Unless the data is scrutinized for accuracy, discipline leaders may conceal surplus hours and/or hourly deficits in order to disguise the fact that their discipline may be having difficulty meeting project submission requirements and/or deadlines. Care must be taken to ratify ETCs by either the PM or senior management. To be useful, ETCs must be an honest representation of tasks and effort remaining.

One of the many benefits of routinely preparing ETCs, is the constant attention focused on the original project scope. Periodic reviews of work completed, work-in-progress, and estimates to complete cause the PM to closely compare the original scope with ongoing work. This results in prompt recognition of "out of scope" work and early heads-up that extra fees may be needed to satisfy adjunct efforts or related necessary work, not encompassed or contemplated by the original project scope. Team review of ETCs will provoke a discussion of project scope and a realistic assessment of "scope creep" on the project.

PROFIT BY DESIGN

Scope creep is a deadly disease which can infest a project and eat away at revenues, schedules and profits. When a project seems to wonder beyond the limits of budgeted scope, the PM should call a time out, then call the client. Because a project budget is established using a clear and well-defined scope of work, a project or task which is permitted to extend beyond the limits of that scope will inevitably strain the budget. Scope creep must be prevented to assure accurate ETCs. If the boundaries of the scope are permitted to move and become amorphous, the ETCs associated with the project will have no value. ETCs are measured against an established budget and a specific, well understood scope of work.

The importance of preparing monthly ETCs and the rigors of checking to see if work is progressing as planned, should be conveyed to all levels of staff and become part of the office or firm culture. At least two remarkable benefits occur from frequently communicating with staff about ETCs: 1.) it reinforces the idea that time has value and that each hour represented on a time card is a debit against a project budget; and 2.) all staff members, by their conscious actions to work efficiently, contribute to the profitability of the project and office. Raising the awareness among all staff about project scope, budgets, and profitability goals help staff become responsible and take pride in their piece of the effort. Stripping away the mystery surrounding project budgets, fee estimates, scope deviation, submission requirements, and sharing information between teams and disciplines will generally result in more efficient work and more respect for each member of the team.

Without the feedback mechanism known as the ETC, projects may be in serious trouble and project progress reports won't reflect the problem until an entire labor budget is consumed, well after it becomes too late to take corrective action. When an ETC indicates serious labor over-runs or schedules are slipping, the PM must move swiftly to bring the project back in line.

PROFIT BY DESIGN
Overtime versus "Comp Time"

In the interest of attracting and retaining high caliber staff, firms have experimented with a broad range of "time off" scenarios, where hard work and good performance are rewarded by flexible working hours. Small firms find "comp time" to be an effective way of acknowledging dedication and extra effort on the part of the staff, when client imposed deadlines are met and the rigors of the workplace swing dramatically into those high intensity times. Rewarding good job performance is necessary at all levels within the office or firm, from the clerk in the mailroom up through the senior principal(s).

Small firms seem better able to predict the down times associated with delays between project phases, manpower needed to accomplish specific tasks, and the coordination efforts with consultants, largely due to the limited numbers of projects and staff being managed at any one time. The idea of "comp time" was born of the necessity to quantify and describe that intangible benefit that firm owners bestow on their staff, when they extend the gesture – "take the day off."

The idea behind a structured comp time benefits program is that staff can be rewarded by paid time off, beyond normal vacations, holidays, sick days and personal time. In theory, staff who receive a comp time benefit have worked additional hours, or on weekends, or holidays and put in the extra effort to meet a project deadline, prepare for a public hearing, teach the staff a particular skill or technique, rehearse long into the night in preparation for an interview, or contribute to the well being of an office by devoting their personal time and energy without extra pay. Many firms that administer comp time programs create their own formula for earning comp time credits. How the staff schedule their comp time days off can vary widely and change (over time) depending upon office administration and the ebb and flow of work-in-process. It is presumed that earned comp time will be taken when events in the office and demands of projects subside.

PROFIT BY DESIGN

Larger firms and multi-discipline A/E firms have also experimented with comp time programs. To a greater or lesser degree, they can be effective perks when recruiting new staff or retaining hard working existing staff.

Overtime pay within the A/E service community is also widely interpreted and/or misinterpreted. Although the U.S. Labor Department requires "overtime pay" at prescribed overtime rates (usually 1.5 times hourly wage) few firms understand the regulations or how they apply to A/E firms. The basic, unmistakable legal supposition expressed in U.S. Labor Department regulations, is that supervised labor, performing routine and repetitive tasks, must be paid overtime if they work overtime hours. (Insert the DOL citations)

A comp time policy and program carries certain very serious ramifications for any firm (large or small) that has subscribed to an accrual accounting methodology. These ramifications must be well understood by senior management, as the costs to support such a benefit can be surprisingly high. Owners and managers must be willing to absorb the drain on firm revenues and forecast the amount of time that staff will take, as their comp time allotment. Controlling comp time is difficult in a large, multi-disciplined firm.

In the context of a typical earned revenue model, "comp time" is really an 8 hour working day that a staff member takes off, with pay. The obligation to pay for the non-productive 8 hour period is something the firm plans for and expects as an element of the comp time benefits program. The 8 hours of time off is still paid for by the A/E firm, with all the ancillary benefits (social security, FICA, life insurance, and routine carry costs). The staff member still gets a paycheck, representing full time payment for the unproductive 8 hours that get posted to the books. Q=Where are these comp time hours posted? A=To overhead (of course). Unproductive, unbillable regular working hours become part of the indirect costs of the office. The beauty of an earned revenue system is that the staff hours are either billable, or they're not! There are no other options. Staff time is either billable directly to a project, or it is an indirect expense. Any hour of time not charged to a client's project is, (by default) carried on the books as an overhead cost.

In the normal course of business, an 8 hour day for any technical staff person would be predominately "billable" time. Examples of this were presented in this book in the chapter titled "Macro-Management." Even if only 6 out of every 8 hour working day is truly "billable" to a job, the net result of a comp time day taken is that none of those comp time hours are billable . . . . and yet they cost the firm money. How much money? More than meets the eye! For every hour of unbilled technical labor not attributable to a project the firm "loses" that direct payroll hour and the unbillable overhead and profit normally earned on that hour! This is a major point that many firms fail to visualize when creating elaborate, (or event simple), comp time scenarios.

To illustrate this point clearly, a direct hourly wage of $50 paid to a senior architect would normally earn $172.50/hr. at a 3.15 multiplier (the multiplier includes all overhead and profit). The loss to the firm of that unbilled staff hour (the comp time hour) is $222.50, because the $172.50 rate could not be charged to a client AND, the firm still pays the direct rate ($50) in the form of salary or wage to the employee. That's a loss of 4.15 times direct cost in real terms!

Comp Time Cost

$172.50 (unbilled labor hour @ 3.15 multiplier)
+ 50.00 (direct salary cost)
$222.50 (total loss to firm per hour)

If staff time is not being posted to a project, and no revenue is being earned, the hidden impact of the financial loss can be dramatic. Using the above example, an 8-hour day off in the form of comp time costs the firm $1,780. This is a reduction of earned revenue and profit.

Another typical case worth studying is offered up by a firm that believes a comp time program can be an effective substitute for overtime pay it would normally provide its non- professional (non-licensed) employees. In an earned revenue system, where each technical hour is planned and allocated to a project, a decision to employ a comp time program, in lieu of an overtime formula is incorrect and costly. An example of this will illustrate the point:

If a junior staff member earns a direct hourly wage of $20/hr. and the billable rate to a client at a 3.0 multiplier is $60/hr., then allowing that employee to take "comp time" as a reward for good performance costs the firm $80/hr. (the impact of the unbilled hour plus the direct staff wage carry cost expense). On the other hand, if that same staff person were "paid" at legally applicable overtime rates (say 1.5 x direct wage), the cost to the firm to get the extra effort out of the staff member and reward them with extra pay is only $10/hr. This staff member would earn a total of $30/hr. in direct payroll and the firm continues billing the client at the established $60/hr. rate. Losing the $10 per hour to a valued member of the staff and compensating staff for their extra effort is far more desirable to the firm than losing $80 per hour to offer the staff comp time.

At technical staff levels, history indicates that incentive compensation and overtime pay is more important to the employee than time off. At senior staff and professional/managerial levels, comp time may make greater sense as supervisory employees are not entitled to overtime pay, and their rate of compensation does not necessarily depend on time devoted directly to projects. For staff considered entirely "overhead" by virtue of their job assignment, i.e. marketing, office management, accounting, human resources, managing principals, etc. . . . , comp time may be the best non-cash method for acknowledging outstanding performance, attracting and/or retaining valued employees.

The creation of a comp time program must be well considered and the financial impact on the entire firm (all staffing levels and operations) should be evaluated. An ill-conceived program, though well intended, can ruin a firm within a year. Our earlier example can be extrapolated into a larger firm model to indicate the potential downside on a broader, firm-wide scale:

If 40 technical employees are permitted to accumulate up to 100 hours of annual comp time (each) as an element of a firm-wide comp time program, and the average hourly direct payroll rate for these 40 people is $40/hr., the 4,000 hours of potential comp time liability for the firm will cost $160,000 annually in direct payroll expense and another $480,000 ($160,000 x 3.0 multiplier) in unbilled revenue. So, the total "cost" of supporting a comp time program of this nature, in a medium size firm with 40 technical staff, is $640,000.

> 4,000 hrs. (total accumulated comp time debt)
> $40 (average hourly payroll rate)
> $160,000 (total comp time debt to staff)
> plus
> $160,000 (direct cost)
> x 3.0 (normal multiplier)
> $480,000 (lost billings)
>
> $160,000 (direct cost)
> +480,000 (lost revenue)
> $640,000 (total annual comp time cost)

The rational and prudent firm owner or principal will evaluate the idea of comp time (and the financial burden on the firm) in the context of how much profit the firm is making or plans to make. Reflecting back on the earlier discussions in "Macro-Management" if the average billable hourly rate is $172.50, and the firm earns 15% profit from that hour of billed revenue, then $22.50 (the profit), times 1294 billable staff hours per employee (the actual number of hours a staff person might bill), times 40 technical staff members, results in a total anticipated annualized profit of $29,115 per technical staff member or $1,164,600 in total "profit." The owner or managing principal will ask the obvious question . . . . "Can we afford to reduce our earned profit by $640,000 per year to support a comp time program?" In this scenario, banks and shareholders are going to be much more supportive of and interested in the annual business plan that shows potential gross profits of $1,164,600 than the plan that shows the same work effort and projects generating only $524,600 in gross profits. This comparison is over-simplified to dramatize the potential cost to a firm of making what some personnel feel is a kind and rational compensatory time offer, in exchange for extra time worked. Despite the cost, many firms embrace a comp time plan and encourage staff to take time off during slow times.

The dilemma for the prudent strategic thinking business leader is the determination of clear priorities and goals for the firm. Is it better to attract and retain staff by offering a unique (but expensive) "Comp Time" program versus the higher gross profit potential and the flexibility to pay cash bonuses from a larger profit pool? Are the staff more interested in a bonus check at the end of the year or time off for outstanding performance throughout the year? Would a carefully crafted overtime pay program for certain levels of staff, combined with an incentive bonus plan for senior employees make more sense? Questions such as these must be asked and answered with empirical data. The emotional response is usually much less rational than a response based on real cost data.

Decisions about overtime vs. comp time policies should be by-products of strategic discussions and a thoughtful business plan. Management deliberations about overtime pay policies must first recognize labor standards and compliance with federal labor laws. Then, alternative policies for granting time off as part of an incentive compensation program should be carefully considered and evaluated based upon their potential impact on cost and culture.

Collections and DSOs

A/E firms are fueled by cash flow. The constant need for cash is driven by payroll, expenses and operational costs. In a professional service business, there are very few assets and little or no real property against which loans can be secured. The ability to collect cash and accumulate a sufficient supply of cash to meet obligations is a critical aspect of firm survival and viability.

In an A/E business, cash is not collected until after billings are submitted to clients for work performed. This means that the A/E business is usually paying for goods and services to benefit the client before invoices are sent to the client. Therefore, a credit line of some magnitude is required to finance the work effort until the client tenders payment for billed work. The A/E firm advances both cash and labor effort in the expectation of being reimbursed by clients. This financial "float" can last for many months.

After bills have been issued, appropriate attention must be given to collecting the funds as an aspect of firm operations. The longer payment lags behind the billing cycle, the more debt the firm takes on through its credit line. Preparing bills and sending them out promptly helps to minimize the out of pocket financial investment of the firm. A credit line is essential to keep the firm operating while debts are being collected.

Collections are vital to the firm's success. Establishing a methodology for assuring timely collections will help improve cash flow and give comfort to lending institutions that support the firm. One of the first elements of an effective collections program is the assessment of a client's creditworthiness as a risk to the firm. Just as the bank which extends a line of credit to the A/E firm takes care to evaluate the payment history and credit worthiness of the business, the A/E firm must evaluate and scrutinize the owner or client's ability to pay for services to be performed by the A/E team. Having a valid contract is one thing. Having a valid contract with a client who already has the means to pay the bills or credit sufficient to meet his obligations under the contract is quite another thing. It takes additional effort on the part of A/E firm principals and owners to get to know and understand the creditworthiness of those who become clients.

One way to accomplish this is to ask the client for evidence that funds are available to support the design contract. Letters of credit, lines of credit or bank balances should exist to cover the basic fees outlined in the Owner/Architect Agreement. Creditworthiness is a major factor in the management decision to proceed with a particular project. If there is any question as to the client's ability to pay bills, then caution should be exercised. The owner of the A/E firm, (or senior management) must be prepared to make hard decisions and pass over a project if appropriate funds or credit lines are not in place as the design effort begins.

When economic times are hard and banks are lending less money to support design and construction activities, the decision to say "no" is particularly hard. If the firm needs the work in order to survive, exceptions sometimes occur to the basic rules of creditworthiness. When credit risks seem to be worth taking, outstanding balances and unpaid bills must be closely monitored. Periodic contact by telephone with a questionable client or a client with growing uncollected balances on account should be planned. Losses from bad debts pile up in an economic recession. The cautious A/E firm owner will minimize losses by requiring retainers up front and remaining in constant contact with clients in order to stay visible and in the forefront when funds become available from which the client may pay his bills.

In extreme cases, it may be necessary to stop the design effort and suspend work on a client's project. Shutting the job down, even on a temporary basis, is usually effective in causing prompt payment of some portion of the outstanding balance. However, this also places the relationship with the client in jeopardy. Discussions with the client about the consequences of delayed payment against billings should precede an actual work stoppage. However, the client must clearly recognize that failure to pay bills carries a consequence.

Incentives to encourage prompt payment of bills can be built into a contract. Charging of interest for all fees more than 30 days past due is one such incentive. If interest on outstanding balances is to be charged, it should be discussed thoroughly during contract negotiations and fully detailed in the contract. A commonplace dispute is the date from which interest begins to accrue against an outstanding account. Clarity of interest terms is important. Both parties to the contract should understand when interest is being applied. From the A/E's point of view, interest charges should be substantial in order to encourage prompt payment. Agreed upon interest rates should be greater than those the A/E's bank is charging for funds borrowed against the A/E's line of credit, up to the maximum rate permitted by law, without risk of violating usury restrictions.

If cash flow within an A/E business is highly dependent upon billings and collections, then it seems logical to suggest that more frequent billings will result in more rapid and more frequent payments from clients. Billing clients on a more frequent basis may help reduce the A/E's need for borrowed funds. Thus, the A/E's line of credit with one or more banks may be preserved for emergency situations when clients simply fail to pay in a timely manner.

Progress billing is only the first part of a strategy to improve collections and reduce the collection cycle. A follow-up system that requires a client's attention to amounts due should be devised. It is not enough to bill promptly and then wait to receive a check for these costs 60 or 90 days later. Assertiveness and strategic attention to amounts due will allow the A/E firm to continue practicing architecture and engineering without fear of becoming a banking business or a secondary project finance office.

Perhaps the most aggravating part of running and A/E practice is the collections process. Delinquent accounts receivable can mount and cause the firm to close its doors with debts to banks and unpaid creditors, all due to the failure of clients, to pay in a timely manner. This is especially true during recessions or in difficult economic times when delayed payment becomes the rule, rather than the exception. When interest rates are high and credit tightens, the collection of money takes longer and becomes more expensive in real dollar terms. Being proactive about collecting fees is the key to financial stability and long term survival. Cash is king in a shakey economy.

Various methods have been developed to keep tabs on billings and receivables in an A/E business context. One such method is the calculation and tracking of the number of Days a Sale is Outstanding (otherwise known by the acronym DSO). Firms of varying size use DSO calculations as comparative indictors of cash flow and aged accounts receivable. Firms will calculate DSOs differently, and there is no universally accepted method, consistent among all firms and every application. However, DSOs become empirical measures of the time a firm must wait to deposit money into its bank account based upon client payments.

Many firms calculate DSOs from the date of an invoice is prepared to bill a client for services rendered in the prior period. Other firms may calculate DSOs based upon the postmark that is applied to the envelop containing the invoice. Still others begin a DSO calculation by using time sheet data entered at the end of a pay period when the number of hours devoted to all jobs is routinely posted into the accounting system.

Whichever method or variation in method is applied, the firm must evaluate the data, understand its significance and use it to improve the collections process. The particular method is not as important as selecting a method that can be applied consistently, with improved collections.

Evaluating DSOs
The first step is to decide how the DSO calculation will be established and used. For example, if the beginning point of a DSO calculation is the date on which time sheet data is entered into the accounting system, this becomes a key date for a determination of how many days it will take to collect funds from the client on which project time (represented by these time sheets) was devoted. If 100 hours was spent on a particular client's job in a given time sheet period (the combined efforts of several employees), then the clock starts ticking from the moment the time sheet data enters the accounting system. Of course, the client does not yet know that these funds are

due. The first time the client is made aware of a payment coming due, is when he receives the invoice several weeks or even a month later.

One important aspect of this issue is the fact that fees have been earned and funds are due from the client many days or weeks prior to a bill being sent to the client. A DSO calculation would include all of those days when the fees have been earned prior to the issuance of the invoice and all of those days following the invoice up to the day when the check is deposited into the A/E's bank account. Therefore, one form of DSO calculation is to add the days from the recording of a timesheet up to the billing cycle with all those days subsequent to the issuance of the bill but prior to the client tendering payment. This is done on a project by project basis. Then all of the projects are either averaged together or averaged on a weighted scale (based upon the dollar volume of the projects).

To illustrate this, if a project has 100 person hours of unbilled project time in a particular week and it is 14 days before the bill is issued, the fees represented by those 100 hours are already outstanding by 14 days. Then, if it takes another 60 days (typical) for a client to deliver a check in payment for those fees, the total DSO calculation for that 100 hours of project effort is 74 days. This calculation can vary, if the unbilled portion of the DSO formula involves more than one payroll or timesheet cycle. For example, if billings are compiled and issued one time each month, and time data is entered into the accounting system weekly, this amounts to 4 time periods per monthly billing cycle.

Using our example, if 100 person hours were devoted to a particular project in each of the 4 weeks prior to billing, the average DSO for the unbilled labor is 14 days (the midpoint of the 4 week period). If the labor effort is greater during one or another of the weekly time periods, then this changes the average or median point. If the 100 hours were devoted in the first week, then no other time were posted for the remaining 3 weeks prior to the billing, then the DSO (unbilled) would be at least 21 days and possibly 28 days depending upon when the bills are issued in relation to when time sheets are routinely recorded. If the client pays the bill in his customary 60 day cycle, the DSO for this particular project will be either 81 days, or 88 days, or something in between.

Work-In-Progress (WIP)

```
| Month 1 | Month 2 | Month 3 | Month 4 | Month 5 |
   ↑         ┊         
 BEGIN       ┊      CLIENT BEGINS
 WORK      SEND     PROCESSING BILL
           BILL     ←————————————————→
        CALCULATE              90 DAYS        COLLECT
          BILL                 (AVERAGE)      MONEY
                     FLOAT
              (FIRM FRONTS ALL $)
 |←————————————————————————————————————→|
 $10k/EMP.
 PER MONTH
```

The A/E Float

When DSOs have been determined for each project, a simple average is computed to establish the historical DSO performance level for the office, profit center, or firm. Using this method of calculating DSOs will produce a DSO factor of from 60 to 90 days, depending upon individual project and client performance.

After the empirical data is compiled and used in this way to establish the overall DSO performance, the information should be communicated to principals, project managers and key project staff. Whatever the record of DSOs and payment history has been, a goal should be established for each project to improve its DSO rating. This will be easier on some projects. Others, particularly those with large bureaucratic functions, will be less likely to improve.

When certain agencies within the federal government began using automatic payment systems and electronic fund transfers, DSOs on certain federal projects were dramatically reduced. With this in mind, asking all clients to provide regular and progress payments electronically is beneficial. Agreements to provide electronic funds transfers should be stipulated in the Owner/Architect contract.

Strategies to reduce DSOs and improve collections on all projects should be discussed openly with project managers and other key project personnel. It should become part of the A/E firm culture to closely monitor DSOs as an indicator of the financial success of both projects and project managers.

This concept of DSO calculation and quantifying the amount of time needed to realize payment for services rendered points up the logic behind asking for and receiving large retainers when contracts are signed. A minimum retainer might be considered that amount sufficient to cover the cost of the first DSO cycle on a new project. If the client fails to pay the first bill within a predictable window of time (established by DSO ranges on similar projects), then it is time to contact the client and use the retainer to offset incurred costs. It is important to recognize that if this decision to take the retainer and credit it toward incurred project costs occurs in the 90th or 100th day of working on a project, the incurred costs may vastly exceed the amount of the retainer. Enough retainer funds to cover 2 or 3 billing cycles should be sought.

DSO ranges for project types and DSO targets for aggressive collections should be well understood by senior project managers. Incentive rewards are often provided in cases where a project has a chronically bad (large) DSO history. In such cases, bringing the DSO data back into a reasonable range, or achieving a deliberately established low target should be compensated in some fashion to underscore the importance of prompt payments (good collection efforts) to the firm. The PM, the accounting office, the collection agency and the bank may all become part of collecting delinquent accounts.

When the DSO formula has been developed and well understood throughout the firm, the case can be made for accelerated billings. In order to offset that portion of the DSO average attributable to unbilled labor or work-in-progress

PROFIT BY DESIGN

DSOs (Days Sales Outstanding)
From the time hours are posted on the time sheet...The revenue has been earned and compensation is due.
Client may not be aware of fees owed for 30-45 days.
Client may take 90-120 days to pay!

Typical DSO calculation:
  Average Days of Project WIP   = 15 days
  Actual Days to Collect after Bill = 63 days
  Total DSO = 78 days

(WIP), advanced billings should be considered. In view of the A/Es constant need for cash to meet payroll and expense obligations, finance projects and the interest cost of securing external funds, it is undesirable to defer billings for any length of time. There is no hard and fast reason to delay billings until after the close of an accounting period for the prior month. Billings can be and should be generated at least as often as prescribed by the terms of the Owner/Architect contract.

There are many ways to accelerate billings. Several of the most commonly discussed reasons to bill a client more frequently than once per month are:

Basis of Billing
1. If a progress billing is based upon an estimated percentage of completion of the work (segments, activities, phases), the estimated percentage complete is available at any time and a progress billing may be issued outside of a normal monthly billing cycle. Such progress billing can even be issued in advance of completing the segment or phase of the work represented by the bill.
2. If a progress billing schedule is set in the contract indicating that fees are due at the beginning of each

segment or phase of the work, then the A/E can control how many segments or phases are being worked on at any particular time, thus justifying the bills for one or more phases in advance.

3. If progress billings are permitted based upon achieving certain specified milestones or levels of percent complete, these events must be reported to the billing office by project management staff just as soon as possible when the condition of billing has been satisfied.

4. If progress billings are based upon actual costs incurred by the A/E, either at an interval tied to percent complete or as the basis for billing on a cost-plus type of contract, then project managers should be tasked with setting early cut-off dates for all incurred costs and make special strides to have all invoices, project expenses records and consultant fee invoices generated early. This will help the finance office in preparing a client invoice that is timely, complete and more accurate (reflecting more realistic costs incurred to date).

5. When cost-plus contracts exist and estimated billings are permitted, estimated bills should be generated to a high side estimate, with subsequent adjustments based on actual cost taking place at a later date. In this manner, estimated costs (and fees) could be billed on a monthly basis and additional billings (even those with credits) will be sent at a later date when actual job cost data is accumulated.

6. Long term, complex projects involving dozens of consultants and multiple phases of the design effort occurring in parallel should provide for billing at the beginning of each concurrent phase of milestone and as each consultant is engaged. This is much more desirable than the reverse, waiting until a phase (or phases) is complete when a consultant's work has been totally performed.

7. Another time when advanced billings might be permitted is when a close relationship exists between the A/E and the client. In a case where a billing cycle is not established by contract, efforts should be devoted to building a relationship between the A/E's accounting staff and the accounts payable staff in the client's

office. If the relationship exists, advanced billings and a polite phone call to draw attention to the bill may be well received.

Another way to reduce DSOs and improve the collection effort is to coordinate the A/E's billing cycle with the client's payment cycle. The A/E should explore and learn about the internal accounting practices of a client sufficiently well to submit bills in advance of a client's monthly closing cycle. If the client's payment cycle is monthly, then knowing the key dates and processes with the client's accounting office can save up to 30 days in a DSO calculation context.

Aged Accounts Receivable
Collections and DSOs are inextricably linked to an analysis of aged accounts receivable. The A/E firm's accounting system should provide an aged analysis of accounts receivable balances on a periodic basis of at least once per month (preferably twice per month). Each A/E firm should develop a timetable for reviewing aged accounts receivable along with an action plan for making collection calls or taking more aggressive collection actions. At the very least, the following types of information are necessary to assist in the control, evaluation and collection of balances due and overdue:

Name of Owner (or Client)
List of Invoices and Open Balances (by project) Name of Project Manager
Invoice Date
Original Invoice Amount Balance Due on Invoice
Aging of Progress Billings (30, 60, 90, 120 days) Analysis of Retentions
Status of Project (Active or Inactive)
Comments (a field of information to describe special circumstances or latest information gleaned from client contact)

Through such information, senior management can identify: 1) the amounts due on each contract as well as the total amount due from each owner; 2) the project manager responsible; and 3) the overdue balances for both progress billings and retentions.

The analysis of aged accounts receivable is an essential tool for determining what action to take to draw attention to the overdue account and provoke a payment (even a partial payment). It is worth noting at this juncture that just one seriously overdue project, with large overdue balances, can distort the DSO calculation for an entire office or firm. Constant vigilance is needed to collect overdue accounts.

Firms that make a concerted effort to collect overdue funds are generally more successful, more secure, and more credit worthy. If the bank which provides a line of credit for the A/E firm's use sees a high percentage of aged receivables being converted to cash, the bank will take this fact into consideration when making future loan decisions. Remember, the value of an A/E practice is not in equipment or furnishings. The employee assets are "walking assets" that can easily walk out the door. The only tangible assets against which a bank may feel comfortable loaning money are the accounts receivable (AR). The stronger the likelihood of collecting aged receivables, the better the asset.

Noncurrent account balances should be carefully studied, investigated and discussed before decisions on next steps. Collection procedures might include monthly statements, dunning letters, phone calls and personal contact with owners. Some collection efforts may be conducted in a golf cart, others over the lunch table, and still others with aggressive calls from a collection agency or attorney. Whatever the method, careful review and discussion of the proper course of action is critical.

Lengthy collection delays or partial payments from clients may be indicative of a misunderstanding. Project managers must be made aware of delinquent payment so they can politely inquire of the status of payment during scheduled job review meetings where the client or client's representative is present. In the event excessive delays or currently due progress billings continue to plague specific projects, the A/E firm's senior management should consider the feasibility of assessing interest on overdue balances. In extreme cases, stopping the work and/or withholding work products may yield the desired result.

Using empirical data concerning the amounts of money due, the length of time it is overdue, the creditworthiness of the

PROFIT BY DESIGN

client and customized billing practices can markedly improve cash management and cash flow. Establishing aggressive DSO targets for each contract will help instill a sense of responsibility in the project staff and improve awareness of earned revenues and profits.

PROFIT BY DESIGN
Relevance of Backlog

The design business is both cyclical and sensitive to economic change. An A/E firm must plan ahead to survive. Economic conditions worldwide can cause severe swings in available design commissions. The architectural and engineering fields are vulnerable to interest rate adjustments, construction starts, consumer confidence, School Board decisions, Congressional budget actions, regulatory initiatives, labor disputes, project cancellations and a host of other less significant factors that influence the general business climate. When loans become more expensive, less money to undertake design and construction projects is borrowed by owners and clients. When consumer confidence is low and the economy is sluggish, business owners and investors become conservative; less likely to initiate new projects and/or assume new risks.

When the political and regulatory climate is favorable, owners have an easier path to new project approval. Local politics, even at the County and Municipal levels, have a tremendous impact on the willingness of investors and developers to seek and obtain permission to begin new construction projects. Many variables must be right, when viewed from an economic, political and business perspective.

The volume of "work on the boards" can vary significantly from month to month (or even week to week) depending upon the firm size, general economic conditions, geographic location, and the virility of the marketing and sales effort within the A/E office. Measuring and predicting the work out ahead is partly an empirical exercise (based upon real contracts and other known conditions), and part subjective, based upon intuition, judgment and educated guesswork. Stability of the firm or office is linked directly to the accuracy of predictions about future business volume, revenues and profits. All three must be assessed and predicted with reasonable accuracy.

There are many definitions of backlog in use with the A/E community. Surprisingly, each firm tends to modify the true definition and broaden the method for determining the dollar volume of new work ahead. This makes for a complicated task when attempting to compare notes and backlog on one firm with the next. What some firms consider backlog, other firms consider merely a business opportunity or prospective job. Little consistency exists in the A/E field about the term backlog as a description of the basic condition of work logged on the books, which the firm will get back to in the future. This backlog becomes a vital part of the plan for an A/E firm's maintenance, survival, growth and evolution.

So, what is backlog? A useful definition widely understood in the profession is the quantity of work not yet initiated or undertaken, evidenced by ratified contracts (real written agreements), expressed in gross or net fee dollars. This is a somewhat more refined definition, specific to the A/E profession. Another well accepted definition is found in Webster's Dictionary: "Backlog: 1.) a large log of wood forming the back of a campfire or hearth fire, 2.) a reserve that promises continuing work and profit [for a business], 3.) an increasing accumulation of tasks unperformed or materials not processed." (Webster's Third New International Dictionary of English Language – Unabridged © 1993). The relationship between the unburned log in the back of a hearth and the uninitiated work on contracts which have been accepted by the firm should be clear. The work is there, evidenced by contracts with clients, but efforts to execute the work have not commenced. Backlog is the future of the firm or office. The work is signed-up and contracts have been fully ratified, but staff and consultants have not yet performed any of the contracted work.

An important aspect of backlog is that it is never static. Each day, staff performs more work on projects, leaving less work in the backlog for the next working day. Concurrently, new projects are being pursued and won, adding, new work to existing backlog, constantly replenishing the supply of future work. When times are good and business opportunities are plentiful, backlog should grow at a faster pace than that of performing work. Growth in backlog implies a healthy firm and permits decisions to be made about personnel expansion, specialization and overall firm growth. Declines in backlog (also known as the failure to win new work) require the development of contingency plans for staff reduction, expense reduction, surplusing space and equipment, and (if things get really slow), the ultimate dissolution of the firm. The rate at which backlog diminishes is important to the timing and sequencing of decisions to reduce staff, close an office, terminate leases, borrow money and/or fold the business entirely.

A healthy and viable A/E office is always adding new backlog as it burns through scheduled work. Many firms calculate what is commonly called a burn rate and attempt to compare the rate at which current work is being performed with the rate at which new contracts are being added to the backlog. This is a valuable forecasting tool, based in common sense, because it is important to know how long the current staff can be retained with only current work in the backlog. If the current burn rate is higher than the rate of new business coming in the door (for a sustained period of time), then senior management should take action to enhance new business development or reduce the burn rate by employing fewer staff.

There should be no mystery about a firm's backlog at any specified moment in time. Like the analogy of the log in the back of the hearth, senior management should be able to visualize and recognize the work ahead based upon the security of a contract or some other written commitment from an owner or client. There should be no guesswork. Speculation and the inclusion of soft commitments (usually verbal) and/or tentative projects can be fatal. The log in the back of the hearth is real, it can be seen, held, evaluated, protected, controlled and placed on the fire at the discretion of the firm's senior management. Tentative projects and/or estimates of some number of future marketing efforts being transformed into real contracts carries an unacceptably high degree of risk and distorts the truth when trying to assess the health and viability of the firm.

Calculating backlog should be a frequent event. Periodic updates (even several times per month) can be helpful in an effort to identify trends, peaks, valleys and pending potential problems. Evaluating backlog will demonstrate the pulse of the firm, new work in, performed work delivered and all staff actively engaged with work in process. Care must be taken to avoid inflating backlog through complicated and overly ambitious formulas, intended to capture and include some reasonable percentage of future work. Discipline in the approach to backlog determination is critical. The firm must employ consistent calculation methods and resist the temptation to overstate the description of the future. Variables should be held to a minimum. The statement of backlog should include a clear and concise written explanation of how the calculation was derived, complete with a disclosure of any pending contracts or tentative commitments included in the final figures.

Banks and lenders view backlog as a true and significant indicator of the A/E firm's strength within the marketplace. The amount of backlog stated and booked can be translated into some percentage of market share within the local area. Banks will compare A/E firms to determine which one or two might be stronger than all others. Financial Institutions will favor doing business with those firms possessing the strongest backlog and evidencing the brightest future. In a free enterprise system, some firms will succeed and others will fail. The larger the market share (evidenced by backlog), the more dominant the firm is as a competitor in the local or regional marketplace. Accurate statements of backlog should indicate the actual amount of work the firm expects to perform within a specified period of time, with bonifide, signed contracts to substantiate the backlog claim.

It is risky business to add some portion of the unknown to the backlog calculation. Yet, many firms deliberately add potential new work as an element of the backlog calculation. Usually based on experience with repeat clients or predictable events, firms can be tempted to add anticipated work (not yet under contract) to backlog. Regardless of the firm's history or track record in wining new work, the "don't count your chickens before they hatch" filter needs to be cast over all entries in the backlog ledger. Firms which routinely include some percentage of proposals issued in the preceding 30 days (or preceding quarter), run the risk of artificially adding value to the firm's total worth, when those values really don't exist. This can complicate the backlog determination and distort the overall value of the firm to the high side, presenting both an overly optimistic view of the firm's future and creating false confidence about the viability of the business. When a prospective purchaser arrives on the scene and begins to explore the notion of purchasing the firm or office, the very first level of evaluation is the credibility of the backlog statement. To be useful in planning and budgeting, backlog must be real.

While it is useful to keep data on the probability of new work resulting from proposals, business development, referrals, and repeat clients, these "hit rate" statistics should be evaluated separately from genuine backlog. Some firm's call this the business development backlog. With little doubt, some percentage of projects pursued will lead to signed commitments. However, such information is still in the realm of speculation and can cause suspicion in the minds of those who review the backlog statement. Banks, lenders, shareholders, investors, employees, consultants and even some interested clients would much rather know what is real and under contract.

Similarly, stale projects sometimes creep into the backlog statement. Old projects awarded months or years ago are suspect if they remain in the backlog too long. Even after the excitement of a new win, the negotiation of scope and fee, and after the ink has dried on a real professional services contract, the project may be placed on hold and/or terminated through no fault of the A/E firm. Occasionally, large projects are terminated and just stop before any work begins. It is possible for a significant project to be carried as backlog for several years before work actually gets underway. Therefore, senior management must scrutinize each entry in the backlog statement to estimate when the new work can commence. A tremendous backlog, with millions of dollars in contracted fees, provides great comfort to management and staff if the work is immediate and/or imminent. This same tremendous backlog doesn't mean nearly as much to projections of revenue, profit and staffing if all the effort is a year or more out into the future. In calculating backlog, all projects must be scrutinized and certain projects (regrettably) may need to be purged from the data base and de-booked to eliminate them from the realistic work projection. Just as "honesty is the best policy," reality is the best measure of backlog when decisions concerning risk, loans, cash flow and staffing projections (people's jobs) hang in the balance.

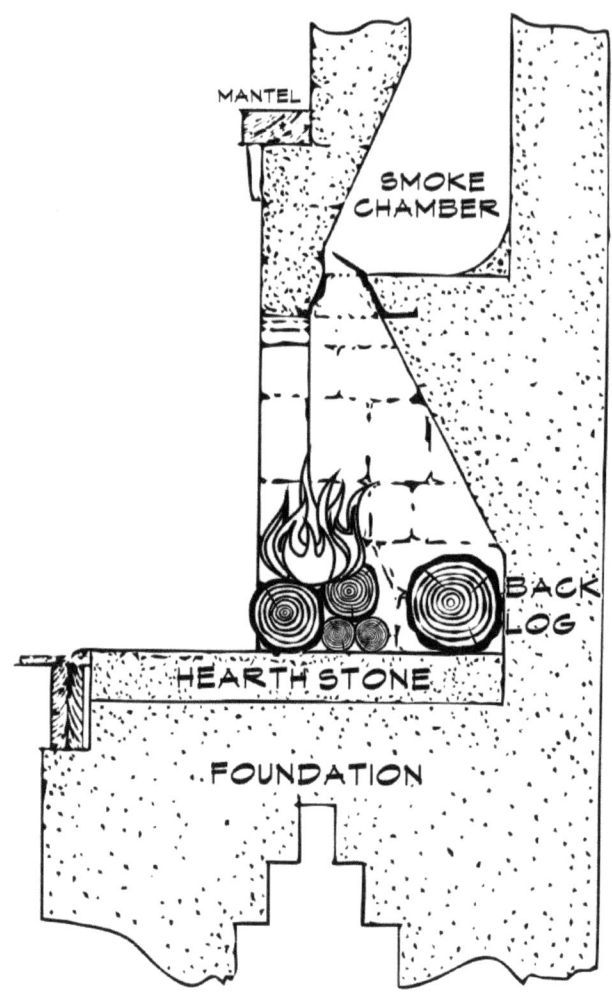

backlog (noun)
Synonyms of backlog
1 : a large log at the back of a hearth fire
2 : an accumulation of tasks unperformed or materials not processed

backlog (verb)
backlogged; backlogging; backlogs
: ACCUMULATE

source: MERRIAM-WEBSTER DICTIONARY

PROFIT BY DESIGN
Break Even Analysis

In order to determine at what point during the course of a business year an A/E can break even, several important pieces of data must be known. These essential parts are Fixed Expenses, Variable Expenses, Total Expenses, Total Revenue (Sales) and Profit Goals. From the annual business plan (see description of a business plan elsewhere), revenue and profit goals have been established for the current and/or future fiscal year. In order to monitor progress toward meeting established goals, a system must be devised to assist management with necessary mid-course correction decisions. The idea is to measure how well the firm or office is progressing and at what point revenues exceed total expenses.

One simple method to monitor progress toward meeting established Business Plan targets is with a break-even chart. Such chart may contain many types of financial information.

The simplest form of break-even analysis provides a means to determine the required sales volume (expressed in gross revenue) to meet all direct costs, payroll costs, and overhead costs. The point at which the volume of revenue is sufficient to pay all expenses and generate a profit (any profit) is the break-even point. A break-even chart also can be used to measure or estimate the profitability of various levels of revenue, beyond the break even point.

To construct a graphic break-even chart specific to the firm, the following items must be known:

1. Fixed Expenses. These are the expenses that will be incurred whether or not any work comes into the office. Examples of fixed expenses are rent, memberships, licenses, telephone charges, electricity, leases on vehicles and equipment, software licenses, purchase of supplies and/or furniture, and depreciation.
2. Variable Expenses. These are expenses that change with changes in sales volume or revenue. Examples of variable expenses are salaries, bonuses, consultant costs, supplies necessary for specific projects, incidental

PROFIT BY DESIGN

costs for project execution, sales commission (if any), reproduction, photography and computer software specific to a particular job.

3. Total Expenses. This is the sum of all fixed expenses and variable expenses.
4. Gross Revenue (Gross Sales). This is the dollar value of all work sold or commissions contracted and performed.
5. Profitability Target. This is the total number of dollars the firm expects to earn during the course of the year after all expenses have been paid. This figure comes from the business plan where specific targets have been set for gross revenue, net revenue and total profit.

Design professionals are visual people. It is best to communicate the idea of a break-even analysis by constructing a chart to illustrate specific points, dollar volume and variables. An easy method for producing a graphic break-even is illustrated below, using a hypothetical A/E firm, small in size, with modest revenue and profit goals.

Examples:

Basic Information
1. The A/E firm plans to contract and perform $2.0 million of new work in the coming fiscal year.
2. Fixed expenses attributable to keeping the office operational and functioning are $500,000, including all rents, estimated phone charges, utilities, equipment leases and depreciation.
3. Variable expenses for staff salaries, consultants, and supplies attributable to performing the work will be $800,000.
4. Total expenses are all fixed expenses plus all variable expenses, or FE + VE = TE. In this example, $500,000 + $800,000 = $1.3 million

Creating the Chart:

The first step is to create a vertical and horizontal axis (ordinate and abscissa) at some convenient scale large enough to be read. Place the $2.0 million revenue target at the top of the vertical

PROFIT BY DESIGN

axis and divide the remaining length of the vertical axis into convenient whole dollar amounts from $0 to $2.0 million (say $100,000 increments). The next step is to draw a horizontal axis the same length as the vertical axis. The next step is to draw a horizontal line equal to the dollar amount of the fixed expenses ($500,000). Then, draw another horizontal line at the planned revenue (sales) figure ($2.0 million). Next, draw a 45 degree line from zero (0) up to the planned revenue line. Where the diagonal line intersects with the planned revenue line, draw a vertical line back to the horizontal axis. A square is formed.

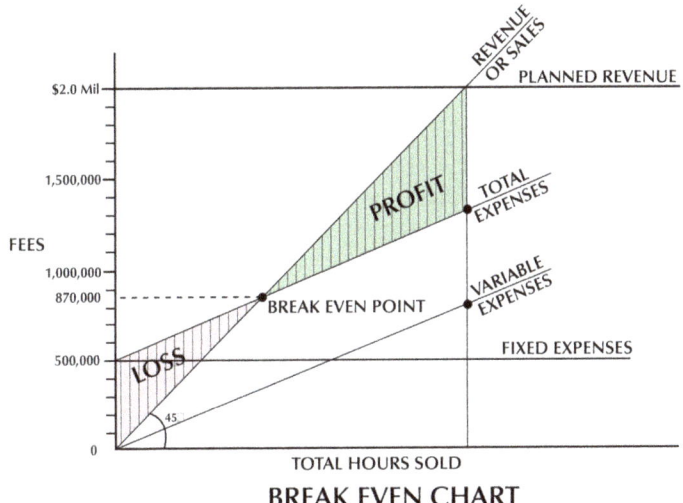

BREAK EVEN CHART

Then, draw a diagonal line from zero (0) across the square to the opposite corner and label it "Revenue" or "Sales."

Plot the total expenses along the right hand vertical axis ($800,000). Then, draw a line from the fixed expense line at the left hand vertical axis, across the chart to the plotted point on the right hand vertical axis, and label it "Total Expenses."

The intersection of the revenue (sales) line and the total expense line is the break even point. If another line is drawn back from this point to the left hand vertical axis, it will indicate the total sales volume required to break even (in this example, $870,000). The area below the break even point that falls between the revenue line and the total expense line represents loss; the area between these lines that fall above the break even point is profit. To evaluate the variable expenses, plot the total variable expenses along the right hand vertical axis and draw a line from zero (0) to this point. At any given sales volume, it is easy to determine expected total expenses, profit, variable expenses and (of course) fixed expenses. It is not necessary, however, to include the variable expenses line to monitor only break-even and profitability factors, as shown in the example.

This basic chart can be used to estimate expenses, profit, and sales volume throughout the year. With this chart, it is reasonably easy to determine what the total expenses and profit should be at any revenue volume along the sales line. To use the chart in this way, draw a horizontal line from the revenue amount in question over to the sales line. Then draw a vertical line at this point and read the total expenses, and profit. Senior management and any other users of this chart may compare planned revenue figures with actual performance. In this way, a simple and fast determination of whether the business is on plan can take place. If business plan goals are not being met, corrective action is necessary.

Using the same chart created above, to determine what the profit level should be at $1.1 million in sales revenue, draw a horizontal line from the $1.1 million point to the sales line. At this intersection draw a vertical line down to the horizontal bottom axis. Now, read the total expense as $950,000 at the point where the vertical line interest the total expense line. The profit is indicated (and calculated) as $150,000. Profit is the Total Revenue (Sales) minus Total Expenses (P + ? R - ? E) or (P = S-TE). Therefore: $1.1 million - $950,000 = $150,000 profit. The variable expenses at this sales/revenue volume are $450,000.

The break-even point also can be calculated by formula. This method is used when the only information is desired in the break-even figure. The formula is:

Break-event point (BEP) = **Fixed Expenses / 1 − VE/S**

For the example just discussed:

$$BEP = \$500{,}000 / 1 - 800{,}000 / \$2{,}000{,}000 \text{ or } BEP =$$

$$\$500{,}000 / 1 - .4$$

$$\text{or } BEP = 500{,}000 / .6 = \$833{,}000$$

This is slightly more accurate than the graphic solution (depending upon the scale and accuracy of the chart). Approximately the same figure is derived in each case. The disadvantage of the formula is that performance cannot be as readily monitored as with the chart. The chart reveals more information even if only an approximation.

The break-even analysis (using charts or calculations) provides a simple tool and relatively easy method to check progress against established goals and milestones. Many computer programs now exist to assist with such evaluations. In its simplest form, this tool is used to establish the relationship between revenue and costs, with profit being the difference between the two.

Management uses a break-even analysis to determine what it can expect in profits from various levels of productivity and work effort. This type of analysis also is helpful when considering the acquisition of a new piece of equipment or adding staff.

It is advisable to create a break-even point for every major investment, including expansion or acquisition of another office. Establishing a time frame for expected returns (profits) from an investment is an important element to the success of any business. Within the design professions, the more quickly a break-even point can be reached, the more attractive the investment. As has been stated elsewhere in this text, profit is something that should occur with each and every billable hour attributable to a client's project. Even so, the break-even analysis demonstrates how much revenue is necessary (the total earnings including profit) before sufficient income is generated to offset all fixed and variable costs. There are many factors to take into consideration in predicting the break-even point. However, the goal is to include all known costs, fixed and variable, and remove as many unknowns as possible. Computer programs and interactive accounting systems are widely used by larger A/E firms to monitor progress against business plan goals on a weekly and monthly basis.

PROFIT BY DESIGN
Internal Audit/Internal Control

The larger an A/E firm becomes, the more important it is for management to install an internal auditing system to periodically evaluate compliance with established procedures. The idea behind internal audits is to provide assurance to the Board of Directors (or other governing body) that internal procedures and controls are sufficient to meet the firm's financial objectives. The internal audit is a much different type of audit than a year-end or periodic financial audit. Many large A/E firms employ a full time, internal audit staff tasked with investigating and reporting compliance with a variety of procedures back to the Board of the Directors or CEO. Teams of internal auditors may actually visit each office within the A/E firm and explore various aspects of: 1) the reliability of financial reporting, 2) efficiency of operations, 3) compliance with internal policies and procedures, and 4) compliance with applicable laws and regulations governing the A/E business, including contract performance laws and regulations.

Internal audits within an A/E business entity have at least three specific goals:

1. to establish and review the effectiveness of internal controls to safeguard assets
2. to ensure compliance with established corporate and administrative controls, including accounting standards
3. to evaluate the effectiveness and efficiency of conducting business within a specific office, area, region, city, or related to specific project type.

Underlying the need for internal audits is the assumption that consistency of operational control between offices, projects, and project managers is important to the firm's business plan and profit objectives.

To the extent possible, the internal audit team should function as an independent and objective body, with reporting authority directly to the Board of Directors or CEO. In this manner, operating outside of the normal accounting office functions, a system of checks and balances is created which helps improve the effectiveness of procedures, minimize risk, and assure investors (shareholders and bankers) that corporate objectives are being met.

Controlling assets within an A/E firm is much simpler than in other types of businesses. Because an A/E has relatively few fixed assets, emphasis is placed on controlling the cost of personnel assets (walking assets), cash, contracts, and accounts receivable. Fixed assets must be included, but are less significant than other types of assets on which the business depends.

The professional nature of an A/E business and the relatively small amount of supplies and equipment needed to perform work makes risk of loss to fixed assets (computers, printers, copy machines, furniture paper supplies) relatively small. By comparison to the construction contracting business, where reliance on machinery and equipment is much greater, the A/E business presents fewer opportunities for assets to walk away or be lost at some remote site. The tracking and assignment of fixed assets in an A/E firm is a relatively simple task.

The second basic objective of an internal audit system is to assure that the A/E firm is operating its business in compliance with laws, regulations, guidelines and procedures. A determination of compliance with laws and regulations involves a review of internal accounting methods, specific contract requirements and other external technical mandates as they pertain to such things as government contracting, tax reporting, the SEC, and other regulatory entities. Guidelines and procedures usually involve an assessment of internal practices particular to the corporate culture, developed by the firm over some period of time. Written corporate policies and procedures are distinct and separate from state, local and federal laws; generally accepted accounting principles (GAAP); union labor agreements and other requirements not within the company's direct control. The internal audit is intended to assess the firm's operation methods and procedures to determine if they are effective, adequate and consistent as they related to external (legal) requirements and internal (policy) requirements.

The third goal of an internal audit system relates directly to project management and the role of the project manager in the day to day operation of the business. If a particular project or project manager has overlooked or failed to follow some established firm-wide procedure, the internal audit will reveal this and encourage corrective actions. The internal audit should evaluate whether or not a project manager is making optimal use of corporate assets (including labor) to produce the planned return on investment anticipated from a specific project or contract. The auditor should explore the project manager's decision-making process and challenge actions taken at various phases of a project. This effort is partially a test of sensibility and logic. The audit will compare the project manager's written work plan with actual performance. An internal audit should reveal those projects which are in compliance with internal procedures and those project managers who are fully utilizing the resources at their disposal in an efficient manner. Another goal of this aspect of an internal audit is to be instructive to project managers, pointing out ways of improving overall job performance and project profitability.

Firms that are large enough to use internal auditors should make staff and directors aware of the process by which audits will be conducted. If the internal audit function is a recurring operation, then it is useful to show the reporting authority of internal auditors on a firm organizational chart. If the internal audit reports are provided directly to a board of directors or CEO, this will reinforce the serious nature of internal procedures and the audit function. Internal auditors should have no vested interest in the outcome of the audit. Objectivity is key to the success of the audit and reliability of an audit report.

The internal audit function may be performed by a single individual, or an audit committee. Whichever the case, the auditor must have the authority to explore all records, documents, time cards, processes, procedures and details of contracts, subcontracts, expenditures, allocations and work in process. The draft audit report should be discussed openly with the project manager and the auditor should place considerable weight on the views and concerns of a project manager before a final internal audit report is delivered to senior management.

Elements of a Successful Internal Audit Program

When creating an internal audit program, the following basic attributes should be apparent to everyone involved:

1. The internal audit function is intended to improve firm efficiency and profitability.
2. The role of an internal auditor is important with primary responsibility to the Board of Directors or CEO.
3. The audit function is not bureaucratic, requiring secondary reporting relationships and additional paperwork on the part of an office or project manager.
4. The audit function is both informative and instructive. The internal auditor should use the results of the audit to help a project manager improve efficiency.
5. The audit is authoritative, based on actual data, time records, accounting information and verification that procedures have been followed. The internal auditor must be prepared to stand behind the audit.

In smaller firms, the necessity for an internal audit function is less obvious. When only one or two project managers are handling most projects, they can easily compare notes and discuss efficiency related to their work. Office policies in small firms are usually much less rigid and can rapidly change. Very small firms rarely even document their procedures or invent them as necessity dictates.

In larger firms, independent reassurance about the safety of investments is one driving force behind a strong internal audit function. With the number and size of projects in larger firms dramatically increasing, hands-on control by senior management is often impossible. The owners of the A/E firm, shareholders, and the financial institutions providing operational and project financing require independent reassurance.

There are no government regulations that specifically identify the internal controls required in an internal audit. The U.S. Securities and Exchange Commission (SEC) has guidelines for internal control relating to publicly held companies. Publicly owned architecture and engineering companies are rare. However, they are subject to the same rigorous public reporting requirements as are IBM, General Motors, General Electric and others.

One of the largest concerns of an internal audit is the firm's basic accounting system. Does the accounting system provide the basic information needed by project managers and operational personnel? Does it adequately consider project planning documents and compare actual and planned performance? Is the accounting system capable of determining profitability on a weekly or monthly basis? A major focus of the internal audit will be on the A/E firm's accounting system. The accounting system should be evaluated to determine if it contains certain minimum attributes, such as:

- Written policies and procedures
- Proper timekeeping procedures
- Separation of duties
- Periodic reconciliation of accounting data
- Recording and use of budgetary data
- Adequate audit trails
- Management authorization of critical transactions

Beyond the basic accounting system, the internal audit will investigate compliance with a variety of additional procedures, developed over time by the firm for internal control. There internal procedures might involve:

- Protection of Original Contracts
- Filing Procedures/Organization of Project Files
- Existence of Project Work Plan
- Existence of Office Business Plan
- Handling of Consultant Agreements
- Labor Allocations and Reconciliations
- Business Development ("Go"/ "No-Go" Procedures)
- Internal approvals, review & signature procedure
- Minimum project submission standards
- Graphic and reporting standards
- Transmittal/Correspondence records
- Standardized insurance/contract protection clauses

An internal audit can be approached in several different ways. The "complete" audit would assess at least 3 aspects of operations and office accounting. These 3 different approaches are:

1. **Contract Audit**
2. **Functional Audit**
3. **Procedural Audit**

The contract audit is intended to explore an A/E firm's largest, most significant projects. In theory, these large projects are the source of most firm revenue and profit. The audit will provide assurance that accounting practices and internal controls are adequate to maintain some established minimum level of project performance and profitability. The auditor will focus on a particular contract, and assess relevant factors such as percentage complete, income recognition, direct costs, overhead, cash flow, estimates to complete, profitability and the relationship the project manager might have with the owner or owner's representative.

The functional audit addresses the operational aspects of the office or firm. The many functions that make up the operational side of the business such as proposal development, fee estimating, planning, scheduling, contract accounting, purchasing, payroll, accounts receivable, inventory control, accounts payable, overhead allocation, utilization, shared labor, labor reconciliation, billings and collections are all explored evaluated and summarized in the functional audit. This approach to internal auditing is not project or control specific.

Procedural audits are those involving the firm's written procedures. The auditor will assess the adequacy of written procedures, such as may be found in a personnel manual, and test these procedures to determine if they are being followed. An A/E firm may have a broad range or written procedures relating to such things as time recordation, purchasing of supplies, continuing education, lunchtime seminars, expense reimbursement, credit card use, public representation, contact with the media, project recordation, etc. Any guidelines or procedure developed and adopted by the A/E firm to govern or regulate routine conduct, as may be found in project management manuals and design guidelines are all fair game for a procedural audit.

A thorough internal audit addresses all three of the above areas. The audit will be planned well in advance and announced to staff or the office involved. Sometimes, the audit is planned but no notice is given, allowing the audit team to arrive by surprise. This "ambush" form of audit usually points up those internal procedures not well understood or following consistently by various levels of staff. An ambush audit carries with it certain perceptions and risks that may be unhealthy to the firm's corporate culture. If the impression is given that Senior Management does not trust or respect the personnel in a particular office, this can lead to internal unrest, contempt for procedures and high staff turnover.

Audit Reports

At the conclusion of an internal audit, several steps must be taken before issuing a final audit report. First, the auditor should share the general findings and conclusions of the audit with an involved project manager or office manager. In part, this provides for some due process and affords the project or office manager an opportunity to explain or rebut any negative findings. In some cases, deviations from established procedures are acceptable, with adequate justification and explanation. This follow-up session allows the key personnel to clarify specific points. In this way the final audit report can present a complete picture, including the staff's own description of procedural anomalies, for the benefit of senior management, the audit committee and/or the CEO.

In addition to a summary of the audit's focus, methodology and findings, the final audit report should introduce recommendations for improving procedures and processes. If problems are identified in the report, corrective actions should be prescribed and fully communicated to those who must implement changes.

Most internal audit reports will set forth details of an identified deviation, prescribe corrective actions, assign responsibility for corrective actions and set forth a time table to implement changes. This usually requires a follow-up audit near the end of the time allocated for the remedies.

The follow-up audit normally will involve just a single person (perhaps as member of the internal audit team) who will revisit the office to determine the adequacy, effectiveness, and timelines of remedies implemented at the site.

Recommendations that result from an internal audit will address specific improvements and provide discussion of:

- Responsibility
- Nature, timing and extent
- Scheduling
- Process
- Implementation Technique(s)
- Desired Objective(s)

Auditors assigned to perform an internal audit must be objective, non-biased and able to evaluate actual operations based upon a set of facts compared with established procedures. An audit of this nature cannot be based on speculation, interpretation or conjecture. If established procedures are not well documented or well understood among the involved staff, this fact must be stated and senior management should take immediate steps to fully document, update, and explain procedures it intends to enforce. An internal audit process helps reinforce the importance of an A/E firm's business plan and profit objectives. Awareness of periodic internal audits will cause staff to accept the emphasis placed on achieving planned profits. The internal audit system may be used to educate staff and assure broad recognition among all levels of staff that established policies and procedures are important and contribute to the profit objectives of the firm.

PROFIT BY DESIGN
Profit through Cost Reduction

Perhaps it is too obvious – spending money and committing the resources of the firm eats into profits. It's one thing to earn revenue, and quite another to spend it. The profit conscious manager will be aware of all costs and take steps to minimize spending at all levels of the company. Each individual expense, whether project related or not, represents an opportunity to enhance the bottom line of the financial statement. Spending reductions, renegotiating supply agreements, shifting from purchase plans to lease plans, modifying work hours, creating a second shift for staff, scrutinizing postage and turning the lights out when the conference room is not is use . . . . are all areas to be explored (along with dozens of others) in the interest of improving profits.

Effective managers must determine if spending money to make money will generate more profit than not spending the money at all . . . . A/E firms must generate profit to exist, so spending money is something to be undertaken only when there is a high degree of certainty that a return on the investment will be gained. It costs money to operate a business. Alternatives exist to almost every expense (including rent) and the creative principal or senior manager will challenge each expense category in the ledger and determine how costs can be reduced, deferred, offset with income, or eliminated all together. For each expense there should be a tangible gain for the office.

Profits and people are often viewed as competing needs in a service oriented business. People are those walking assets that good firms must attract, cultivate, motivate and depend upon to generate work and satisfy clients. Spending money on items that will enhance these people assets and protect them from the urge to wander down the street is tricky, but necessary.

Costs, at all levels, must be scrutinized, but decisions to reduce costs, eliminate programs or benefits, or change the working conditions of employees should be approached delicately and with a view toward trading some cost reduction for another more motivational idea.

PROFIT BY DESIGN

Without question, design professionals are creative thinkers. That same creative and analytical energy can be channeled toward involving employees in cost reduction strategies. A design challenge can be cast down to teams of employees with the ultimate goal of yielding perpetual profit improvement.

Because they have been trained to recognize and appreciate systems and processes, they will welcome the creative task of devising new methods within the firm for reducing costs, maximizing efficiency, and improving profits. Employees can be an important part of the profit enhancement strategy. Soliciting ideas and proposals from teams of employees can yield remarkable results, and gain a sense of ownership among staff who see their ideas implemented.

There are literally dozens of ways that an A/E firm can reduce expenses or offset expense with new income. Using the firm's expense ledger as an outline is the first step in the process of scrutinizing each capital outlay. The expense ledger should be reviewed and the simple question why? should be asked for each expense item. However, the process shouldn't stop there. Additional questions such as "how do we generate income with this line item?" should be asked.

For example, one of the largest expense items for any A/E firm is that of rent. Rent is a necessary expense and a lease usually exists to commit the firm to this expense over a fairly long period of time. So, how does the firm minimize this cash outlay? How does the office get the biggest bang for the buck (generate income) from this expense? What can be done to offset some significant portion of this rental expense? Ideas can include things such as: multiple shifts for employees (reducing the rented area necessary to have all staff in the office during a 9-5 work day); time-share of conference rooms by neighboring businesses for a small fee); subletting areas not currently needed to conduct firm business; development of an office "laboratory," where employees become students and pay a small fee to learn new technologies or have exposure to new materials (this works well in reverse too . . . . where product manufacturers and proponents of new technology are assessed a fee for the opportunity to teach or introduce a new technology); isolate reproduction, plotting and printing services and subcontract for those services on a long term basis which would include equipment and space costs (rent) being carried by the service provider; allow a cellular phone company to rent antenna space on the roof or upper floor; centralize project files and eliminate redundant filing and library space, allowing more workareas, conference rooms or sublet areas, etc. These few ideas can be explored and cost models can be run to estimate rental cost reductions and offsets to basic rent outlay.

Another expense category relating to labor and personnel overhead costs can be offset (in part) by requiring managers to work longer hours. If overhead salaries are fixed (constant) and more benefit to the firm can be derived by managers working a 45-60 hour week (as compared with competitors), then the net result can be reduced overhead expense (fewer managers needed, fewer manager office areas needed, more space for revenue generating employees and corresponding efficiencies in payroll cost, insurance and benefits). Of course, management might be reluctant to accept such a policy. Yet, creatively assessing the "normal" working day might lead to specific recommendations about the working hours of certain managers and senior staff. Flexible hours for various levels of staff might be instituted and achieve the same or similar result as reduced management expense.

There are simple and relatively minor improvements to be discussed as cost reductions are sought. Such items might include: Contracting with an automated payroll service (reduce a time consuming staff task); having employees take advantage of direct deposit for paychecks (less time away from the office); convert the office time sheet system to an automated electronic time keeper system which appears on the CRT screen with recurring data already imbedded – to save time completing time records; provide a centralized mail delivery center (near the coffee room or repro center) instead of paying a staff member to deliver mail.

Another related idea for offsetting rental expense is to assess fees to clients or particular projects that may require special services or equipment. If the project involves model making and the model shop is dedicated to that project or client for some prolonged period of time, then why not charge the rental expense of that space off to the project? Similarly, if a large government project requires the firm to have a site security clearance and the work to be done in a isolated, secured area (a SCIF), why not charge a premium for the dedicated space and equipment to the specific project or government client (above and beyond normal hourly rates, fees and overhead)? These are generally allowable costs on federal contracts.

In certain types of A/E firms, such as interior design, additional revenue can be generated through sales commissions attributable to furniture and other products selected and specified. Thus, in addition to design fees, additional revenue is earned in the form of commissions, coordination and handling fees. Depending upon the jurisdiction and/or attitude of the firm about such secondary commissions being derived from product favoritism, indirect (yet equally tangible) benefits can be developed by the firm accepting donations of products and education services from suppliers and product manufacturers.

Other attractive cost saving ideas relating to personnel costs (payroll burdens, FICA, FUTA, vacation, paid holidays, sick leave, bonuses, 401(k), short and long-term disability, group medical, etc.) can be derived from offering staff higher basic compensation (direct salary) in lieu of certain benefits. Certain categories of benefit are optional to employees, but mandatory for the firm. Certain other benefits are flexible and allow the employees latitude to offer various levels of contribution or tiered benefits. If additional cash were offered to employees instead of some benefits . . . (provided the additional compensation was less costly to the firm than those benefits), the firm reduces cost for benefits and the staff earns greater pay.

For example, developing incentives to reduce absenteeism will pay benefits to the firm almost immediately. If the goal in an A/E design practice is to maximize the number of billable hours charged to projects in a given year, losing hours to sick time and personal time will result in lower profits. Incentive plans should be linked to productivity improvements (both an individual and team basis). Reductions in absenteeism must be measurable and compared with some specific prior performance period. Incentives could manifest in vacation bonuses, an extra paycheck or some portion thereof, gift certificate, free parking space for a month, or some other noticeable (public for all to see) reward. Reducing absenteeism reduces overhead cost to the firm, even if a new form of overhead cost (a less costly form of incentive) replaces the absenteeism cost.

Other less significant but still important personnel related cost-saving ideas include:

- Determine if new hire training qualifies for Targeted Job Tax Credit (TJTC) whereby a certain percentage of training expense (overhead carry for personnel) is refunded or reimbursed to the company.
- Explore child care service costs and tax benefits for employers who offer such a program for staff benefit.
- Establish a vacation policy which requires vacation time to be taken and used within the same year it is earned. If vacation time is carried over into the following year, salaries may (and probably will) go up. It will be even more expensive to the firm for an employee to take his/her earned vacation time next year or the year after, rather than right now.
- Develop a vacation and sick time buy-back program whereby employees can "sell" their earned vacation and sick time back to the company (at a reduced rate).

Still other cost cutting opportunities exist within most A/E offices, if management is alert and diligent. Such relatively minor cost reduction measures as renegotiating long distance carrier service, or cell phone rentals or pager agreements can all add up to real dollars and a margin of reduced cost that will add profit to the bottom line.

Additional types of costs that typically occur and recur in A/E firms should be evaluated:

- Renegotiate rates, terms, delivery and payment schedules with vendors that provide goals and services.
- Update e-mail, fax and copy equipment. Put controls in place to assure corporate use only (non-personal) of

company owned and leased equipment.

- Negotiate all telephone and long distance communication contracts to achieve the best possible plan or package. Remember, business is a two-way street. Data concerning outgoing calls is usually less than half of all telephone or fax activity. If it helps to play the "numbers game," the total call activity generated by the business may far exceed the volume of just outgoing calls. In an A/E business, this is particularly true. A single call out to inquire about a new product or to contact a contractor may result in dozens of calls coming back in the other direction.

- Develop and enforce a long-distance telephone policy that holds staff accountable for any personal long-distance calls they initiate from the office phone system.

- Install a computerized phone tracking system to allow all project related calls (incoming and outgoing) to be charged off to the project. Capturing project related phone expense can add significantly to billings, and help reduce overhead by noticeable amounts.

- Analyze utility costs to determine peak usage of power, lights, heating, cooling, etc. Ask the utility company to audit power and utility costs for gas, electricity and water (they will normally do this for free) and ask their advice on spreading or reducing utility costs. Equipment rotation, staggered equipment start-up, replacement of out- of-date equipment, running plots and prints during off hours, etc., can all result in lower utility expense.

- Use less artificial light during daylight hours and only enough task light at night to support production activities. The use of CRTs and computer drafting allows light to be turned off most of the time in studios and open office areas. Plotters and printers can be set to run in the evening when demand for power is lower and personnel in need of plots are more relaxed.

- Explore a fixed monthly retainer for legal expenses, rather than engaging a lawyer on an as needed basis. If legal services become necessary on some routine basis, seek out a lawyer who specializes in design contracts and construction law, understands the A/E business and is willing to work a fixed number of hours each month at a lower than normal hourly or daily rate.

- Use less expensive lawyers or collection agencies for small collection actions. They will normally perform the work for some percentage of the outstanding debt, but will not require up front cash outlay or monthly fees.

- Assign a senior level individual within the firm to the role of negotiator and "heavy" during all disputes. Let someone in the firm other than the PM, principal in charge, or Name Principal to play this role and empower him/her to settle all disputes in a timely manner. It is better to negotiate and settle than to litigate and lose.

- Prepare press release and public announcements using in-house staff in lieu of a public relations firm.

- In more significant advertising programs, seek out a relationship with an agency or partner that will share in development costs. If an agency is selected, get the agency to take the risk for a percentage of resulting revenues. This approach will save marketing dollars and minimize the risk of large scale advertising.

- Develop an "in-house" magazine for periodic communications with past, present and future clients. Sell advertising space in the company newsletter or magazine to offset the cost, resulting in reduced marketing costs and/or inexpensive advertising.

- Challenge insurance providers and level of coverage. Change insurance carriers periodically to cause competition for the firm's business.

- Use an independent travel agent for business travel plans, as they generally can find the best deals – and research the variety of discount plans available at their cost.

- Review monthly expenditures for hotel rooms and meals to support staff members traveling between offices. It may be that leasing an apartment near the office, (complete with maid service) is more cost effective than paying hotel rates.

- Develop and enforce polices for travel and expense approval prior to the actual trip. Advance travel authorization can help control travel costs and cause the employee to demand the best possible available rates.

- Evaluate whether excess property and equipment can be sold or leased to reduce carrying cost. If outdated computers and equipment are part of the excess property inventory, invite staff to purchase items no longer of value to the firm, or donate them to take a tax deduction for fair market value.

- Insist that gasoline and repairs for both personnel and corporate automobiles be purchased via credit card so that mileage and fuel consumption can be tracked.

- Keep car allowances and parking benefits to an absolute minimum.

- Insist on the same level of service (and at the same low prices) as vendors and suppliers are providing to the competition. Be diligent and check vendor/supplier costs frequently. Negotiate new, lower rates for goods and services whenever new information about a better deal becomes available.

- Evaluate bank fees and have banks compete for the

privilege of working with the company.

- Recycle paper for communication, drawing and specs. Waste paper is a huge bi-product of an A/E business, and reusing certain types of waste paper can reduce supply costs.

- Determine whether the company can benefit by relocating to another area, i.e. within the confines of the same metropolitan area. Investigate possible benefits (including tax benefits) for:
  a. relocating to a state or city "enterprise zone"
  b. new business job credits
  c. research and development tax credits
  d. tax credits for rehabilitating an older office building
  e. sales and use taxes for certain types of services and products.

- Explore a variety of business development and entertainment expense programs that can be carried by staff (or teams of staff in the form of clubs) and removed from the firm's expense ledger.

The ideas and suggestions above are only a small sampling of possible ways to reduce cost within a typical A/E practice. There are hundreds more! The place to begin is on the balance sheet, which identifies all categories of expense (general and specific). During the life of a firm, expenses can become so routine and expected that firms fail to scrutinize their cost/value relationships. Aggressive cost review and detailed investigation of all categories of expenses can result in bottom line benefits equaling or exceeding earned profits. Strategies to save money and avoid cost are every bit as important as strategies to generate revenue and produce profit.

PROFIT BY DESIGN
Facilities Management Outsourcing

The requirements of today's A/E business environment demand that we continue to search for more efficient and cost effective methods to conduct our business. Reducing overhead costs attributable to reproduction and printing helps achieve greater profit.

This chapter is dedicated to minimizing the overhead cost traditionally associated with reprographics, plotting, and printing. This is provided as practical advice to shift costs onto project accounts where the costs can be recovered. As pointed out in earlier chapters, reproduction expense can consume valuable firm resources. Charging reproduction and plotting costs back to the project for which these services are required is the issue.

Facilities management is a concept that arose from the high overhead costs associated with printing that exists in most A/E offices. The realization came to be that A/E firms (outside of the reprographics industry) would never be able to achieve the same quality, speed, and cost effectiveness in their offices as could professional printers. This is because reprographics companies have expertise in the systems necessary for output, can purchase machinery and consumables less expensively, and employ a pool of trained staff to draw upon to produce the work.

There has been a surge of interest in the past few years regarding facilities management and repro centers. In addition, project accountability became the most compelling reason to outsource a firm's internal printing needs. Firms are being asked to produce a wide array of services for their clients, often without compensation or a way of recovering the expense. Without the sophisticated systems and techniques used by printers to track all costs, many reimbursable dollars went unaccounted for. A better way to track printing expenses was needed.

PROFIT BY DESIGN

The following are some of the characteristics common to facilities management (FM), the outsourcing of an A/E company's internal print shop operations:

- The wages and the overhead associated with reprographics and office support staff are eliminated; they are supplied by the reprographics firm. This eliminates the payroll expenses of the current printing overhead.
- The ability to accurately account for every plot and print produced in-house eliminates plotting and printing waste. Every print and plot is coded to a project with project numbers.
- A firm's CAD Manager no longer has to devote valuable time to managing and maintaining plotting functions; they are performed by the reprographics firm.
- Technical staff and designers produce billable hours rather than spending time plotting and printing. Professional A/E time is dedicated to performing A/E services.
- The production of valid third-party invoices for reimbursement is done automatically.
- Accurate tracking for all printing and plotting means that all reimbursables are captured and identified with an income producing revenue stream.
- Highly trained FM manager(s) dedicated to operations will free up A/E staff to produce billable hours rather than manage print work.

Reprographics as an A/E Profit Center

The common way that firms regard printing is as an expense to the bottom line, much like salaries, supplies or rent. This has been the case for many years for nearly all A/E firms. In recent years, a trend toward outsourcing printing work formerly being performed by a firm's office staff has taken hold. The noticeable change to the firm's operation is the shifting of capital expenses from the firm's overhead to the company to which the work is outsourced.

The typical way a firm handles in house printing is to first research, and then finance printing equipment. Next the new equipment pieces must be attached to the Local Area Network (LAN), and employees are assigned to be responsible for its operation and upkeep. All of the work stations affected must be updated to handle the software involved. The capital costs are in the equipment, the equipment's consumables, the maintenance on the equipment, the servers and connections to the LAN and the employee's time that is spent managing the entire process.

After the steps have been taken to purchase the equipment and systems, the work has just begun. With regular maintenance, software upgrades, troubleshooting, coordinating in-house printing systems, networking, queuing, etc. even a modest sized firm can pose a tremendous reproduction challenge. In addition to these expenses, the company is now saddled with the fixed costs of a piece of equipment for typically five years (or more), regardless of how obsolete the equipment model becomes.

The costs that are the most difficult to contain are the ones that cannot be tracked. When a firm buys equipment, it first takes the time of someone in the firm to research, purchase, and finance the equipment. As a limited purchaser of printing equipment, they will be given retail pricing for the equipment, service, and supplies with no volume discounts. If the equipment is to be integrated into a LAN environment, it is possible that an inexperienced systems integrator or end user may be required to perform installation tasks. This self-integration can be one of the greatest causes of poor quality and inefficiency even with high quality equipment. The cost of machine obsolescence begins the moment equipment is purchased, leading to the cycle repeating itself.

The primary purpose for producing work in house is for the clients' benefit. Immediate access to prints and graphic materials is desired. Each print must be religiously tracked so cost can be assigned to, and eventually reimbursed back to the client. Doing so can be an extremely difficult task. Missing opportunities for reimbursement while the work is being done can result in great losses to a firm.

PROFIT BY DESIGN

If a firm is large enough, they may elect to hire their own employees for the sole purpose of operating a print center.

Since the primary business of the firm is not printing, selecting the right employees will be a continual challenge. Then training and having temporary personnel as backups when an employee is not available can be problematic.

In a nutshell, in-house printing requires a firm to outlay capital for equipment, systems, and personnel. The result of this outlay can be substandard quality, poor efficiency, misallocation of employee time, wasted prints, and uncaptured reimbursables. Firms lose money on reproduction and graphics. . . . The question is, "How much?"

One solution to this overhead cost dilemma is to find a reliable outsourcing provider. Companies like Pitney-Bowes, Ridgeway's and ABC Imaging of Washington, Inc. offer solutions to some of these challenges. An outsourcing equipment team is expert at purchasing equipment. The equipment, which is usually purchased at wholesale rates, is first shipped to the provider for testing. After quality certification, the equipment is placed at an FM location. The equipment team is also expert at coordinating the IT systems and servers which are necessary for each piece of equipment. They provide and update any systems necessary at the client's site. The maintenance is also performed by the provider with staff on call (24 hrs. per day) for any equipment failures. The equipment and systems are purchased and placed in a provider's FM facilities at no charge to the firm.

Providers like ABC Imaging have Facilities Management divisions that completely manages the entire FM process. The FM's are staffed with experienced operators. After mutual agreement on employee selection, the Primary FM Manager(s) and their backups operate in the client's office at no charge for direct labor. They are responsible for stocking the machinery with consumables, and coordinating offsite printing projects with other provider locations. The FM is linked to other off site printing equipment to assure A/E printing schedules are met. This is also done at no charge.

The remainder of the FM service is in the form of support of the managers that are placed in offices. There is a management team, coordinating all of the activities and ensuring backup personnel are available. There is an equipment team, that is ready to respond to equipment and systems issues. Finally, there is an accounting team, which provides the order processing that turns the work performed into a seamless and steady stream of invoices.

With the correct systems, equipment, and personnel in place, the FM service provides a dramatic improvement in quality. In addition, these procedures are performed efficiently, the firm's architects, managers, IT personnel, or other key employees no longer have to spend time coordinating internal or external printing. They focus on their own billable work.

It is clear that the FM provider is outlaying capital necessary to purchase or lease, install, network and run the expensive in house printing operations of the A/E firm. This is already a cost savings to the firm of tens of thousands of dollars. The key to the FM system, and how it turns routine printing from a cost to a profit, is in the capturing of all of the print jobs and properly assigning them for reimbursement. Even if a firm was able to do this as accurately as the FM provider, they would still be merely attempting to recover the costs that were paid. This is the most challenging part of the entire process. Collecting data on the hundreds of prints, faxes, copies, and messenger jobs performed throughout the course of a month is a business unto itself. To convert all of this data into invoices for numerous clients can be a task overwhelming to even the most sophisticated accounting departments.

The FM provider is usually experienced at capturing this data. Much of the data may be easily presented to a firm as third party invoices for client reimbursement. Even though the work is produced in the A/E's office, it is an arms length transaction. The A/E firm can avoid the intense scrutiny of clients pouring over invoices for printing that has been produced in support of their projects. This approach to cost recovery is not unlike retaining an independent expert or consultant to provide printing and reproduction services, much the same as other specialty consultants an A/E firm might hire.

PROFIT BY DESIGN

All that is necessary for the A/E firm is to include the sorted printing project invoices along with regular invoices for payment as "back-up". On top of that, the FM will provide the A/E firm with a discount for all of the invoiced work done. The amount that is charged to a client on the invoice minus the amount that the FM has been discounted for the invoiced work is a clear profit to your firm.

Facilities Management programs have been developed to save A/E firms tens of thousands of dollars per year. All of the costs associated with printing are absorbed by the provider and manipulated into an invoicing structure. The provider can make a profit because of the economy of scale involved in running an in house printing operation as an extension of its own facilities, and because of the volume of work that is done in the office. An A/E firm makes a profit because there are no longer costs associated with in house printing. Instead, all work is captured and assigned to a project. The firm achieves a profit on the discount that the FM provides for the work that is invoiced to individual clients.

Elements of Facilities Management

There are several successful FM providers who have been running successful Facilities Management operations for many years. From this experience, they have learned to continually improve the processes and techniques of operating FM installations. Today, providers specialize in coordination of all the different activities that make up daily printing operations.

Past history has demonstrated that Facilities Management Programs will show immediate cost saving advantages in the following areas:

- automated tracking of all work done on site.
- appropriately track costs for all reimbursable and non-reimbursable work.
- Proactive management of work creates the highest level of customer service.
- IT support, provided by the FM staff, keep in- house printing systems running, and aligned perfectly with work sent out.

- flexible pricing and professional hardware selection.
- improved efficiency of printing operations.
- provides a one-stop-shop at a location convenient to the A/E (on-site).
- 24-hour per day continuous operations at select locations to meet all A/E firm needs to accommodate the most difficult schedules.
- customized project billing (one invoice per project per period, digital or hard copy) simplifies an otherwise complex process.

Specific, profit related benefits are realized by A/E firm's when the take time to analyze the cost of equipment, supplies, and personnel associated with in-house printing. Reducing overhead by eliminating cash outlay for reproduction equipment is a significant step. Why should the A/E firm purchase or lease repro-graphics equipment and be forced to study and become expect on technical printing matters? If the decision is made to outsource through an FM services provider, then detailed accounting of equipment use and numbers of prints is possible. Even check prints (often the source of incredible waste within an A/E office) can be accounted for and assigned to a particular project. Cost recovery for all printing necessary to perform the work becomes plausible.

In a macro sense, if an A/E firm is budgeting 5% to 10% of its entire project fee for copies, prints, paper, supplies and reproduction, why should these project costs exist only on the expense side of the ledger. If the lion's share of these costs can be tracked, accounted for and reimbursed under an agreement with a client, significant profits can be added to the bottom line.

Facilities Management services provided by organizations such as ABC Imaging of Washington, Inc. are highlighted here as a clear and present example of how outsourcing works to the benefit of A/E firms. ABC's program is but one of many. There are other competing reprographics companies attempting to provide similar services. When the goal of an A/E firm or office is to reduce overhead, capture all project expenses, avoid up front equipment purchase and provide high quality work the FM concept works.

PROFIT BY DESIGN
Once Through Process

In the struggle to achieve efficiency of process and conserve resources within an A/E firm, empirical data suggests that project budgets are usually insufficient to cover the complete range of services and disciplines needed to accomplish contracted work. Expressed another way, the work effort usually expands to consume more than the available budgeted hours. Designers usually complain that inadequate funds were allocated to cover programming, conceptual design, preliminary design and design development. Project architects and engineers contend that the design phases consume far too many hours and a disproportionately large part of the total project budget, leaving insufficient funds for engineering and construction documents. Construction managers and/or field staff often assert that the construction administration phase is short-changed because project budgets and fees are consumed in earlier phases, before actual construction begins. These (and other) chronic expressions of dissatisfaction with fees and budgets lead to internal squabbles among and between staff. Competition among disciplines and the project team for greater numbers of budgeted hours results. There never seems to be enough time to adequately perform the work to the satisfaction of all team members.

Competition between phases of the design process and between involved disciplines is common place. The battle for larger project budgets is fought first with the client during negotiations, then internally with the project staff. Project Managers must arbitrate these legitimate concerns and control the design process with strong leadership, sound judgment and by employing strategic, efficiency-driven management techniques. It is necessary to recognize that fee agreements are based on performing professional A/E services for a specific client, with a clear scope of work, within an established schedule, for a calculated number of hours which comprise the budget.

The A/E business evolves around the selling of time at an established (and well justified) cost per hour. The cost per hour includes overhead and planned profit. If the work effort

PROFIT BY DESIGN

expands beyond budgeted hours without additional fee, profits are diminished and less revenue is earned per hour. Once the scope, fee and schedule have been established, the A/E diligently performs the contracted work and tries to achieve efficient use of time within each phase. As each phase progresses, decisions and next steps become more clear.

The entire negotiation between an owner and the A/E is predicated on the owner needing professional services and the A/E firm agreeing to perform those services for fair compensation. Underlying the assumptions on which a services and fee agreement is based is the idea that the A/E will perform the work one time, in an efficient manner. The Owner does not intend to pay for mistakes, false starts, redundant efforts, mis-steps are carelessness on the part of the A/E. When the linear design process commences, the expectation is that logic and sequential execution of the work will result in an acceptable solution and product. The process is expected to be linear, logical, sequential, efficient, progressive, and devoid of repetition. The design sequence, therefore, must be delivered as a Once Through Process in order to achieve planned profits.

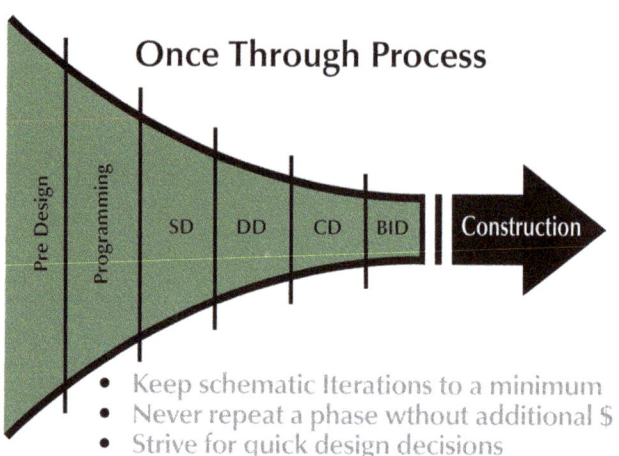

The Phase-Service Matrix helps illustrate the many categories of service within the sequential phases of the design process. The matrix implies that a project may not proceed into the next subsequent phase of design until the current phase has been fully performed and the client has approved the work.

PROFIT BY DESIGN

PHASE/SERVICE MATRIX

PHASE 1: PRESIGN SERVICES	PHASE 2: SITE ANALYSIS SERVICES	PHASE 3: SCHEMATIC DESIGN SERVICES	PHASE 4: DESIGN DEVELOPMENT SERVICES	PHASE 5: CONSTRUCTION DOCUMENTS SERVICES	PHASE 6: BIDDING OR NEGOTIATIONS SERVICES	PHASE 7: CONSTRUCTION CONTRACT ADMINISTRATION SERVICES	PHASE 8: POST CONSTRUCTION SERVICES	PHASE 9: SUPPLEMENTAL SERVICES (9a)	PHASE 9 (CONT'D): SUPPLEMENTAL SERVICES (9b)
Project Administration	Project Administration	Project Administration	Project Administration	Project Administration	Project Administration	Project Administration	Project Administration	Special Studies	Leasing Brochures
Disciplines Coordination/Document Checking	Disciplines Coordination/Document Checking	Disciplines Coordination/Document Checking	Disciplines Coordination/Document Checking	Disciplines Coordination/Document Checking	Disciplines Coordination/Document Checking	Disciplines Coordination/Document Checking	Disciplines Coordination/Document Checking	Renderings	Expert Witness
Agency Consulting/Review/Approval	Agency Consulting/Review/Approval	Agency Consulting/Review/Approval	Agency Consulting/Review/Approval	Agency Consulting/Review/Approval	Agency Consulting/Review/Approval	Agency Consulting/Review/Approval	Agency Consulting/Review/Approval	Model Construction	Computer Applications
Owner-supplied Data Coordination	Owner-supplied Data Coordination	Owner-supplied Data Coordination	Owner-supplied Data Coordination	Owner-supplied Data Coordination	Owner-supplied Data Coordination	Owner-supplied Data Coordination	Owner-supplied Data Coordination	Life Cycle Cost Analysis	Materials and Systems Testing
Programming	Site Analysis and Selection	Architectural Design/Documentation	Architectural Design/Documentation	Architectural Design/Documentation	Building Materials	Office Construction Administration	Maintenance and Operational Programming	Value Analysis	Demolition Services
Space Schematics/Flow Diagrams	Site Development Planning	Structural Design/Documentation	Structural Design/Documentation	Structural Design/Documentation	Addenda	Construction Field Observation	Start-up Assistance	Quantity Surveys	Mock-up Services
Existing Facilities Surveys	Detailed Site Utilization Studies	Mechanical Design/Documentation	Mechanical Design/Documentation	Mechanical Design/Documentation	Bidding/Negotiations	Project Representation	Record Drawings	Detailed Construction Cost Estimate	Still Photography
Marketing Studies	On-site Utility Schedule	Electrical Design/Documentation	Electrical Design/Documentation	Electrical Design/Documentation	Analysis of Alternates/Substitutions	Inspection Coordination	Warranty Review	Energy Studies	Motion Pictures and Videotape
Economic Feasibility Studies	Off-site Utility Schedule	Civil Design/Documentation	Civil Design/Documentation	Civil Design/Documentation	Special Bidding Services	Supplemental Documents	Postconstruction Evaluation	Environmental Monitoring	Materials and Systems Testing
Project Financing	Environmental Studies and Reports	Landscape Design/Documentation	Landscape Design/Documentation	Landscape Design/Documentation	Bid Evaluation	Quotation Requests/Change Orders		Tenant-related Services	Special Disciplines Consultation
	Zoning Processing Assistance	Interior Design/Documentation	Interior Design/Documentation	Interior Design/Documentation	Construction Contract Agreements	Project Schedule Monitoring		Graphic Design	Special Building Type Consultation
		Materials Research/Specifications	Materials Research/Specifications	Materials Research/Specifications		Construction Cost Accounting		Fine Arts and Crafts Services	
Project Development Scheduling	Project Development Scheduling	Project Development Scheduling	Project Development Scheduling	Special Bidding Documents/Scheduling		Project Closeout		Special Furnishings Design	
Project Budgeting	Project Budgeting	Statement of Probable Construction Cost	Statement of Probable Construction Cost	Statement of Probable Construction Cost				Non-Building Equipment Selection	
Presentations	Presentations	Presentations	Presentations	Presentations				Project Promotion/Public Relations	

Once Through Process

PROFIT BY DESIGN

With new projects becoming increasingly more complex and sophisticated, the range of professional services needed to accomplish the work expands. Developing a comprehensive Phase/Service Matrix, representing all conceivable service categories and disciplines is nearly impossible. Yet, standardizing the matrix and using this tool to manage the execution of the work within each phase is crucial. The idea is to avoid backtracking. At the end of each phase, the PM should reconcile the work effort with budgeted hours for that phase and make a determination as to the adequacy of the work effort. If all services have been satisfactorily performed and the project is ready to advance into the next subsequent phase, owner approval is all that is needed to endorse the advance to the next step. The process must move forward and the sequence must be linear.

Problems occur when budgeted hours are not adequate to fund the work within a particular phase. If more work is required than the budget allows, a deficit is created in one phase, at the expense of another. Any redundancy of process or repetition of steps within a phase will result in just such a deficit. If the deficit occurs early in the overall design process, each subsequent phase will be taxed to compensate for early problems. The client has agreed to pay for a professional effort "once through."

A Once Through Process implies that all steps within each phase and all sequential work will advance logically and follow the plan originally charted by the Project Manager. There can be no room for error. If the PM cannot maintain control over the project and perform the work in accordance with his/her own work plan, the project is doomed from a financial perspective. Controlling the flow of the work is paramount. Resisting pleas from discipline leaders, consultants and project team members for more hours and greater portions of the fee becomes both an art and a discipline unto itself.

The Once Through Process is therefore imperative to the financial success of any project. The following concept diagram illustrate how the Once Through Process overlaps the Phase/Service Matrix. Quite simply, the process depends on constantly advancing the process toward the conclusion

PROFIT BY DESIGN

Phase Service Matrix

Once Through Process

Once Through Process

of each phase, obtaining necessary approvals from clients, owners, and/or review authorities, then proceeding efficiently through subsequent phases. At all times, the PM must resist the pressures of iterative planning and design efforts. Herein lies the essence of a basic conflict between design gestalt and management. Designers strive to produce many design concepts and test improvements to a design through repetition. Designers entice a client or offer a broad spectrum of potential design solutions in order to learn priorities and preferences from the client and/or user. The design time to consider other options, ideas, and generate multiple design solutions is costly.

Use of Design Guidelines
In the above diagram, the mouth of the funnel at the kick-off stage in a typical project can be large and ill-defined. The loosely established boundaries of the process at the far left become more clearly defined and narrower in scope as the process advances. The efficiency of the process depends largely on the PM's ability to avoid backtracking and/or duplicating steps or phases within the process as it sweeps toward the conclusion of a project. Progressive flow of the work and momentum toward the finish line is essential to achieve profitability goals:

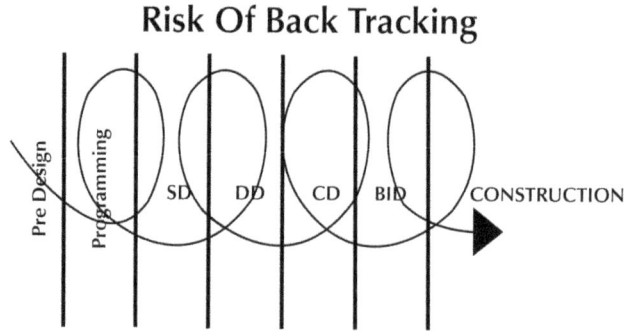

- Iterations are expensive
- Projects can spin out of control
- Client's get frustrated
- Firm loses money

If the process becomes diverted at any stage, profitability suffers. If the process stagnates or becomes suspended, anticipated (future) profits may never be realized.

PROFIT BY DESIGN

One successful method to prevent a project from being sidetracked or flowing into a backwater of iterative cycles is to employ design guidelines. Design guidelines help define more clearly the goals and objectives of the project such that the boundaries of the design process can be established and narrowed within well understood project limitations. This is not to say that the creative design process is hindered or constrained. The idea behind using design guidelines is that more of the available conceptual, and schematic time can be spent productively on potential solutions more likely to satisfy project requirements and owner preferences.

Quantifying the increase in profitability resulting from the use of design guidelines can be complicated. The graphics/charts above illustrate the concept of defining more accurately project requirements at early stages in the design process (pre-design and schematic design), in order to more quickly eliminate design options which make little or no sense, or hold less promise for tangible solutions.

Design Guidelines are developed using a team approach, with each major discipline and consultant participating in the early documentation of project goals, objectives and limitations. The client is a critical player in this process of defining project ambitions. So too is the review of feedback on the client's program from involved A/E professionals. In its simplest form, a design guideline is a restatement of the client/owner's project program, (sometimes with intuitive responses) annotated by the entire A/E project team. The more detailed the design guideline, the better understood and more clearly defined project goals and objectives will be for the entire A/E Project team and the owner.

Design guidelines often help transform unrealistic client and design team expectations about a project into tangible and workable potential solutions. The best guidelines contain an outline of what the client expects the project to become including pre-conceptions about image, cost, longevity, use, construction schedule and materials. When compared with a design teams' view of these same issues, remarkable contrasts develop which precipitate an agenda for clarification and refinement of the overall project program.

PROFIT BY DESIGN

To prepare a design guideline, a meeting involving the client and key members of the A/E's design team should take place so that the client may (convey) to the team his ambitions, ideas, goals and limitations. Such items are usually well understood by the client or owner, but far less well communicated to the A/E team. An enormous amount of design time, effort, iterative conceptual planning, illustrations and fee can be consumed in the early stages of design trying to achieve a common understanding of project goals among the players. The PM should never allow the design process to begin in earnest (and invest valuable professional time) without seeing eye to eye with the client and without the client having complete confidence in the fact that the A/E design team shares the same set of motivations and ambitions for the project. The Once Through Process depends on clear communication.

Following a kick-off meeting, with the client during which the client's ambitions and goals are shared and questions from the A/E team can be asked, the design team adjourns (sometimes for days or weeks) to synthesize the client's program and develop a draft design guideline. This draft becomes the agenda for a subsequent meeting with the client to feed back to the client interpretations discussed by design team members. This meeting many manifest itself as a working session, complete with tracing paper, markers, lap tops, calculators, and reference materials as the entire A/E team communicates its interpretation of the client's needs and goals back to the client. This session should be well attended by senior members of the A/E team with all disciplines and major consultants represented. The session may take several hours or several days, but the value to the project is immeasurable.

At the conclusion of the second design guideline session, all decisions, interpretations, opinions and a revised client program should be recorded and circulated for final review and concurrence by all parties. The best design guidelines are well organized and thoroughly detailed, sometimes including a conceptual design and an outline set of desired construction materials in the form of a skeletal (outline) material specification.

With an owner/client approved set of design guidelines,

the A/E team can then be confident that professional time invested in each step of the process will be well spent. With better project understanding and many early design decisions established in the guidelines, minimal wasted effort, false starts and speculative concepts will be explored in vain.

The value of design guidelines can be seen first in a reduction of person hours invested in up front iterative design schemes and, later, a corresponding reduction in competition between later phases of the design process. By utilizing guidelines, the PM can more accurately plan and manage the hours required to fulfill requirements within each phase.

Part of a design guideline should address and describe deliverables (in detail) at the conclusion of each design phase. In this way, all project team members may focus on the physical components of each set of deliverables. The client will know what to expect at the end of each milestone. This tool also provides the PM with a basis from which to allocate design and production time.

An inherent benefit of a design guideline strategy is derived from the involvement of more senior and seasoned design professionals in early stages of the project to participate in early design and engineering decisions. The earlier that senior design and technical talent can be focused on the project (as in design guideline preparation), the more rational and economical the design solutions will be. Less time will be expended in trial and error type cycles with less experienced staff attempting to obtain new-experiences and "go to school" at the expense of the project budget.

Although it may seem counter-intuitive, using more experienced A/E team members at the early stages of design (even at most higher salary and expense rates) helps keep the project from going astray. As early design decisions are made and directions become more clear as to material and specification details, senior staff can withdraw and oversee the production effort. Getting greater numbers of people involved in the early stages of design is desirable, but they must be the correct people . . .

. experienced and forthcoming with their ideas and conceptual recommendations.

This idea of streamlining project production is consistent with a Once Through Process. As the work processes and the flow/stream narrows in the Once Through Process diagram, so too the number of staff involved in the production of documents decreases. What may seem contrary to the traditional design process approach which involved greater numbers of employees and disciplines as the work processes, is, in fact, crucial to achieving planned profits.

As has been the case on far too many projects in an incalculable number of firms, as the deadline approaches for 70%, 90% or 100% C.D.s, the "kitchen sink" is thrown at the project. This is often the case toward the conclusion of each phase or major project milestone. Avoiding this tendency to call in the cavalry as deadlines approach is important. When panic sets in and PMs begin pulling staff from other projects and work-in-progress, chaos results. Profits cannot be controlled when the design process is in a periodic state of chaos.

The following diagram conceptually illustrates the contrast between the traditional approach to linear design delivery and a streamlined/integrated approach involving senior discipline leaders up front at the design guideline and kick-off stages.

Design guidelines and early design decisions, with collective buy-in from the owner/client and A/E team members, can dramatically reduce wasted efforts and preserve project budgets so that adequate effort can be deployed at each stage in the process. Involving more senior discipline leaders early in the process results in more rapid, early design decisions. Making design decisions quickly, with owner concurrence, preserves budget for the production of higher quality construction documents.

Allocating design, engineering and production resources carefully, deliberately and in the proper sequence are

PROFIT BY DESIGN

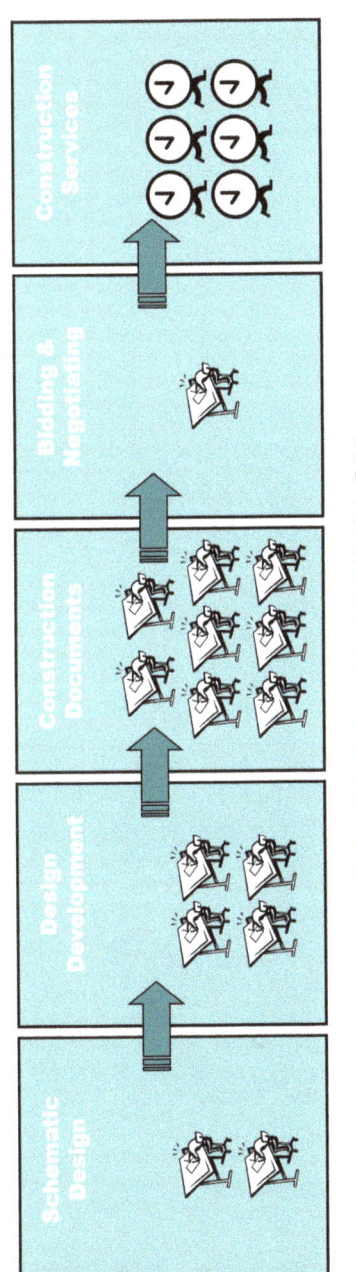
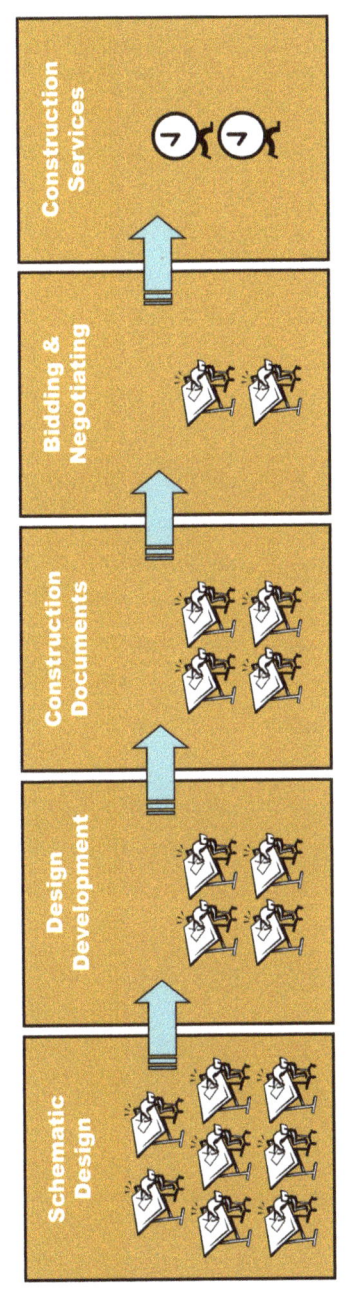

Once Through Process 175

PROFIT BY DESIGN

characteristics of the Once Through Process. Correctly using design guidelines and being vigilant about staffing budgets, revenues and profit are key elements of the process.

PROFIT BY DESIGN
Planning for Negotiation

Negotiation is second nature for most owners and managers. In fact, most business owners negotiate with customers, employees, suppliers, lenders, spouses and children on a daily basis. Many books and magazine articles have been authored on the subject of negotiation. Very little of that guidance is focused specifically on the architectural and engineering business community.

Recently, a text entitled Architect's Essentials of Contract Negotiations, by Ava J. Abramowitz was published by John Wiley & Sons. In addition to the advice and approach described herein, further details about negotiations can be explored in that book.

Two more good sources of advice and commentary on negotiating (written with A/E firms in mind) are the Architect's Handbook of Professional Practice (Thirteen Edition), published by the AIA, and A User's Guide to Federal Architect-Engineer Contracts, by James B. Goodowens. These two books contain concise recommendations for preparing to enter into negotiations which clients, suppliers, creditors, staff and consultants. Many suggestions first put forth in these documents are expanded and restructured in this chapter, to simplify preparations for negotiations.

Beyond these well known sources of information is a more obscure publication entitled Hammer& Tongs, Tools for Negotiation in the Construction Industry, by Christopher L. Grant. This brief 38-page document contains simple, yet refreshing ideas on how to prepare and conduct an important negotiation.

This chapter attempts to capture the basic steps in planning for a negotiation with emphasis on the notion that all negotiations are important. Each victory at the negotiating table, no matter how small, whether with clients, suppliers, vendors, bankers or staff, leads to improved profits and better financial performance.

PROFIT BY DESIGN

Just as every business should have a business plan, and every investment portfolio should be derived from an investment plan, a negotiation should never be entered into without a negotiation plan. Laying out the goals and objectives of each negotiation and clearly expressing the steps and sequencing of issues, proffers, and concessions are key to preparing for a negotiation.

Negotiations are frequently combative, argumentative and frustratingly unproductive early in the session. Then, as each party's views and opinions become clear to the opposing side, a more productive and more congenial atmosphere evolves. Some negotiations require multiple sessions, frequent meetings and discussions on smaller components of the overall program, and even some "grandstanding" to add emphasis and drama. Other negotiations are brief and informal. Some are even conducted by telephone or with e-m ail without contentious meetings or protracted compromise of scope and fee.

The idea of a negotiation is to achieve an agreement that is acceptable to both parties. All negotiations are unique and each is characterized by one party being slightly more (or less) satisfied than the other. However, ultimately, they both agree and a deal is born. Most successful negotiations result in a deal that is desirable to one or both of the parties. Yet, a negotiation that results in no deal is also a successful negotiation. If no compromise in scope or fee is possible and no middle ground can be reached through a series of steps and concessions on both parts, then an agreement to disagree is still a successful negotiation.

Preparing for negotiation is similar to preparing for battle. This battle is intellectual combat on many levels. At the negotiating table (the battlefield) a strategy and a series of tactics are employed to engage the opposition and maneuver the opponent into a position of compromise and concession. The strategy is an overall negotiating plan, with clearly outlined objectives and a set of predictable events laid out in an expected sequence. Tactics are smaller, (more specific and more variable) and sometimes contingent upon certain preceding events.

Strategy is critical to a successful negotiation. Tactics are important too, and the skilled negotiator will have mastered both aspects of the game. As the battle unfolds over the negotiating table, tactic after tactic will be set in motion (like the volley on a tennis court) until the skill level and strength of the opposition is known. Learning the strengths and weaknesses of an opponent is an important aspect of successful negotiating.

Some negotiators will place emphasis on strategy over tactics; putting more value in the overall battle plan than the arsenal of arguments or the sequence of shots fired. Others will take the opposite approach, and place heavy emphasis on a precise sequencing of discussions, resolving each microscopic issue on a prepared agenda, in exact order until all elements have been resolved.

According to Chris Grant's book Hammer and Tongs, . . . "The outcome of a given negotiation is determined principally by the relative strategic power of the parties." This implies that both parties develop and deploy a strategy at the negotiating table, and one party will prevail over the other. One party will have greater strategic power than the other. This could manifest itself as: a.) a better strategic plan, b.) better and more skilled negotiators, c.) greater resolve to persuade the other party, or d.) some better combination of these three things. Planning for a negotiation, therefore, requires: developing both strategy and tactics; involving skilled negotiators; and being persuasive at the negotiating table.

Architects and engineers usually enjoy the highest rung on the design and construction ladder. As such, A/E firms are usually first to argue their case with a client (any owner) as a project gets underway. Most clients will not yet have finalized a project budget, talked with a contractor, negotiated with a bank, obtained financing, met regulatory requirements, or even engaged legal counsel prior to discussing a potential project with an architect or engineer. This means that the client is likely to be both cautious about these early discussions and ill-prepared to negotiate scope and fee.

The experienced A/E firm and the well trained negotiator representing the design firm usually have a distinct strategic advantage over the client as a negotiation commences. The client is ignorant (unknowing) about the nuances of the design process and the elements of A/E practice. Negotiating fees to support and pay for these activities is not something routine for the owner or client. The A/E is much more knowledgeable about architecture and engineering practice – and much better able to estimate fees and costs necessary to execute the work. Knowledge is power and the strategic advantage in the beginning of every negotiation with a client should rest with the A/E.

On the other hand, the client may be a large corporation or federal government agency with decades of experience negotiating A/E contracts. This levels the playing field and presents a serious strategic hurdle for the A/E to overcome. If the client is more experienced than the A/E at architectural and engineering contract negotiations, the strategic advantage goes to the client and discussions over the negotiating table are likely to be animated, emotional and intense. The client may be less receptive to instruction by the A/E.

The design and construction industry has certain characteristics that distinguish it from other large segments of our national economy. The number of providers and suppliers of goods and services is one such special characteristic. This industry comprises many small companies that actively compete for their part of the market share. Competition among architects, engineers, contractors, subcontractors, suppliers, manufacturers, and the increasing number of specialty consultants is intense. Being selected to perform the required work or design the client's project is a huge accomplishment which may take months to achieve. The honor and prestige of being selected is so great that negotiations may be tainted by goodwill and the contract may produce inherent losses as a consequence of poor negotiations. The idea that a client may terminate a negotiation and move on to the next A/E is a point often raised to support the client's low budget, overly ambitious schedule, or lack of clarity about scope and level of service.

The A/E negotiator must be aware of the client's potential ultimate decision to walk away from the table and terminate discussions. With this in mind, the A/E negotiator usually tries to retain the client's interest and desire to complete the negotiations.

According to Grant, an appropriate strategy for negotiation is based on bargaining power. A strategy must be weighed against some other acceptable, alternative outcome. One such possible alternative is failing to negotiate a deal and losing the commission. If the A/E firm can afford to have the negotiation of a contract fail, then there is bargaining power. Such power can be viewed as an offset to the client's similar bargaining power, which is . . . . "let's go talk to the competition." If the A/E firm has a low back log, or has made business decision to branch out into a new building type, then the firm may not be able to walk away from the design opportunity. In this case, the A/E has little or no bargaining power.

Negotiating A/E fees and contracts can be hindered by the absence of factual data from which to establish a negotiating position. The factual data that comprises part of any negotiation position (at a minimum) includes to hourly rates, indirect costs, reproduction costs and quantifiable aspects of overhead such as telephone charges or the purchase of new software specific to the project. Nearly everything else put forward in a negotiation requires qualitative thinking, speculation, judgment and guesswork.

The number of employees assigned to the project, their utilization, the number of drawings estimated to be in the set, the size and scope of the specifications, the number of pages and level of detail in a construction cost estimate, and the schedule by which the various stages of design will be achieved are all judgmental, requiring discussion and ultimately an agreement. There are many variables in the way an A/E firm will approach a project. Different A/E firms may employ vastly different approaches to the same project, with widely differing schedules and costs. This can be illustrated by the fact that no two A/E firms will produce the same number of drawings in a set of C.D.s.

The Architect's Handbook of Professional Practice contains concise recommendations for negotiating an agreement with a client. In the AIA Handbook emphasis is placed on being careful with proposals and written claims of expertise, capability and fee. Often, proposals become part of a contract. Other times, the proposal represents the basis for a negotiation from which only downward departures are acceptable to a client. When pursuing a particular project, the A/E firm must evaluate the form of a proposal and determine the risks (if any) in making assertions or claims about credentials, staffing, schedules, consultant team members and fees.

The basic components of an agreement between the owner and architect are well established in the various AIA Standard Forms of Agreement. Every clause in a contract is subject to negotiation. Therefore, a standard contract may be used as an outline to conduct a contract negotiation. This may be appropriate on smaller, less complex projects where scope and other conditions are clear to both parties. As stated earlier, a skillful negotiation will involve clear objectives to be accomplished during a negotiation and a strategy for achieving the goal. It is not generally a good idea to follow a pre-printed standardized "agenda" to conduct a sophisticated negotiation. No two negotiations are alike.

The AIA sets forth six suggestions to guide architects toward proper negotiations. These steps include:

1. Establish Project Requirements
Prepare a written statement of project requirements with minimum criteria including: project use, site, levels of quality and amenity; role of the project; scheduling constraints; target date for completion; budget; sources of financing; and anticipated key project team members.

2. Describe Project Tasks and Assign Responsibility for Each
Key to a successful negotiation is a clear understanding of who will be responsible for what task throughout the entire design and construction process. Owners have responsibilities to provide certain data to the A/E team and to

perform various tasks along the way, in the interest of their project. The A/E has specific tasks to perform, some of which are contingent upon the owner's ability to perform. A successful project results from the design and construction process proceeding smoothly, with both parties to the contract performing their respective roles in a timely and professional manner. Both parties should identify the administrative, design, construction, and facility operation tasks that must be undertaken to achieve project objectives. Both parties should then identify the services required for the project and who will be responsible for each.

3. Identify Schedule Requirements

This involves a determination of project schedule and milestones as well as any special scheduling constraints that might exist on the part of the A/E. Each project task defined above should be placed on a timeline, with specific assignment of responsibility, and a duration must be estimated for every task. In preparing for a negotiation, the A/E must be particularly careful in this step because a number of variables beyond the A/E's control could impact the project schedule. Such things as project financing, zoning approvals, plan reviews, consultant work schedules, public hearings, neighborhood meetings, client review times, the number of supplemental review submissions, etc. can delay completion of the project. Clarity of schedule and responsibilities along with a recognition of events that could unavoidably after that schedule, is necessary for a successful negotiation and reasonable contract.

The best project schedules allow enough time for decision making. The A/E should ask critical questions before committing to a schedule such as: "Is the schedule reasonable?"; "Have I allowed enough time to prepare each submission?" "Will the owner have enough time to adequately review each submission?"; and "Will the regulatory agencies have sufficient time to review and comment on submission for approvals and permits?"

4. Establish a Basis for Compensation

Of all the many ways to develop and prepare a fee proposal, none is more reliable than a precise calculation of man hours, labor costs, indirect costs, consultant fees, expenses, contingent costs and profits. Whatever choice is made at this juncture with regard to developing a proposed project fee, be certain that it is both logical and defensible. One of the most embarrassing moments for any negotiator representing the A/E side of the table is for the question "why?" to be asked by the opposing side. There must be an answer and the explanation should make sense. Postulating fees for complex architectural and engineering projects cannot be done properly by applying a percentage of the construction cost to the owner's budget. Both figures may be wildly in error and neither may be rationale or defensible.

5. Select a Form of Agreement

This final step may be the simplest. The AIA and several engineering societies publish a wide range of standard contracts which may be easily modified and tailored to suit a particular project type and/or client type. Such standard agreements are widely accepted within the industry and tested in courts of law throughout the United States. These contracts are usually tied to the AIA-201 General Conditions of the Contract for Construction which helps establish clear sets of responsibilities for the Owner, the A/E, and the Contractor.

Beware of all non-standard forms of agreement prepared by the owner or the owner's attorney. Scrutinize every agreement before entering into negotiations. Raise objectives about the form of contract and specific contract terms before the negotiation to assure thorough discussion of contract clauses before any agreement is signed and ratified. Planning a negotiation includes knowing what form of agreement will be used to retain and commit design services. If the form of agreement is not a conventional standard form of agreement, then a portion of the negotiation should be dedicated to discussing all contract terms and conditions. Even though this is tedious, the detailed discussion of contract terms will usually point up opportunities for additional services and/or reasons to justify additional compensation.

6. Develop the Strategy

It is expected that an A/E will establish a bottom line fee below which the firm will not venture during a negotiation. It is appropriate to define this number and discuss the minimum scope of services that can be purchased with this minimal fee. There must be a bottom line scope of services that corresponds to the bottom line fee. Then, the A/E must be prepared to walk away from the negotiating table if it becomes clear during negotiations that the client expects more work for less money. The bottom line must be the bottom line and the proper conclusion to a session wherein the client attempts to reduce the compensation to a level below the bottom line, is to terminate discussion and leave the project in the hands of the owner.

Each side in negotiation will view the project, process, schedule and value of the design services differently. Even two or more A/E firms will view the project differently and approach the fee negotiation from discordant vantage points. There is nothing unusual or wrong with this. A major part of the negotiation must be devoted to talking about the scope, process, schedule and nuances of the proposed project. The idea is to interest the client in understanding the A/E's point of view. Education is part of negotiation. Benjamin Franklin said in Poor Richard's Almanac: "If you would persuade, speak of Interest, not to Reason."

Each side in a negotiation will have separate views and expectations about what is meant by a "successful negotiation." From the client's perspective, a successful negotiation is one in which the owner is able to achieve its project requirements in a timely and acceptable manner and at the lowest possible cost. From the A/E's standpoint, a successful negotiation is one which assures that the firm will be paid for all costs incurred along the way, have the opportunity to produce an acceptable design product in a timely manner, and provide a reasonable profit for all these endeavors. Normally, the client is not concerned about whether or not the A/E makes a profit. Conversely, the A/E is not concerned about its fees being the lowest. Most other elements in the negotiation are shares and both parties are concerned about quality, time, and the venture's overall success.

If the client is a government entity, negotiations are noticeably different. Government clients are, in fact, concerned with the A/E's profitability. Such items are regulated and guidelines exist to assist government negotiators in arriving at a fair and reasonable profit. Other procurement and contracting laws (particularly at the federal level) place limits on the A/E's "allowable costs." On federal projects, this concern for allowing

PROFIT BY DESIGN

a prescribed profit and regulating allowable overhead and indirect costs provides balance and the illusion of fairness in the payment of fees. Such laws and regulations complicate both the fee proposal and negotiation process on federal and other government jobs.

Planning for negotiation and developing the appropriate strategy means the A/E negotiating team must apply reason and depend upon some methodology used to predicate the fee. The client will need to know and understand that methodology. The client will be reassured to learn that great care was taken in the analysis of his/her requirements and development of the proposed fee. Even if the client is initially shocked by the proposed level of compensation, it is important to demonstrate to the client (private or government) that a high degree of care and precision was used to calculate the fee. This indicates that the same high level of attention will be devoted to the client's project throughout the design process.

A typical negotiation involves several sequences of events that should be understood in advance of submitting a fee proposal:

First, the written and submitted A/E fee proposal usually represents the highest possible fee that the A/E can expect to earn for the prescribed scope of services. This figure will differ (sometimes substantially) from the "bottom line" fee, below which the A/E will walk away from the project. Then, there is the "middle ground" where some compromise will occur through discussions with the client, and (hopefully) an argument will emerge on an appropriate fee for a clearly understood (and probably revised) scope of services. Therefore, part of the A/E's methodology in preparing for a negotiation is to establish these figures and the range of all appropriate agreement.

Second, the A/E must recognize the client's interest in and curiosity about the basis for the written fee proposal. Every detail set forth in the A/E's fee proposal must have back-up sufficient to withstand the client scrutiny. All man-hour estimates, disciplines, sheet counts, consultant costs, review meetings, presentations, indirect costs, special services, reproduction expenses and any other out-of-pocket expenses and profit should be justified by data, calculation, prior project experience and empirical facts to substantiate the A/E's view of the project must be available for discussion. The client has the right to understand how the proposed fee was developed and why the A/E has requested the specific level of compensation. Then, the client will attempt to compare the A/E's methodology and expectations with his/her own. It is likely that the client invested far less time and effort attempting to estimate the designer's fee.

If the client is a federal agency, a more detailed government cost estimate was prepared for the purpose of comparison and negotiation. The client will need to be educated and persuaded that certain aspects of the fee proposal are justified and reasonable. This process can take hours, days or even weeks depending upon the complexity of the project and/or the sophistication of the client. This process of education, persuasion and discussion will result in a set of issues being resolved and a list of issues being unresolved. Usually, the client requests additional time to consider the "unresolved" items. If the client takes a more aggressive posture and simply refuses to consider the disputed elements, it is wise for the A/E to request a time out. Knowing when to call time out and reflect on the discussions is an important element in the overall negotiation strategy. Finally, the negotiation closes with an agreement and a handshake. If the process has been successful for both parties, there is a feeling of satisfaction on both parts. A team has been formed and the project may nowproceed with enthusiasm from all parties. Don't forget to obtain a written agreement following negotiations. The third factor is flexibility. For a negotiation to be successful, several conditions must exist. The A/E firm must be willing to negotiate. Flexibility is key. Don't expect the client to simply agree to the proposed fee as submitted. It would be unproductive for the A/E to enter the negotiation with a steadfast . . . "this is our fee, take it or leave it" attitude. Parameters for the give and take on specific items must be established and well understood by the A/E's negotiating team.

The fourth important aspect of any successful negotiation is for both sides of the debate to recognize that they need one another. The A/E needs the work and desires to have both the client and the project added to its portfolio. Conversely, the client needs the A/E, either because of special skill and experience, or because the client believes that this particular A/E can perform the work in unique way, with particular sensitivity to the client's issues and concerns.

Another condition that must exist is that both sides are ready to negotiate. Before the actual face to face negotiation meeting, all homework must be done, all data should be compiled and both sides have an organized list of questions and issues as the basis for beginning discussions. Hesitation on the part of either party or reluctance to set a negotiation date is usually the result of one or the other party being inadequately prepared.

When negotiations begin, both sides must be aware that they have common interests and common goals. If the A/E and the client do not want to work together, then going forward is futile. When common interests outnumber and outweigh the disputed aspects in the negotiation, the process will move forward and closure will be achieved, albeit at a slow pace. Both sides must be willing and able to overcome the small differences in perspective on both scope and fee and accept compromises and suggestions from the other side. Both sides must desire to arrive at closure on scope, fee, and contract terms.

Finally, a successful negotiation can only be achieved by each side letting go of certain biases and special interests. The desire to reach an agreement must exist on both sides. One party cannot be less committed to this end than the other. If the A/E negotiating team senses that the project is not really important to the client, evidenced by the client's laissez-faire attitude or cavalier response to specific scoping questions, then the A/E should back away and reconsider the project. The client may not be serious about moving forward.

Negotiations should always be conducted using a team approach. One person should be designated as the lead negotiator. However, a team of at least two and preferably three or more professionals should be sent to each negotiation. This is necessary for a variety of reasons including:

- it assures the A/E side that issues are being perceived accurately (two sets of eyes and ears are better than one).
- it demonstrates interest on the part of the A/E about the client's project.
- it provides a witness to all compromises, concessions and decisions.
- it allows someone to take notes and attempt to document the discussions.
- it provides a meaningful sounding board for private discussions that may become necessary during a time out.
- it permits a "good guy-bad guy" scenario to play out.

These days, it is virtually impossible to vest all knowledge of process, procedure, discipline, coordination, consultant coordination, design and operational issues in a single individual. Professionals selected to join a negotiating team should be principals, project managers, discipline leaders, and/or key consultants with a large part of the scope and fee at stake. Never send in a single professional to explain a multi-discipline complex proposal. The client will have difficulty accepting a single person as a credible authority on all aspects of the work. In addition, whether the client is a private corporation or a government agency, the client's

team will likely comprise technical experts in several of the key disciplines who are interested in meeting their counterparts and discussing details of the program. This face to face meeting of project counterparts is important to the relationship.

Prior to ever reaching the negotiation table, a good negotiator will collect all of the necessary data to substantiate every element of the fee proposal. The negotiator must study the scope and cost parameters of the proposal to fully understand those aspects of the work which are "fixed" (mandatory) and those portions of the work which may be optional or contingent. The lead negotiator must be able to explain the relevance of each line item in the proposal and be able to comment on sequencing and the interdependence of various tasks.

PROFIT BY DESIGN

The good negotiator will have several additional attributes to bring to the table (beyond being studious). First, the negotiator must be patient. He/she must be part teacher, part economist, a public speaker, and recognize the need to remain calm and composed throughout the negotiation, no matter how aggressive or indignant the other side becomes. The slow, methodical approach to a negotiation will yield much more satisfactory results than rushing to accept the first counter-proposal volleyed by the client.

Based upon having done the homework, the lead negotiator should be well prepared to discuss any and all real issues precipitated by the negotiation. Being prepared for just about anything the client may throw at the A/E's team is a necessary precaution and will provide better assurance that the ultimate deal is fair and reasonable. In addition, the good negotiator will have the ability to think on the run and create alternative approaches to settle differences or overcome an impasse. Often, there are many alternatives available to the A/E negotiator other than that of accepting a major concession. Lastly, the lead A/E negotiator should be professional at all times and project the image of a leader. The client will respect the entire negotiating team if the lead negotiator is leaderly, in command, professional, courteous, patient, and smart.

When the day for negotiations is set and the A/E's negotiating team has been selected, a strategy meeting needs to take place to discuss the fee proposal, variables in scope and fee, establish negotiating parameters, develop tactics and rehearse the anticipated sequence of events. This is similar to preparing for an interview, but the focus is on "winning the client" because (presumably) the A/E has already won the job.

At this all important preparation meeting, a list must be established of all remaining questions for the client that may have cost and fee implications. This becomes a useful prop in the actual negotiating session. Then, the team must determine which aspects of the scope and fee are non-controversial. It is usually obvious that some portion of the scope is well defined and well understood by both parties. This list of "clear" and "fuzzy" aspects of the scope should be developed but remain concealed from the client as part of the A/E's negotiating arsenal. Finally, it is critical for the team to review all of the fee elements in the original fee proposal and establish both a bottom line and the acceptable range for each key function (whether that is by phase, by discipline, or by some increment of time). Remember, the written fee proposal itself represents what the team originally estimated the cost of the project to be. Establishing ranges for expected compromise must not be revealed to the client without a corresponding reduction in scope or some other concession in deliverables and/or schedule. Offering to simply reduce the price at the opening of negotiations is tantamount to telling the client that your original fee proposal was wrong. This will draw the entire fee proposal into question and cause suspicion about the credibility of all submissions from the firm from that moment forward.

The negotiation itself will unfold in many possible ways. The A/E should never attempt to control the negotiation or be perceived as manipulating the client toward some pre-conceived goal. The good negotiator will be very subtle and quite cautious about the sequence and timing of any concessions and/or engagements over specific tasks and costs.

As a rule, let the client lead the session and establish the pace of negotiations. This is both courteous and wise. The more the client says in the opening few minutes of a negotiations, the better equipped the A/E's team will be to respond or adjust the anticipated sequence of issues, questions and ideas. This is where patience has value. Allow the client to ask if there are any questions about the scope before the list comes out. Allow the client to reveal his/her expectations about cost and as many details of the fee as he/she will reveal before attempting to respond or rebut. The more the client exposes a negotiating posture, the better able the A/E team will be to deploy logical tactics and use the props prepared in advance.

If the client asks for questions or clarifications in the first few minutes, deploy the list of questions prepared earlier, but express them gently and downplay their significance in the fee proposal. After all, the written fee proposal is already on the table along with the presumption that the A/E understood the scope before preparing the fee estimate. Cautiously get the client to respond to the questions and engage the client in some discussion about a technical aspect of the scope. This will set the entire group at ease and get the client talking again. The more the client talks, the more likely he will be to reveal some part of his negotiating strategy or position.

If the client opens the session with a written counter-proposal and lengthy explanations about how the A/E's fee proposal is astronomical compared to the available budget, stay calm. Let the client talk as long as he/she will, then, an appropriate response is to ask for a recess or a few minutes for the team to evaluate and discuss the counter offer. This is perfectly normal and, in fact, the wise thing to do. Don't stare like a deer in the headlights at the client's counter-offer wondering how the decimal point on the bottom line moved an entire digit. Ask for a time out. Regroup and consider the options.

As quickly as possible after a time out or after the client has elaborated on some technical aspect of the scope, get the client to either present his/her expectations of cost in detail or ask the client to compare his/her estimate of each task with the original A/E fee proposal. The idea is: a) keep the client talking, and b) let the client define areas where there is no dispute, i.e. where it appears that the component fee elements are close. Each time the sides in a negotiation agree that something is not disputed, a partial agreement is reached. Both sides become vested in that portion of the negotiation, and it allows both sides to feel that progress is being made.

If the client opens the session by asking for a review of the original fee proposal to be conducted by the A/E head negotiator, the leader needs to be prepared to discuss scope, sequence and details of the fee. However, this is an opportunity to raise both the list of pre-prepared scope clarification questions and/or attempt to overstate the areas where agreement is expected. If the client interrupts at any juncture and voices an objection to a particular item – stop, hear him/her out, get the client to talk as much as possible about the objection, then say . . . "Very well, let's set that aside and come back to it." Do this as often as the client has an objection to raise. Let the list of items to be revisited build until it is clear that portions of the work are already agreed to . . . . and others are not. Defining that which is not at issue will advance the process and create the impression that progress is being made. It will also signal to the client that disputed issues may be far less significant when compared to the list of non-disputed tasks.

The next phase of the negotiation will be to discuss in detail each controversial item. This is where patience, sound judgment and alternative thinking come into play. If the client asks for price concessions on any disputed item, be certain to propose a reduction in scope or a modified A/E effort, or a change in schedule (or some combination of the three before agreeing to a price reduction. Never reveal the "bottom line" to the client without associating that figure with a skeletal scope of work that corresponds to the minimal fee. Only reveal the bottom line figure if an impasse has developed and discussions cannot move ahead.

The astute lead negotiator will proceed along these lines and reach as much of an agreement as possible on all other portions of the project, isolating those areas where no middle ground has been found, then – request another time out. This time, both sides should take away a specific list of those items contested and agree to return to the table at some early convenient date.

Normally, an agreement can be consummated within the first one or two negotiation sessions. During the recesses and/or times outs, the A/E negotiation team must become creative and do what design professionals do best – solve problems. When negotiations resume, the A/E needs to be prepared to put forth one or more creative ways of reducing scope, combining submissions, short-cutting a client review by suggesting "on-board" meetings in the office, or some other novel idea that will allow the client to see a functional or process benefit and help reduce cost. Being pro-active by suggesting alternatives will continue to show the client that the A/E is interested in performing the work. However, to the extent possible, keep the client talking and engaged in the discussion of alternative approaches. The idea is to interest the client in what the A/E can provide and persuade the client into agreeing to a particular approach for a reasonable fee.

PROFIT BY DESIGN

Don't attempt to beat the client over the head with bundles of paper and historical data demonstrating that the costs included in the original proposal are correct and well justified. Persuade through interest and use creativity to maneuver the client into a position where signing the final agreement is an exciting event, not a chore. One of the most important aspects of firm profitability is to negotiate a proper fee up front and be certain that a reasonable profit is expected from the negotiated contract sum. If concessions are made that impact direct labor rates, indirect costs, or minimum expected profit, you can't make it up on volume, or by creative management.

When a successful negotiation results in a deal, with both sides content with scope, fee and contract terms, celebrate. Make the signing of an agreement a significant event. Both sides should be pleased with the outcome and excited about the project moving forward.

PROFIT BY DESIGN
Profiting from Federal A&E Contracts

There is a certain mystique surrounding federal design contracts and the ability to make money as a provider of architectural and engineering services. For decades, many firm owners have believed that federal A/E contracts were less profitable than similar work in the private sector, due to regulatory restrictions, rigorous submission requirements, and subcontracting limitations. This notion, though appearing valid on the surface, must be studied and dispelled.

Prior to a decision to pursue federal A/E contracts, consideration should be given to various risk/reward scenarios and a comparison of profit potential on such work.

Practice Sectors/Regulations

• Private Sector	Unregulated
• Institutional Sector	Somewhat Regulated
• Federal Sector	Highly Regulated

Risk/Reward

• Private Sector	High Risk/High Reward
• Institutional Sector	Modest Risk/Modest Reward
• Federal Sector	Low Risk/Low Reward

There are two primary, legally binding sets of rules that frame the procurement of A&E contract fees are concerns contracting with the federal government. These two relevant acts of Congress are: P.L. 92-582 (commonly known as the "Brooks Act") and Federal Acquisition Regulation (FAR) 15.903(d)(1)(ii). The first one describes the process by which the federal government will announce available contracts and solicit credentials for federally funded design and construction projects. The second regulation stipulates that "for architect-engineering services for public works or utilities, the contract price or the estimated cost and fee for production and delivery of designs, plans, drawings and specifications shall not exceed 6% of the estimated cost of construction of the public work or utility, excluding fees." This is the famous "6%" fee limitation usually held as a ceiling on federal A/E design contracts. This limitation was first established back in 1939 under 10 U.S.C. 4540.

In theory, an architect-engineering contract cannot be awarded if the total, cumulative contract price, including options, exceeds 6% of the total estimated costs of construction to which the design services pertain. On the surface, this seems both clear and restrictive. However, after many years of redefinition and experienced negotiating, and after several paradigm shifts involving bundled consultant services and an ever expanding network of disciplines involved in the art and science of construction, the line has been drawn between "basic" A&E services and those excluded from the 6% fee limitation. Any architect or engineer venturing into the realm of federal design work must know where this line is drawn and how to negotiate the largest possible fee, to cover necessary project costs.

The following are widely accepted examples of service categories and types which, for the purpose of this 6% fee limitation only, are not considered an integral part of the design, production and delivery process. Basic design services include only those disciplines and services directly and unarguably part of the creative process of designing and the necessary documentation of information needed to construct the design. Supplemental services, or service categories that may be precedent to the creative act of design, and/or not important to the production of construction documents are not considered restricted by the 6% rules. Such excluded services and service categories are:

- Field and topographic surveys, property, boundary, utility and right-of-way surveys
- Subsurface explorations and borings, soils and materials testing and resultant reports
- Feasibility studies and other investigations
- Flow gaugings, model testing
- Preparation of design development criteria
- Preparation of general and feature design memoranda
- The services of consultants, where not specifically applies to the preparation of working drawings and

- specifications
- Preparation of environmental impact assessments, statements, and supporting data
- Title II services (those required during construction)
- Models, renderings, or photographs of completed designs
- Reproduction of designs for review purposes
- Travel and per diem allowances in connection with excludable services.

In addition to the items listed above, other efforts that may be performed by an A/E firm, but are not considered restricted by the 6% statutory limitation are standard designs or prototype designs. These items are not specific to a particular site and, often times it is difficult to generate an estimated construction cost for a standard design which must be further refined and site-adapted prior to actual construction. Even though plans and specifications are developed for a potential project, the effort is not aimed at construction of a particular facility. Because of this important fact, the 6% statutory limitation cannot be applied to such efforts.

The impact of the statutory fee limitation on the cost of A/E contracts could be the subject of another entire book. However, the overarching approach to federal A&E contracts resulting from the limitation involves listing all of those services covered by the 6% fee – and all those service categories required to accomplish the work, but not covered under the 6% fee limitation. A common practice which has evolved along these lines is known as the Front Side/Back Side Analysis. The front side services are all those required to be performed prior to the basic design services that are covered by the 6% fee limitation. Similarly, the back side services are all of those required to be performed after the construction documents have been issued. There are even minor service categories requisite to the basic design and construction documents process, but can be classified as outside of the basic services umbrella.

One well known source of A/E contracting advice cites the rules for conducting a front side/back side analysis quite well.

PROFIT BY DESIGN

"The determination of compliance with the 6% statutory limitation is a simple process. Once the final agreement on price has been achieved, including options, the costs related to excludable elements are then deducted from the price. The resultant price is them divided by the estimated constructive value of the proposed project and the resultant percentage portrays the relationship of design costs to construction value. Not only must the negotiated value comply with the 6% statutory limitation, the original government estimate developed prior to negotiations must fall under the limitation, otherwise negotiations will never commence. So, prior to beginning the negotiation process, the government must evaluate whether the project can be designed to accommodate the statutory limitation. If it cannot, the public announcement must be cancelled and the proposed project sent back to the criteria development stage, or the project must be reduced in scope in order to accommodate the requirement."

From page 340 Federal Architect/Engineer Contracts.

Presuming that a project is correctly budgeted and fully authorized to proceed, it should be clear that the agreed upon fee will be substantially higher than the 6% limitation on basic design efforts. After all, the A/E is performing work precedent to and subsequent to basic design; therefore, additional compensation is necessary and expected. Certain projects will involve all or most of the excluded services categories listed above, and can drive the total A/E compensation figure well into a range of 12-14% of total estimated construction cost. In such cases, the 6% fee limitation could amount to only a fraction of the required effort and negotiated fee. The astute architect or engineer will not only know these rules and how they apply to the project in question, but will make it clear to the government representative fees beyond the 6% limitation will be required. Obviously, this discussion occurs well in advance of the fee proposal and negotiation to make certain that the government's representative has properly scoped and budgeted the project.

The unknowing A/E or inexperienced project manager can find him/herself in a serious pickle if the 6% rule is misapplied to the entire project budget without regard for the other efforts

PROFIT BY DESIGN

required.

PHASE/SERVICE MATRIX

	PHASE 1: PREDESIGN SERVICES	PHASE 2: SITE ANALYSIS SERVICES	PHASE 3: SCHEMATIC DESIGN SERVICES	PHASE 4: DESIGN DEVELOPMENT SERVICES	PHASE 5: CONSTRUCTION DOCUMENTS SERVICES	PHASE 6: BIDDING OR NEGOTIATIONS SERVICES	PHASE 7: CONSTRUCTION CONTRACT ADMINISTRATION SERVICES	PHASE 8: POST CONSTRUCTION SERVICES
	☐ Project Administration	☐ Project Administration	☐ Project Administration	☐ Project Administration	☐ Project Administration	☐ Project Administration	☐ Project Administration	☐ Project Administration
	☐ Disciplines Coordination/Document Checking	☐ Disciplines Coordination/Document Checking	☐ Disciplines Coordination/Document Checking	☐ Disciplines Coordination/Document Checking	☐ Disciplines Coordination/Document Checking	☐ Disciplines Coordination/Document Checking	☐ Disciplines Coordination/Document Checking	☐ Disciplines Coordination/Document Checking
	☐ Agency Consulting/Review/Approval	☐ Agency Consulting/Review/Approval	☐ Agency Consulting/Review/Approval	☐ Agency Consulting/Review/Approval	☐ Agency Consulting/Review/Approval	☐ Agency Consulting/Review/Approval	☐ Agency Consulting/Review/Approval	☐ Agency Consulting/Review/Approval
	☐ Owner-supplied Data Coordination	☐ Owner-supplied Data Coordination	☐ Owner-supplied Data Coordination	☐ Owner-supplied Data Coordination	☐ Owner-supplied Data Coordination	☐ Owner-supplied Data Coordination	☐ Owner-supplied Data Coordination	☐ Owner-supplied Data Coordination
	☐ Programming	☐ Site Analysis and Selection	☐ Architectural Design/Documentation	☐ Architectural Design/Documentation	☐ Architectural Design/Documentation	☐ Building Materials	☐ Office Construction Administration	☐ Maintenance and Operational Programming
	☐ Space Schematics/Flow Diagrams	☐ Site Development Planning	☐ Structural Design/Documentation	☐ Structural Design/Documentation	☐ Structural Design/Documentation	☐ Addenda	☐ Construction Field Observation	☐ Start-up Assistance
	☐ Existing Facilities Surveys	☐ Detailed Site Utilization Studies	☐ Mechanical Design/Documentation	☐ Mechanical Design/Documentation	☐ Mechanical Design/Documentation	☐ Bidding/Negotiations	☐ Project Representation	☐ Record Drawings
	☐ Marketing Studies	☐ On-site Utility Schedule	☐ Electrical Design/Documentation	☐ Electrical Design/Documentation	☐ Electrical Design/Documentation	☐ Analysis of Alternates/Substitutions	☐ Inspection Coordination	☐ Warranty Review
	☐ Economic Feasibility Studies	☐ Off-site Utility Schedule	☐ Civil Design/Documentation	☐ Civil Design/Documentation	☐ Civil Design/Documentation	☐ Special Bidding Services	☐ Supplemental Documents	☐ Postconstruction Evaluation
	☐ Project Financing	☐ Environmental Studies and Reports	☐ Landscape Design/Documentation	☐ Landscape Design/Documentation	☐ Landscape Design/Documentation	☐ Bid Evaluation	☐ Quotation Requests/change Orders	
		☐ Zoning Processing Assistance	☐ Interior Design/Documentation	☐ Interior Design/Documentation	☐ Interior Design/Documentation	☐ Construction Contract Agreements	☐ Project Schedule Monitoring	
			☐ Materials Research/Specifications	☐ Materials Research/Specifications	☐ Materials Research/Specifications		☐ Construction Cost Accounting	
	☐ Project Development Scheduling	☐ Project Development Scheduling	☐ Project Development Scheduling	☐ Project Development Scheduling	☐ Special Bidding Documents/Scheduling		☐ Project Closeout	
	☐ Project Budgeting	☐ Project Budgeting	☐ Statement of Probable Construction Cost	☐ Statement of Probable Construction Cost	☐ Statement of Probable Construction Cost			
	☐ Presentations	☐ Presentations	☐ Presentations	☐ Presentations	☐ Presentations			

FRONT SIDE — 6% FEE — BACK SIDE

PROFIT BY DESIGN

Another significant myth pertaining to the 6% limitation is that redesigns must be treated as lost effort. This is not the case! When the scope is changed by the government's representative or the scope is altered because the project was poorly scoped in the beginning, the extra effort needed to modify the design must be compensated to the A/E, even if the overall estimated cost of construction does not change. "Lost effort" does not include redesigns when the scope is modified. Such efforts on the part of the A/E are separately estimated, negotiated and agreed upon in advance of performing additional work.

The notion that the A/E was responsible for all redesign work without additional fee was dispelled in 1985 by amendments to the Defense Federal Acquisition Regulation (DFARS).

Prior to 1985, when a change order was issued to an A/E contract that was under the 6% limitation provision, the efforts of redesign were was treated as lost effort and deducted from the relatable design value used to calculate the statutory limitation compliance. A construction value was calculated for the lost effort and was deducted from the established construction value of the project. At the same time, the construction value of the new work was calculated and added to the construction value of the project. This represented a very simple and accurate method of always determining the construction value of a given facility and how that facility design stood relative to the statutory limitation provision. At the same time, the architect-engineer that was responsible for the design always had an accurate construction value incorporated into his/her contract whereby he/she could be judged under the FAR clause 52.236-22, Design Within Funding Limitations. As is the case with most things in government that work well, this regulation has been changed several times.

In August 1985, the Defense Federal Acquisition Regulations Supplement (DFARS 36.606-(72) changed the way business was conducted. This change stated that where redesign is required and the contract is modified, the following method shall be used to insure that the 6% statutory limitation is not exceeded.

1. The estimated construction cost of the redesigned

features will be added to the original estimated construction cost.
2. The contract cost for the original design will be added to the contract cost for redesign.
3. The total contract design cost obtained will be divided by the total construction cost obtained and the resulting percentage may not exceed the 6% statutory limitation (for those items limited by the 6% rule).

Remember to correctly estimate the requisite design effort. A "front side/back side" analysis will clarify the portions of the project which are limited under the 6% rule. Isolating these services and adding the fees required for other services not limited by the 6% rule, will usually result in a fair fee.

Most federal agencies will establish wage, overhead, and profit limitations on certain types of design contracts. This is the case with delivery order type contracts (or indefinite quantity type contracts) where a specific task or scope may not yet be known when the contract is awarded. Multi-task delivery orders may extend out over many years, and be very active (many task orders) or dormant for long periods of time. The formula for generating profits with such task orders include:

- negotiate a reasonable wage rate for all categories of direct labor to be purchased under the contract;

- establish an overhead rate that includes all costs associated with servicing the contract through the office structure. (Note: most agencies have definitions for "unallowable overhead" and care must be taken to properly define and account for legitimate overhead costs);

- negotiate a profit rate that is fair and appropriately the same as the firm would earn if the work were being provided to other clients (public or private);

- when task orders are issued and fee estimates are prepared, be certain that the scope is clear, well defined, limited to a quantifiable work effort or time period and that adequate fees are estimated for all categories of labor required;

- negotiate well and with conviction. Make certain the government's representative is aware that you know and understand the rules, how the 6% limitation is applied, and that you are carefully watching the scope.

- Manage the project to be certain that time frames are met and all submissions are complete. Don't let the project drift and make certain that out of scope items and extra work are brought to the attention of the client, with a request for additional compensation before the services are performed.

When approaching a federal project which is highly regulated and subject to rules and restrictions well beyond projects in the private sector, it is important to remember that budget constraints are most likely an attempt to posture for future negotiations. The ploy of the government is often to consider the 6% limitation as broadly applicable to all disciplines, services and tasks related to a project. Of course, this is incorrect, but a first encounter with the government negotiator will reveal whether the pending negotiation will be framed by constant references to the 6% limit. It is easy for the government's representative to assert that proposed fees are too high – referencing the 6% limitation – but this usually means that the government has not undertaken a careful analysis of the project scope and budget. When a government negotiator introduces a budgetary limitation, it generally means that little initiative has been taken to analyze the scope, or that the government's project manager has lost control of the process, and has taken an easy way out. If budget constraints are a real problem, then the scope of work is too broad to be accomplished with available funds. If the scope of work is too broad, then it must be reduced or options must be cut. It is wise to avoid projects which purport to be limited by available funds. Budgetary constraints are sometimes real and other times artificial.

The following chart compares the relative effort and potential profit of private sector and federal work. This chart generally reflects the fact that it is more difficult to achieve large profits

PROFIT BY DESIGN

on federal work, due to the highly regulated nature of the work, restrictions on "allowable costs", and special circumstances, conditions, submission requirements, and standards which impact the work.

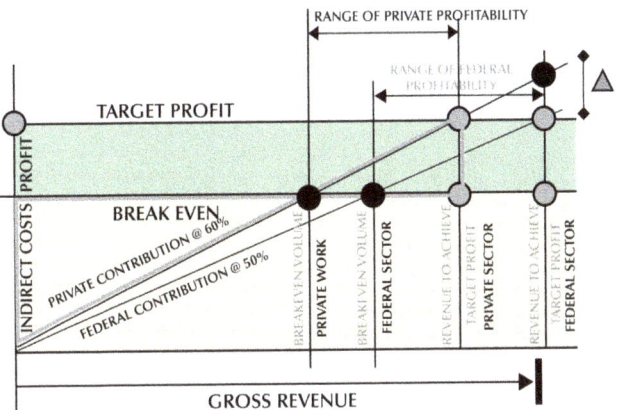

Inter-Relationships **(Private vs. Federal)**

Unlike private sector projects, all federal government projects are regulated as the amount of pure profit permitted to be earned on the work. The government has the authority and staff to audit the A/E firm's financial records and assess penalties if agreed upon profits are exceeded. Reasonable profits are possible in federal A/E contracting. However, it is necessary to know the special rules and conditions which govern federal A/E contracting. Allowable costs and expenses are different under federal contracting rules. Execution of the work can be more complex, requiring multiple progress submissions and many consultants. Rigorous thresholds for minority sub-contracting can complicate fee proposals and work plans.

Profits on federal A/E contracts can be predicted, earned and protected if the A/E understands the rules and how regulated aspects of the design process are impacted.

The actual text of the "Brooks Act" (P.L. 92-582) and a description of the steps administered by most federal agencies in the selection of A/E firms can be found in the Appendix (page 207).

PROFIT BY DESIGN
Federal Procurement Analysis Guide
Developed by Steven L. Biegel for the American Institute of Architects by contract in 2006.

Introduction

Each year the federal government awards over one billion dollars in design contracts, for everything from courthouses to embassies to parking structures to warehouses. The federal facilities that architects design symbolize the "dignity, enterprise, vigor and stability of the American Government" (GSA Guiding Principles for Federal Architecture). Working for the federal government is an excellent opportunity for both large and small architectural firms to raise their profile and build a lasting design portfolio.

However, the process of pursuing and winning federal contracts can be daunting, especially to smaller firms. And the recent adoption of a new form that architects and engineers use to obtain government work has posed obstacles for many firms.

The AIA Guide to Federal Procurement offers practical, up-to-the-minute information on getting into the federal procurement arena. It is intended as a guide for firms which have never performed federal work and those that are transitioning to the new submission format.

The Guide provides a line-by-line summary of the new Standard Form (SF) 330, as well as a comparison between the new form and the former SFs 254/255 submission materials that A/E firms have used for years.

This Guide also provides information on how the government selects A/E firms, how the qualifications-based selection process works, how to register as a vendor with the federal government, and how to search for job opportunities within the federal government.

This guide was updated in 2010 with insights and recommendations from a broad cross-section of AIA members and member firms.

PROFIT BY DESIGN

If you have any questions or comments about the guide or its contents, please contact sbiegel@placedesigners.com.

Steven Lawrence Biegel, AIA, Director of Architecture
PLACE designers inc
Architecture, Planning, & Interior Design

Background

Federal procurement of architecture and engineering (A/E) services has changed dramatically over the past several decades. As these professions expand and become more specialized, so too must the methods of comparing and evaluating firms that provide professional services. Prior to 1975, the U.S. General Services Administration (GSA) and other federal agencies used a very simple Standard Form 251 to evaluate interested firms and individuals electing to submit credentials in pursuit of federal design projects.

The SF 251 was often supplemented by elaborate brochures, color photography and lengthy descriptions of projects previously completed by firms and individuals. In the 1950s and 1960s, with expanding federal services and government bureaucracy, large scale federal projects became more prevalent in the nation's capital and throughout the United States.

As the government expanded, opportunities to design significant and lasting pieces of architecture grew. However, few firms were experienced with federal requirements and procedures. Small firms, in particular those outside of Washington, DC, had little chance of winning significant federal work.

In 1975, GSA issued Standard Forms 254 and 255, replacing the more general SF 251. SFs 254 and 255 were created through an inter-agency committee with advice and input from professional architectural and engineering societies. The SF 254/255 submission process was used extensively by federal agencies, state and local governments, and other institutions as a vehicle for evaluating providers of A/E services. The SF 254/255 process leveled the playing field and provided for a broader spectrum of A/E firms to compete for government design commissions.

As A/E services expanded and became more specialized, and as employees of various firms migrated from one company to another, it became increasingly difficult to assess the capabilities of a particular firm using the SF 254/255 format. In 1994, an effort was undertaken to modify and revise the SF 254/255 submission process.

During many years of debate as to the fairness and utility of the SF 254/255 forms, several issues were identified which prompted concerns among procuring agencies and design firms. These major issues included:
- Attribution & credit for architectural works among firms and individuals.
- How to weigh firm experience against individual employee experience.
- Significance of previous team involvement, including engineers & specialty consultants.
- Relevance of recent similar project experience vs. creative design talent & ability.
- Government desire & mandate to spread the work and allow firms of varying size & composition to compete for and win significant projects.

In response to these and other concerns, an interagency ad hoc committee developed a new Standard Form 330. It was based on the results of a joint federal-industry survey of the existing SFs 254 and 255 conducted by the Standing Committee on Procurement and Contracting of the Federal Facilities Council (FFC) in 1995, and published in 1996 as FFC Report Number 130, entitled "Survey on the Use of Standard Forms 254 and 255 for Architect-Engineer Qualifications."

Both federal and A-E industry practitioners believed that the forms needed to be streamlined and updated to facilitate electronic usage. The objectives of the SF 330 were to merge the SFs 254 and 255 into a single streamlined form, expand essential information about qualifications and experience, reflect current A/E disciplines, experience types and technology, eliminate information of marginal value, permit limitations on submission length, and facilitate electronic usage.

On October 19, 2001, a proposed Federal Acquisition Regulation (FAR) rule for a new A-E Qualifications form was published in the Federal Register (66 RF 53314). The final rule replaced SFs 254 and 255 with SF 330. SF 330 began to be used on January 12, 2004, and became required by all federal agencies on June 8, 2004.

How the Federal Government Selects A/E Firms

The Brooks Act (Public Law 92-582), enacted on October 18, 1972, establishes the procurement process by which architects and engineers (A/Es) are selected for design contracts with federal design and construction agencies. The Brooks Act establishes a qualifications-based selection process, known as "QBS," in which contracts for A/Es are negotiated on the basis of demonstrated competence and qualification for the type of professional services required at a fair and reasonable price. Under Brooks Act procurement procedures, price quotations are not a consideration in the selection process.

This QBS process, as instituted by the Brooks Act, has long been enthusiastically supported by every professional A/E society. There are seven basic steps involved in pursuing federal design work under the Brooks Act:

1. Public solicitation for architectural and engineering services
2. Submission of an annual statement of qualifications and supplemental statements of ability to design specific projects for which public announcements were made
3. Evaluation of both the annual and project-specific statements
4. Development of a shortlist of at least three submitting firms in order to conduct interviews with them
5. Interviews with the firms
6. Ranking of at least three of the most qualified firms
7. Negotiation with the top ranked firm

A brief explanation of each of these steps, along with a description of what is involved in each, follows. The user must be reminded that while the Brooks Act procurement is mandated by law, agencies may modify the procedures slightly, within the confines of the act and the Federal Acquisition Regulation (FAR).

The AIA is a strong supporter of the brooks Act and qualifications-based selection of A/E firms. Read the AIA's QBS Issue Brief.

The QBS Process

1. Public Announcement

The Brooks Act calls for public announcement of opportunities for design contracts. The government posts these on a website known as FedBizOpps.

All intended procurement actions of $25,000 or more, whether for military or civilian agencies, are now posted at FedBizOpps.gov. FedBizOpps.gov does not list procurements that are:

- Classified for reasons of national security
- For perishable items
- For certain utility services
- Required within 15 days
- Placed under existing contracts
- For personal professional services
- Made only from foreign sources
- Not be given advance publicity, as determined by the Small Business Administration

Notices posted to FedBizOpps.gov provide the location and scope of projects and may also contain such information as:

- Estimated construction contract award range
- Project schedule and the date and time limit for receiving replies
- Categories of evaluation criteria and weight factors
- Any requirements for submitting supplemental information

Usually, opportunities for A/E services are listed under the "R" (professional, administrative and management support services) and "C" (architecture and engineering services) sections. However, design opportunities can be included in other sections, such as those for design/build services (listed under "Y," Construction of Structures and Facilities).

2.   Statement of Qualifications

A/E firms with an interest in being considered for design services contracts must submit the required statements of qualifications to each agency with which the A/E wants to contract. The Standard Form 330, Architect-Engineer Qualifications, may be filed each year with a field office of each agency with which the architect intends to do business. This form may be updated and resubmitted at any time. A completed form furnishes the federal agency with general information on the size, capabilities, personnel, and past experience of an interested firm.

Many federal agencies keep SF 330 Part IIs (General Qualifications) on file and review them for prospective design firms if they have a small project hat will not be advertised. The A/E firm can submit this form at the same time as the required project-specific form, the SF 330 Part I, is submitted.

Following the review of the notices on FedBizOpps, if an A/E firm wants to be considered for a specific project listed in it, then it must submit SF 330 Parts I and II. This form is submitted in response to a specific solicitation and, when completed, contains the data relative to the specific project.

When a project is advertised on FedBizOpps, the agency does not notify firms that have previously filed a SF 330 with them. The project advertisements or notices that appear on FedBizOpps are tailored to each specific project, and invite interested firms to submit a new SF 330, along with any supplemental data requested in the announcement. Firms that have a current SF 330 Part II on file with the listed procurement should resubmit it, along with Part I of the SF

330 to be considered for a specific project. Instructions on how to complete the SF 330 are contained in the form.

3. Evaluation of Statements

The evaluation/selection process for A/E evaluation boards composed of members who, collectively, have experience in architecture, engineering, construction, and government and related acquisition matters. The members of the boards are usually appointed from among the professional employees of the agency or other agencies. In some situations, private practitioners sit on these boards if authorized by agency procedures. Of course, when these private practitioners sit on an evaluation board, they or their firms are not eligible for award of a design contract. Usually, private sector board members are "advisors" only, with no actual vote in the selection process.

The evaluation boards then review the statements of qualifications (SF 330). The boards must evaluate the submissions in accordance with the criteria cited in the FedBizOpps notice. For example, some of the criteria in a notice may include the following: professional qualifications and experience of the firm with design of a specific type of project; experience and professional qualifications of the firm's staff to be assigned to the project; location of the main office of the proposing firm and its consultants; overall performance record of the firm; and analysis of the firm's current workload.

4. Development of a Short-list

Following the evaluation of the statements of qualifications, the boards prepare reports that recommend the firms to be named to the short-list. The report ranks at least three of the firms for the purpose of discussing the project with them. The boards are not limited in the number of firms that they can select for these interviews; it is left to their discretion. However, due to the effort and expense of preparing for interviews and more elaborate descriptions of firm capabilities, the AIA recommends that agencies restrict the interview list to 3 firms.

5. Interviews/Discussions With Firms

The interviews usually involve discussions on project concepts and the relative utility of alternative methods of furnishing the required services. Before the interview, some agencies send detailed selection criteria and other information about the project to the firms recommended for further consideration. Under the system established by QBS, the architect-engineer designer does not produce any design product in competing for the project.

Usually these interviews are held at the agency's office. Sometimes, interviews are conducted in the architect's office. Occasionally, and in special circumstances, phone interviews are conducted. The interviews are brief, usually lasting only 30 to 60 minutes.

6. Ranking the "Top Three" Firms

Following the interviews, the boards' reports are presented to the agency head or individual who is designated to act on the agency head's behalf. The reports list, in order of preference, at least three firms that are considered to be the most highly qualified to perform the services. This is considered to be the final selection of the competing firms. If the firm listed as the most preferred is not the firm that was recommended as the most highly qualified by the evaluation board, the head of the agency must provide a written explanation for the reason for the preference. The head of the agency, or that person's designate, may not add names of other firms to the final report. The report reviews the recommendations of the evaluation board and, from that, the agency head makes the final selection.

7. Negotiation with the Top-Ranked Firm

When the final selection is made by the agency head, the contracting officer is authorized to begin negotiations with the top-ranked firm. The negotiations are conducted pursuant to the procedures set forth in the FAR. Usually, the firm is requested to submit a fee proposal listing direct and indirect costs as the basis for contract negotiations. Contract negotiations are conducted following an evaluation of the fee proposal and an audit when the proposed design fee is more than $100,000.

Gatting Started

If a fee is not agreed upon within a reasonable time, the contracting officer will conclude negotiations with the top-ranked firm and initiate negotiations with the second-ranked firm. If a satisfactory contract is not worked out with this firm, then this procedure will be continued until a mutually satisfactory contract is negotiated. The negotiation process will then continue until an agreement is reached and a contract awarded. On a practical note, it is rare that a contract is not successfully negotiated with the top-ranked firm. However, if negotiations fail with all ranked firms, the procurement is cancelled and the process may begin again.

The Six Percent Fee Limitation on Federal Design Contracts

Since 1939, federal construction agencies have been required by law to limit the fee payable to an architect or engineer to six percent of the estimated construction cost. Presently, there are at least four statutes that prescribe limitations on architect-engineer fees, and apply to all civilian and military construction agencies, with the exception of the U.S. Department of State.

Federal agencies have interpreted the statutory fee limitations as applying only to the part of the fee that covers the production and delivery of "designs, plans, drawings, and specifications." The agencies, therefore, consider that the six percent fee limitation does not apply to the cost of field investigation, surveys, topographical work, soil borings, inspection of construction, master planning, and similar services not involving the production and delivery of designs, plans, drawings, and specifications. Most direct federal awarding agencies have, as part of their supplement to the Federal Acquisition Regulation, a list of those items exempt from the six percent fee limitation.

Vendor Registration

The first step in working with the federal government is becoming a registered vendor. Doing so provides your firm with a unique identification number and gives you access to forms and information about contracting opportunities. Registering is mandatory, but easy. Here's how:

1. Data Universal Numbering System (DUNS) Number

Assignment of a DUNS number is free for all entities required to register with the federal government by a regulatory agency, including federal contractors and prospective government vendors. It is a unique nine character ID number provided by the commercial company Dunn & Bradstreet. The process to request a DUNS number takes about ten minutes. Please call the government-dedicated, DUNS number self-request line at 1-866-705-5711 or visit their website. Note that as a result of obtaining a DUNS number, you may be included on Dun & Bradstreet's marketing list that is sold to other companies. However, you can request to be "de-listed" from that marketing file.

2. Central Contractor Registration (CCR)

The CCR is the federal government's primary vendor database. The CCR collects, validates, stores and disseminates data in support of agency acquisition missions. Current and potential government vendors are required to register in CCR in order to be awarded government contracts. Vendors must complete a one-time registration to provide basic information relevant to procurement and financial transactions. Vendors are responsible for updating/renewing their registration annually to maintain an active status.

CCR validates vendor information and shares the secure and encrypted data with federal agencies' finance offices to facilitate paperless payments through electronic funds transfer (ETF). CCR also shares the data with government procurement and electronic business systems. Note that any information shared in a vendor's registration may be shared with authorized government offices. Access the CCR online registration through the CCR homepage and click on "Start New Registration." The CCR handbook describes the registration process and contains a blank template of the full registration and sample letters in the appendix.

3. Commercial and Government Entity (CAGE) Code Assignments

The CAGE code is a five character ID number used extensively within the federal government. The Defense Logistics Information Service (DLIS) administers the CAGE code system and has placed a CAGE code search feature on the internet to help determine if a code has been previously assigned to your company. If not, the CAGE request process is incorporated in the CCR registration; upon activation in CCR, your company will be assigned a CAGE code. CCR is an authorized source for the assignment of CAGE codes. Vendors that require a CAGE code for a Security Clearance or for the assignment of a DODAAC code do not need to go through CCR. They can submit the request on DD Form 2051, "Request for Assignment of a Commercial and Government Entity (CAGE) Code.

4. Online Representations and Certifications Application (ORCA) Implementation

The Federal Acquisition Regulation was amended in December 2004 to require offerors to submit representations and certifications electronically via the Business Partner Network, replacing the paper-based Representations and Certifications (Reps and Certs) process known as Section K. Offerors are encouraged to complete an Online Representations and Certifications Application (ORCA) as soon as possible. To prepare for this requirement and to register in ORCA, vendors will be required to obtain a Marketing Partner Identification Number (MPIN). Vendors create their MPIN in the Central Contractor Registry (CCR). Please note that the MPIN may also be used to access the vendor's accounts in other Business Partner Network (BPN) sites, such as Past Performance Information Retrieval System (PPIRS) and Federal Technical Data System (FedTeDS).

SF 330 Part II (General Qualifications) has been incorporated into the Online Representations and Certifications Application. Submission is voluntary; however, it will increase a firm's visibility in the federal marketplace and may lead to contracting opportunities exempt from public announcement.

Searching for Job Opportunities

In the past, the government publicized contracting opportunities in the Commerce Business Daily. The CBD was published Monday through Friday by the U.S. Department of Commerce, and listed proposed government procurements, subcontracting leads, and contract awards. The CBD has now been replaced by a government website known as FedBizOpps

FedBizOpps.gov is the single government point-of-entry for federal government procurement opportunities over $25,000. Government buyers can publicize their business opportunities by posting directly to FedBizOpps, and commercial vendors seeking federal markets can search, monitor, and retrieve opportunities solicited by the entire federal contracting community. FedBizOpps provides answers to frequently asked questions, defines interface descriptions (i.e. combined synopsis/solicitation, award notice), allows vendors to sign up for the vendor notification service, and links vendors to the latest procurement news and related sites. Some agencies have additional instructions and information on their websites.

FirstGov.gov, the federal government's official web portal, is an excellent place to begin acquiring information concerning selling to the government. The site contains links to GSA schedules, GSA publications for small business, the Defense Logistics Agency Internet Bid Board System, State Procurement Officials, Small Business Guide to Government Contracting Opportunities, Federal Business Opportunities, and much more.

In addition, many local governments, institutions of higher learning and private firms provide bid list instructions on their websites.

PROFIT BY DESIGN

The GSA Standard Form 330

This section describes the sections of the SF 330 Part I (Contract-Specific Qualifications) and Part II (General Qualifications). It also discusses how the SF330 is different from the old SF 254/255 documents.

The GSA's SF330 page has the SF330 in three formats: Microsoft Word and PDF, which you can print; and FormNet.

A more detailed set of instructions for completing the SF 330, provided by the GSA, is available on-line.

SF 330 PART I, A - D Contract-Specific Qualifications	Changes from SF 254/255
A. Contract Information 1. Title and Location 2. Public Notice Date 3. Solicitation or Project Number	Same information as required in SF 255, blocks 1, 2a and 2b. Identifies project and notice date.
This information is required to identify the project by solicitation number and title.	
B. Architect-Engineer Point of Contact 4. Name and Title 5. Name of Firm 6. Telephone Number 7. Fax Number 8. E-Mail Address	Same information as required in SF 255, block 3a, except fax and e-mail are added. Include only one point of contact.
This information identifies the firm (offeror) and primary contact. The contact person must be the legal representative of the firm.	
C. Proposed Team Contractual Relationship (Matrix Format) (check prime, JV partner, subcontractor) 9. Firm Name 10. Address 11. Role in This Contract	Same information as required in SF 255, blocks 3, 5 and 6. The older SF 255 format listed data not necessary for consideration of team.
This information describes the total team, location of each firm on the team, and their proposed role on the contract.	
D. Organizational Chart of Proposed Team (please see example below)	Not required by SF 255, but usually included by A-Es. No specific format or software is required.
Organizational charts are required but may vary in style and format.	

PROFIT BY DESIGN

Agency — Quality Control, Project Manager, Principal-in-Charge — A, M, E, P, C	
SF 330 PART I, E Contract-Specific Qualifications	**Changes from** **SF 254/255**

E.   Resumes of Key Personnel Proposed for This Contract (Complete one Section E for each key person.)
12.   Name
13.   Role in this Contract
14.   Years Experience
a.   Total
b.   With Current Firm
a.   Firm Name and Location (city and state)
b.   Education (degree and specialization)
c.   Current Professional Registration (state and discipline)
d.   Other Professional Qualifications (publications, Organizations, Training, Awards, etc.)
e.   Relevant Projects (no more than five unless specified by agency, a. – e.)
a. through e.
(1) Title and Location (city and state)
(2) Year Completed
  Professional Services
  Construction (if applicable)
(3) Brief Description (brief scope, size, cost, etc.) and Specific Role (check if project performed with current firm)
	One page per person, instead of one-half on SF 255. Essentially same information as required by SF 255 block 7, except specific blocks added to describe five relevant projects person performed.
	
	The result of this change is to offer more information about the proposed professional and relevant similar work performed by the individual.

SF 330 PART I, F Contract-Specific Qualifications	**Changes from** **SF 254/255**

SF 330 PART I, G Contract-Specific Qualifications	Changes from SF 254/255
F. Example Projects Which Best Illustrate Proposed Team's Qualifications for This Contract (Present as many projects as requested by the agency, or 10 oprojects, if not specified. Complete one Section F for each project.) 20. Example Project Key Number 21. Title and Location (City and State) 22. Year Completed Professional Services Construction (if applicable) 23. Project Owner's Information c. Project Owner d. Point of Contact Name e. Point of Contact Telephone Number 24. Brief Description of Project and Relevance to This Contract (Include scope, size, and cost) 25. Firms From Section C(Proposed Team) Involved with This Project a. through f. (1) Firm Name (2) Firm Location (City and State) (3) Role The intent of this section is to assess how much experience the firms have working as a team.	Requests information on 10 projects, similar to SF 255, block 8. Expanded to one page per project, which is generally current practice. Description includes scope, size and cost. Asks for other firms on team and their involvement in the specific project.

If a Firm Has Branch Offices, Complete for
Each Specific Branch Office Seeking Work.
12. Solicitation Number (if any)
2a. Firm (or Branch Office) Name
2b. Street
2c. City
2d. State
2e. Zip Code
3. Year Established
4. DUNS Number
5. Ownership
   a. Type
   b. Small Business Status
6a. Point of Contact Name and Title
6b. Telephone Number
6c. E-Mail Address
7. Name of Firm (if block 2a is a branch office)
8a. Former Firm Name(s) (if any)
8b. Year Established
8c. DUNS Number
	Essentially same information as required by SF 254,
	blocks 1-6.

9. Employees By Discipline
   a. Function Code
   b. Discipline
   c. Number of Employees
(1) Firm
(2) Branch
	Similar to SF 254, block 8. Uses code numbers. Sixty-two
	function codes versus 24 on SF 254. Others can be
	added.

10. Profile of Firm's Experience and Annual
Average Revenue for Last Five Years
   a. Profile Code
   b. Experience
   c. Revenue Index Number
(see list of codes on SF 330 Part II)
	Similar to SF 254, block 10, but does not require number
	of projects, and expresses revenues as ranges instead
	of specific dollar amounts. One hundred and sixty
	identified profile codes versus 117 on SF 254. Others
	can be added.

11. Annual Average Professional Services Revenues of Firm for Last 3 Years
(Insert revenue index number shown on form)
   a. Federal Work
   b. Non-Federal Work
   c. Total Work
	Simplification of SF254, block 9. Only requires annual
	average over last three years instead of annual
	revenues for each of last five years. Uses ranges like SF
	254.

12. Authorized Representative a. Signature b. Date c. Name and Title Signature must be in original ink or electronic	Same as SF 254, block 11.

PROFIT BY DESIGN
Automation and Real Time Data

With recent innovations in software interface coupled with a clear demand for immediate information to be made available for project managers, project principals and owners, custom made accounting and project reporting systems have emerged. Design professionals now have a wide variety of business-savvy computer programs from which to choose. Evaluating various programs and making intelligent choices can become a preoccupation (to the point of distraction from the operational helm of the firm). Care must be taken to pre-screen recommendations from hardware and software companies, each eager to promote their products. Selecting the proper program requires detailed analysis of firm needs, available (user-ready) hardware, operating system, sophistication of users, and financial resources. Misalignment of accounting programs and/or project management systems can result in inefficiency, waste, loss of confidence, confusion, embarrassment and losses on the bottom line.

Architects and Engineers are so habitual about providing professional services to clients that they sometimes fail to recognize that they too are clients . . . . in need of professional assistance from an outside source. While they are proficient problem solvers, they sometimes let their propensity toward finding the solution themselves (using their own methods) interfere with sound judgment. Sometimes the quintessential problem solver becomes part of the problem, when the choice should be . . . . "call in an outside expert."

Just like attorneys who might elect to represent themselves in court or physicians who might self-diagnose and prescribe treatment for personal afflictions, A/E professionals should put ego and self-interest aside and refrain from attempting to solve a complex set of financial and management problems for the firm (with the best of intentions) without consulting a qualified outside expert. Leaving the problem-solving switch in the "on" position prevents an external view of the cause and effect relationships which often impede the firm from maximizing profits. If owners and managers within a firm attempt to analyze and self-diagnose the failings of accounting and management systems already in place, a tendency to rationalize prior decisions and purchases, or worse, perpetuation of antiquated management systems may result.

Within the covers of this book, the goal of achieving greater project profitability and the cumulative benefit of achieving greater profits for an entire office or firm over some prescribed period of time is clear. Therefore, this text embraces many types of initiatives to stimulate creative thought about efficiency of process and refinement of business practices. Modern computerized accounting and management systems underlie many of the recommendations for improving operations and increasing efficiency within any office. The choice of computer hardware and software for project management and firm/office management is best made with an eye toward using that system to generate profits by saving labor and reporting time.

The basic objective of selecting and implementing an automated project management and office management system is to achieve greater profits with less labor. Processing information quickly with less labor devoted to data entry, retrieval, interpretation and analysis would be consistent with this objective.

Often, when the selection of accounting and project management systems is left to the accounting and project management staff, there is a lack of resolve toward purchasing and installing new programs and upgrading software that will more fully automate various functions, requiring fewer people to perform specific tasks. An astute A/E business owner will evaluate the potential labor savings afforded by a systems upgrade and be vigilant about the possibility of redundant efforts in both accounting and project management. Automation is intended to replace manual labor.

To generalize, any A/E firm will need to track projects, project numbers, labor costs, expenses, hours devoted to phases of projects, billings, consultant costs, other project data, and project related expenses. Similarly, any A/E firm will have a parallel need to track office wide labor associated with both project and non-project tasks, accounts payable, accounts receivable, supplies, payroll, benefits and the like. These functions do not change between one firm and the next, or vary as the firm expands or contracts with changes in revenue or staff size. Accounting and project management systems have evolved to address each set of these basic functional areas with certain common functions merged into so called interactive or automated multi-function systems.

In an effort to define and describe a least common denominator among the basic management systems needs of A/E firms across the board, the following lists contain both categorical and component level subject areas typical of modern cost/accounting and management systems for architects and engineers.

Project Reporting/Management
Numerical Coding & Reference System (Standard Sub-#s)
Project Progress Report
Project Detail Report Office Earnings Report Project Summary Report
Interactive Project Reporting Timekeeper
Labor Posting Log
Cross Labor Reconciliation Report

Accounting/General Ledger Aged Accounts Receivable
Accounts Receivable Ledger Accounts Analysis
Income Statement Balance Sheet
Interactive General Ledger Reporting Profit Planning Monitor (Report) Trial Balance Statement
Cash Journal Over/Under Report Backlog Analysis
Business Development/Site Projections

Accounts Payable Cash Requirements Vouchers by Project Voucher Schedule
Misc. Unscheduled Expenses

Employee Based Reports Time Analysis
Accrued Time Report (Vacation & Leave) Labor Cross Charge Detail
Payroll and Withholding Summary Incentive Compensation Schedule

Because an A/E firm is really a professional service delivery business, it is simple to recognize that some functions

PROFIT BY DESIGN

among those listed above are specific to the need for project management and control of projects within the office while others are key to the operation of the office, making the chore of directing a business a little easier. The list includes functions to benefit project management and project managers. Other functions are listed to assist office management and management staff. One set of functions improves the design and construction documents process and results is billing to generate revenue for the firm. The other set of functions improves cost management (the necessary evil side of owning and operating an A/E firm). Within the free enterprise system, every business is established with the objective of making money. The life blood of an A/E business is the efficient execution of work that allows for invoices to be issued and fees to be paid. Obviously, profits are derived from generating large amounts of billings with relatively few expenses.

A graphic illustration of this notion that an A/E firm is organized around two parallel sets of management functions is shown below.

Project Management [illustration]
- Requires focus on efficiency (once through process)
- Continual efforts to reduce labor/maximize billings
- Control Project Expenses and Consulting Costs
- Early design decisions/ fewer iterations (design guidelines)

Office Management [illustration]
- Requires focus on efficiency (high utilization)
- Reduce Costs
- Control/Defer Expenses
- Automate Systems/Reduce Labor
- Eliminate O.H. where possible
- Frequent Billing/Attention to Collections

If the idea of generating maximum profit is taken seriously and becomes part of the core values that comprise corporate culture, efforts will be made by project managers to maximize earnings (billings) while office managers strive to control and reduce all other non-project specific costs. It is in the interest of the bottom line to reduce all non-income producing activities and minimize costs associated with overhead tasks. The greatest opportunity for improving the profitability of an A/E office (or firm) results from a combination of concerted effort to improve earnings (increased billings with reduced investment of labor and expense) with simultaneous efforts to reduce overhead costs (decreasing non-billable labor and expense required to perform management functions). Success in either realm will improve profits and allow the firm to make appropriate decisions about growth, specialization, image, training, staff development and profit sharing. Success in both areas provides greatest rewards for staff and management and assures the longevity of the firm.

To facilitate a project manager's ability to perform better and achieve the goal of greater efficiency, programs have been designed to help manipulate project data quickly. Project managers can analyze data organized and formatted to complement the way they work. Variations in management style or concentration on a particular type of project management data can now be accommodated in several automated systems. Project managers can establish budgets, track projects and make decisions on project costs and billing rates. They can set up project reports customized to their needs. Reports may be produced by discipline, phase or activity. Senior project personnel and discipline heads may look at direct labor activity to determine project status, percent complete and make adjustments to labor budgets, consultant budgets, reserves, etc. quickly and with minimal paperwork. Newly available automated management systems offer flexible, interactive and time-saving characteristics in response to the expanding need for immediate (almost instantaneous) project data.

Similar programs have been devised to help A/E firm accounting personnel streamline routine (but heretofore labor intensive) functions. Tedious but essential posting of labor to project accounts can be made dramatically more efficient by facilitating direct posting (automatically) from time sheet entries directly to the project labor account. Unlike manual posting or systems that require multiple (redundant) posting (such as for payroll, project accounting, billing and estimates to complete) newer automated programs are available to ensure that all data entered for a particular project or person (from time sheet entries) is automatically posted in several places and validated throughout the system. Office or firm accounting staff can more readily display, print, download and manipulate data using standardized and/or customized reports.

Among the most progressive and directly applicable automated accounting systems for architects and engineers is that available through the Deltek Corporation, headquartered in McLean, Virginia. Deltek's new "Advantage" financial and project control system for design professionals is among the most widely used and most flexible. Advantage® is the leading project and financial control system for A/E firms in the United States. Over 3,000 firms with an enormous range of accounting needs, rely on the programs and applications contained in the Advantage® package.

Developing a plan to improve project management within an A/E firm or office presumes that a recognized need for improvement exists. An independent expert in project management systems and processes should be sought and retained to evaluate current operations within the realm of project management. As discussed elsewhere in this book, different project managers within an office may embrace widely differing project management practices. Management "style" between managers will vary despite internal efforts to achieve consistency of approach. However, the best opportunities for change, improvement and greater momentum toward an office standard for project management are derived from recommendations of an external, paid consultant.

Assessment and realignment of project management approaches within an office will focus on many (if not all) of the following:

Project Profitability Management Work Plan Derivation
Project Budgeting
Project Reporting Systems Data Integration Scheduling
Time Analysis Expense Analysis

Recommendations for improvements should be sought and expected in one or more of these areas, relying heavily upon the opinions of current project managers and their need for certain types of data. If a need for a certain type of data, or combination of data is demonstrated by a PM, chances are that the PM has already determined that such improvements are necessary to achieve greater efficiency in some aspect of the current system. The following paragraphs briefly describe the content and utility of each relevant project-related data and reporting category.

Project Profitability Management – enables firms to plan and track project profitability by identifying problems while the project is still in progress. By comparing actual and budgeted costs through the life of the project, project managers can stay on top of planning profits and be alerted to deviations in work progress.

Work Plan Deviation – forecasts periodic comparisons between planned work efforts (including labor, expense and consultants) and actual performance. This requires a detailed work plan to be prepared in advance of project initiation (as should always be the case) and schedule milestones to be correlated with labor and expenses.

Project Budgeting – involves project managers in establishing detailed project budgets to suit the nature of the contract, billing terms and deliverables. Budgets may be: based on cost and/or billing rates; developed at a summary or detailed level; updated to reflect changing costs or scope; used to compare percent of work completed to the percent of budget expended.

Project Reporting Systems – provides for reports to be produced whenever they are needed, making feedback available to project managers and other personnel while work is still in progress. A wide range of options is available so that varying degrees of detail or summary information may be included. Options exist to provide more than the 3 standard sort/select fields for the project manager, principal, and client. Up to 30 additional sort/select fields may be created to allow sorts on multiple levels and in many different combinations of data.

Data Integration – involves both integration of project management data, and the input from general ledger posting. A complete audit trail between project control and general ledger maintains data integrity. Automatic posting to general ledger accounts prevents accounting errors, eliminates the possibility of duplicate postings and speeds operations.

Scheduling – is more than milestones and time lines with concurrent and converging tasks. Scheduling provides for automatic reminders to the project manager to issue billings, generate consultant back-up, perform estimates to complete, and even make necessary collection calls.

Time Analysis – uses chargeability ratios for individual staff members or teams to summarize utilization and labor charged to non-billable accounts. Employee time (compensated and uncompensated) is tracked and compared (weekly and monthly) to planned utilization.

Expense Analysis – project detail for labor and expense transactions can be viewed by project, week, or employee. All expense postings and changes to the database in the order data was received are summarized and reported will drill- down capabilities for detail, vouchers and back-up.

Within newer project management and accounting systems, real time reporting capabilities may be expanded to encompass work-in-process, project progress reports, project detail, office detail and applications using interactive graphic display.

When making improvements in project management techniques and systems with an eye toward enhancing profits, attention should be devoted to developing a project budgeting process that demands profitability data when the budget is first established. In addition, for control and monitoring purposes, a system for immediate review of the profitability of all projects currently underway should be devised. Software programs (such as the Deltek Advantage system) are now able to allow customized reporting so project managers can quickly evaluate levels of project profitability in relation to the original profit portion of a project budget. Better and more frequent reports addressing profit at the project level will help focus attention on this all important aspect of running a successful A/E business.

Concurrently, improvements in office management can be undertaken to reduce overhead, control expenses and automate billing, accounts payable and payroll tasks. In the Deltek Advantage Software System (as an example) office management is made easier and less overhead intensive by automating functions within the accounting office. The

Deltek system focuses on seven specific areas of accounting and accounts management in parallel with project management systems improvements. These areas are: Basic Accounting; Billing; Accounts Payable; Payroll; Profit Center Reporting; Timekeeper; and Expense Keeper. Converting an office accounting and financial management function is serious business. Depending on the size of the firm, this conversion task can be daunting. For those firms that elect to go down this road, Delteck's Advantage software has many new and powerful features including:

- a superior reporting environment
- greater flexibility
- easier interfacing to "third party systems" (e.g., human resources, resource scheduling, and internal cost tracking)

Advantage® operates in a user-friendly Windows environment, eliminating the need to memorize codes or keep hardcopy data checklists. Data can be easily accessed throughout the system.

However, Advantage does not have every identical feature currently in CFMS RD Version 5.1 (another commonly used software program). Some features are not in Advantage, or are simply implemented in a different manner. Therefore, it is essential that an A/E firm's accounting staff participate in a thorough planning and implementation process to ensure that the upgrade runs smoothly. This process should include an analysis of the differences between existing software and Advantage, an understanding of the conversion, and training and testing requirements.

PROFIT BY DESIGN

The major phases in the accounting software conversion process include:

1. Planning
2. Hardware and Software Set-up
3. Test Conversion
4. Introductory Training
5. Segment Testing
6. Additional Application Training
7. Final Conversion
8. On-site Consulting/Training Assistance

Planning

The planning process usually lasts one or two days, and is led by an experienced consultant from the software provider. At this time:

- Input is gathered from senior management, accounting, project managers, and marketing regarding their requirements for the new system.
  - The current numbering system for project, task, labor code, general ledger, vendor, client, and employee are reviewed to determine if changes would be beneficial.
  - A demonstration of various new features and new reporting capabilities is provided.
  - A preliminary implementations schedule is developed.
  - The major phases in the conversion process are scheduled. The conversion process requires many steps and needs to be planned in detail.
  - An analysis of product differences is done, and a review of existing custom software is conducted to determine whether requirements can be handled without custom software.
  - The training program is scheduled so that staff is prepared to do the necessary testing.

Hardware and Software Set-up

The hardware and software set-up can be done with or without the assistance of the software provider, depending on the experience and desire of each firm. It is important to have the hardware and software platform properly established at this point, in order to conduct comprehensive segment testing.

Test Conversion

The test conversion allows senior management or the controller to confirm the accuracy of the conversion programs, and to provide a comprehensive test environment. The test database can be used by a firm to become familiar with the program, and to confirm how the firm will run the software on an ongoing basis. The more thorough the testing and experience with the test database, the greater the confidence in a smooth transition to Advantage.

Introductory Training

The introductory training familiarizes accounting staff with the most efficient way to operate the Advantage software to help run the firm. After the training is complete, staff will be able to take the software through its paces and test it thoroughly.

Segment Testing

Segment testing is conducted so that staff become familiar with each program function. Firm leadership must be satisfied that they can successfully run this new application to meet all business reporting needs. Segment testing allows users to gain confidence knowing that performing data entry (e.g., entering timesheets, expenses, invoices, and units nets similar results as obtained in CFMS). Revenue recognition, overhead, allocation, report generation, and interactive billing all need to be tested to ensure that users are satisfied with the outcomes, and any differences are understood.

Additional Application Training

Additional application training supplements the introductory training and is sometimes presented to a broader audience within the firm. The amount of additional training varies by firm based on experience and preference.

Final Conversion

The final conversion represents the actual cut over the new system. All transactions entered after this date will be recorded in Advantage. Timing of this conversion is critical. Issues such as payroll requirements, billing cycle, and report requirements all need to be considered. Many CFMS user firms are upgrading, and it is very important that schedules are followed in order to ensure that the software firm's consultants are available when needed.

On-site Consulting/Training Assistance
On-side consulting and training can provide additional assurance as the accounting office goes live. Having a consultant in the office during the conversion, and at the firm's first month end close can streamline the process and minimize any potential inconvenience.

The idea that profitability is a multi-faceted problem in any A/E office (large or small) is clear. Organizing an approach to improving profitability involves expertise, commitment, financial resources, automation, and instilling a sense of "profit goal" among the entire office and firm staff. Most important is the idea of commitment. Senior management within the firm must desire higher profits and take steps to communicate this desire to the staff. Balancing the objective of improved profits with less tangible, but important goals (such as improving design quality or staff capabilities) requires careful planning and a decision hierarchy to be developed. Whenever the idea of "profit" aligns with the many other cardinal aspects of practice, it must undoubtedly be near the top. Discussions at all levels of staff, formal and informal, in the lunch room and within the studio, should address the notion of profit as a daily pursuit.

PROFIT BY DESIGN

Building Delivery Process

An Overview of the Building Delivery Process (How Buildings Come into Being)

Building construction is a complex, significant, and rewarding process. It begins with an idea and culminates in a structure that may serve its occupants for several decades, even centuries. Like the manufacturing of products, building construction requires an ordered and planned assembly of materials. It is, however, far more complicated than product manufacturing. Buildings are assembled outdoors by a large number of diverse constructors and artisans on all types of sites and are subject to all kinds of weather conditions.

Additionally, even a modest-sized building must satisfy many performance criteria and legal constraints, requires an immense variety of materials, and involves a large network of design and production firms. Building construction is further complicated by the fact that no two buildings are identical; each one must be custom built to serve a unique function and respond to its specific context and the preferences of its owner, user, and occupant.

Because of a building's uniqueness, we invoke first principles in each building project. Although it may seem that we are "reinventing the wheel", we are in fact refining and improving the building delivery process. In so doing, we bring to the task the collective wisdom of the architects, engineers, and contractors who have done so before us. Although there are movements that promote the development of standardized, mass-produced buildings, these seldom meet the distinct needs of each user.

Regardless of the uniqueness of each building project, the flow of activities, events, and processes necessary for a project's realization is virtually the same in all buildings. This chapter presents an overview of the activities, events, and processes that bring about a building—from the inception of an idea or a concept in the owner's mind to the completed design by the architects and engineers and, finally, to the actual construction of the building by the contractor.

Design and construction are two independent but related and

generally sequential functions in the realization of a building. The former function deals with the creation of the documents, and the latter function involves interpreting and transforming these documents into reality—a building or a complex of buildings.

The chapter begins with a discussion of various stakeholders (personnel involved in the design and construction of the project) and the relational framework among them. Subsequently, a description of the two major elements of design documentation—construction drawings and specifications—is provided. Finally, the chapter examines some of the methods used for bringing a building into being, referred to as the project delivery methods. From the owner's perspective, these methods are called project acquisition methods.

The purpose of this chapter, as its title suggests, is to provide an overall, yet distilled, view of the construction process and its relationship with design. Although several contractual and legal issues are discussed, they should be treated as introductory. A reader requiring additional information on these topics should refer to texts specially devoted to them.

1.1 PROJECT DELIVERY PHASES

The process by which a building project is delivered to its owner may be divided into the following five phases, referred to as the project delivery phases. Although there is usually some overlap between adjacent phases, they generally follow this order:
- Predesign phase
- Design phase
- Preconstruction phase
- Construction phase
- Postconstruction phase

1.2 PREDESIGN PHASE

During the predesign phase (also called the planning or programming phase), the project is defined in terms of its function, purpose, scope, size, and economics. This is the most crucial of the five phases, and is almost always managed by the owner and the owner's team. The success or failure of the project may depend on how well this phase is defined, detailed, and managed. Obviously, the clearer the project's definition is, the easier it is to proceed to the subsequent phases. Some of the important predesign tasks are:

- Details of the project's program.
- Economic feasibility assessment, including the project's overall budget and financing.
- Site assessment and selection, including the verification of the site's appropriateness, and determining its designated land use (see Chapter 2).
- Governmental constraints assessment, for example, building code and zoning constraints (see Chapter 2) and other legal aspects of the project.
- Sustainability rating—whether the owner would like the project to achieve sustainability rating, such as the U.S. Green Building Council's (USGBC's) Leadership in Energy and Environmental Design (LEED) certification at some level (see Chapter 10).
- Design team selection.

Building (Project) Program

This includes defining the activities, functions, and spaces required in the building, along with their approximate sizes and their relationships with each other. For a house or another small project, the program is usually simple and can be developed by the owner without external assistance. For a large project, however, where the owner may be an institution (such as a corporation, school board, hospital, religious organization, or govern- mental entity), developing the program may be a complex exercise. This may be due to the size and complexity of the project or the need to involve several individuals—a corporation's board of directors, for example—in decision making. These constituencies may have differ- ent views of the project, making it difficult to create a consensus. Program development may also be complicated by situations in which the owner has a fuzzy idea of the project and is unable to define it clearly. By contrast, experienced owners tend to have a clear understanding of the project and generally provide a detailed, unambiguous program to the architect.

Although the owner must provide the program details to the

architect, it is not unusual for the owner to involve the architect in preparing the program for some architecturally complex projects. In this instance, the architect may be hired early during the predesign phase. Note that the architect's role in the preparation of the building program is not considered a part of the architect's "basic" services, but as an "additional" service, compensated separately [Ref. 1.1].

Whatever the situation, preparing the program is the first step in the project delivery process. It should be spelled out in writing and in sufficient detail to guide the design, reduce the liability risk for the architect, and avoid its misinterpretation. If a revision is made during the progress of the project, the owner's written approval is necessary.

1.3 DESIGN PHASE

The design phase begins after the selection of the architect. Because the architect (usually a firm) may have limited capabilities for handling the broad range of building-design activities, several different, more specialized consultants are usually required, depending on the size and scope of the project.

In most projects, the design team consists of the architect, landscape architect, civil and structural consultants, and mechanical, electrical, and plumbing (MEP) consultants. In complex projects, the design team may also include an acoustical consultant, roofing and water- proofing consultant, cost consultant, building code consultant, signage consultant, interior designer, and so on.

Some design firms have an entire design team (architects and specialized consultants) on staff, in which case, the owner will contract with a single firm. Generally, however, the design team comprises several different design firms. In such cases, the owner typically contracts the architect, who in turn contracts the remaining design team members, Figure 1.1.

Thus, the architect functions as the prime design professional and, to a limited degree, as the owner's representative. The architect is liable to the owner for his or her own work and that of the consultants. For that reason, most architects ensure that

PROFIT BY DESIGN

their consultants carry adequate liability insurance. architect's liability For Work Done By owner-contracted consultant In some projects, the owner may contract some consultants directly, particularly a civil consultant (for a survey of the site, site grading, slope stabilization, and the design of site drainage system), a geotechnical consultant (for investigation of the soil properties), and a landscape architect (for landscape and site design), Figure 1.2. These consultants may be engaged before or at the same time as the architect.

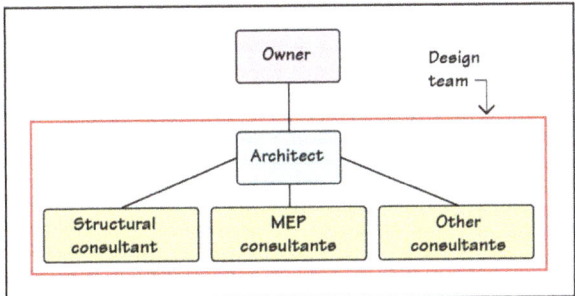

FIGURE 1.1 Members of a typical design team, and their interrelationships with each other and the owner in a traditional contractual set-up. A line in this illustration indicates a contractual relationship between parties. ("MEP consultants" is an acronym for mechanical, electrical, and plumbing consultants.)

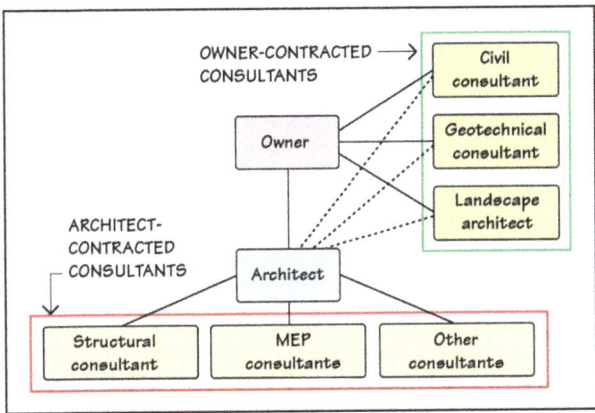

FIGURE 1.2 Members of a typical design team, and their interrelationships with each other and the owner in a project where some consultants are contracted directly by the owner. A solid line in this illustration indicates a contractual relationship between parties. A dashed line indicates a communication link, not a contract.

Even when a consultant is contracted directly by the owner, the architect retains some liability for the consultant's work. This liability occurs because the architect, being the prime design professional, coordinates the entire design effort, and the consultants' work is influenced a great deal by the architectural decisions. Therefore, the working relationship between the architect and an owner-contracted consultant remains essentially the same as if the consultant were chosen by the architect.

Engineer as Prime Design Professional

In some cases, an engineer or another professional may coordinate the design process. This generally occurs where architectural design is a minor component of a large-scale project. For example, in a highly technical project such as a power plant, an electrical engineer may be the prime design professional.

1.4   THREE SEQUENTIAL STAGES IN DESIGN PHASE

In most building projects, the design phase consists of three stages, which occur in the fol- lowing sequence:

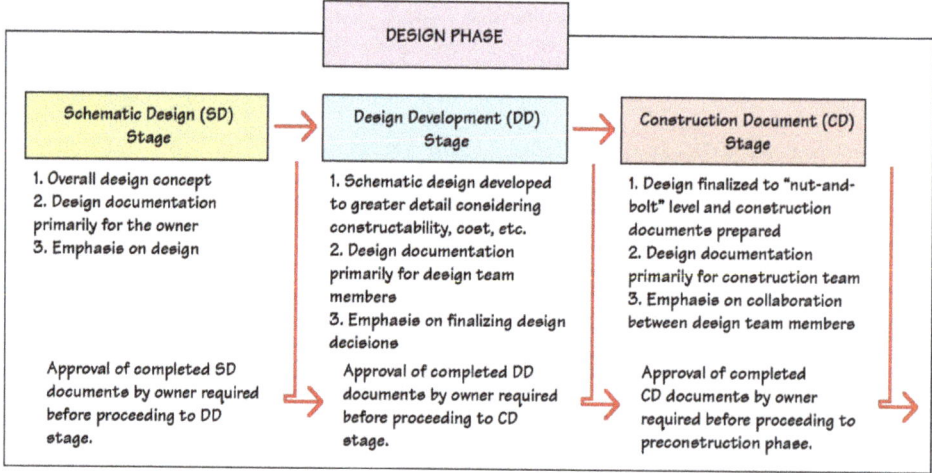

FIGURE 1.3 Three sequential stages (steps) of the design phase and the important tasks accomplished in each stage.

- Schematic Design (SD) stage
- Design development (DD) stage
- Construction document (CD) stage

Figure 1.3 illustrates the sequence and the important tasks accomplished in each stage. Note that at the end of each stage, a written approval from the owner is required before proceeding to the next stage, or from the design phase to the preconstruction phase.

Schematic Design stage—emphasis on Design
The schematic design gives graphic shape to the project program. It is an overall concept that illustrates key ideas of the design solution. The major player in this stage is the architect, who develops the design scheme (or several design options), generally with limited help from the consultants. Because most projects have strict budgetary limitations, a rough estimate of the project's probable cost is generally produced at this stage.

The schematic design usually goes through several revisions, because the first design scheme prepared by the architect will rarely be approved by the owner. The architect communicates the design proposal(s) to the owner through various types of drawings—plans, elevations, sections, freehand sketches, and three-dimensional graphics (isometrics, axonometrics, and perspectives). For some projects, a three-dimensional scale model of the entire building or the complex of buildings, showing the context (neighboring buildings) within which the project is sited, may be needed.

With significant developments in electronic media technology, especially building information modeling (BIM), computer-generated imagery has become common in architecture and related engineering disciplines. Computer-generated walk-through and flyover simulations are becoming increasingly popular for communicating the architect's design intent to the owner at the SD stage.

It is important to note that the schematic design drawings, images, models, and simulations, regardless of how well they are produced, are not adequate to construct the building. Their objective is merely to communicate the design scheme to the owner (and to consult- ants, who may or may not be on board at this stage), not to the contractor.

Design Development stage—emphasis on Decision Making

Once the schematic design is approved by the owner, the process of designing the building in greater detail begins. During this stage, the schematic design is developed further—hence the term design development (DD) stage.

While the emphasis in the SD stage is on the creative, conceptual, and innovative aspects of design, the DD stage focuses on developing practical, pragmatic, and constructible solutions for the exterior envelope, structure, fenestration, interior systems, MEP systems, and so forth. This development involves strategic consultations with all members of the design team.

Therefore, the most critical feature of the DD stage is decision making, which ranges from broad design aspects to finer details. At this stage, the vast majority of decisions about products, materials, and equipment are made. Efficient execution of the construction documents depends directly on how well the DD is managed. A more detailed version of the specifications and probable cost of the project is also prepared at this stage.

Construction Documents stage—emphasis on Documentation

The purpose of the construction documents (CD) stage is to prepare all documents required by the contractor to construct the building. During this stage, the consultants and architect collaborate intensively to work out the "nuts and bolts" of the building and develop the required documentation, referred to as construction documents. All of the consultants advise the architect, but they also collaborate with each other (generally through the architect) so that the work of one consultant agrees with that of the others.

The construction documents consist of the following items:
- Construction drawings
- Specifications

Construction Drawings
During the CD stage, the architect and consultants prepare their own sets of drawings, referred to as construction drawings.

Thus, a project has architectural construction drawings, civil and structural construction drawings, MEP construction drawings, landscape construction drawings, and so on.

Construction drawings are dimensioned drawings (usually computer generated) that fully delineate the building. They consist of floor plans, elevations, sections, schedules, and various large-scale details. The details depict a small portion of the building that cannot be adequately described on smaller-scale plans, elevations, or sections.

Construction drawings are the drawings that the construction team uses to build the building. Therefore, they must indicate the geometry, layout, dimensions, types of materials, details of assembling the components, colors and textures, and so on. Construction drawings are generally two-dimensional drawings, but three-dimensional isometrics are sometimes used for complex details. Construction drawings are also used by the contractor to prepare a detailed cost estimate of the project at the time of bidding.

Construction drawings are not a sequence of assembly instructions, such as for a bicycle. Instead, they indicate what every component is and where it will be located when the building is completed. In other words, the design team decides the "what" and "where" of the building. The "how" and "when" (means, methods, and sequencing) of construction are entirely in the contractor's domain.

Specifications

Buildings cannot be constructed from drawings alone, because there is a great deal of information that cannot be included in the drawings. For instance, the drawings will give the locations of columns, their dimensions, and the material used (such as reinforced concrete), but the quality of materials, their properties (the strength of concrete, for example), and the test methods required to confirm compliance cannot be furnished on the drawings. This information is included in the document called specifications.

Specifications are written technical descriptions of the design intent, whereas the drawings provide the graphic description.

The two components of the construction documents—the specifications and the construction drawings—complement each other and generally deal with different aspects of the project. Because they are complementary, they are supposed to be used in conjunction with each other. There is no order of precedence between the construction drawings and the specifications. Thus, if an item is described in only one place—either the specification or the drawings—it is part of the project, as if described in the other.

For instance, if the construction drawings do not show the door hardware (hinges, locks, handles, and other components) but the hardware is described in the specifications, the owner will get the doors with the stated hardware. If the drawings had precedence over the specifications, the owner would receive doors without hinges and handles.

Generally, there is little overlap between the drawings and the specifications. More importantly, there should be no conflict between them. If a conflict between the two documents is identified, the contractor must bring it to the attention of the architect promptly. In fact, construction contracts generally require that before starting any portion of the project, the contractor must carefully study and compare the drawings and the specifications and report inconsistencies to the architect.

If the conflict between the specifications and the construction drawings goes unnoticed initially but later results in a dispute, the courts have in most cases resolved it in favor of the specifications—implying that the specifications, not the drawings, govern the project. However, if the owner or the design team wishes to reverse the order, it can be so stated in the owner-contractor agreement.

PROFIT BY DESIGN

Relationship Between Construction Drawings and Specifications	
Construction Drawings	**Specifications**
Design intent represented graphically Product/material may be shown many times Product/material shown generically	Design intent represented with words Product/material described only once Product/material identified specifically, sometimes proprietary to a manufacturer Quality indicated
Quantity indicated Location of elements established Size, shape, and relationship of building elements provided	Installation requirements of elements established Description, properties, characteristics, and finishes of building elements provided

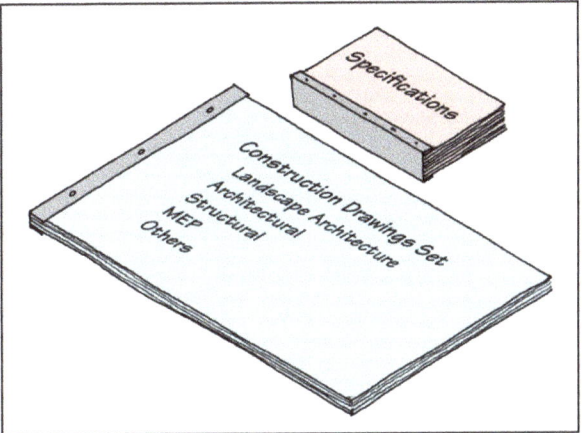

FIGURE 1.4 A construction document set consists of a set of architectural and consultants' construction drawings plus the specifications prepared by the architect and the consultants. The specifications are bound in book format along with other items.

The Construction Document Set

Just as the construction drawings are prepared separately by the architect and each consultant for their respective portions of the work, so are the specifications. The specifications from various design team members are assembled by the architect in a single document. Because the specifications are in text format (not as drawings), they are bound in book format. A few other items are also included in this document at a later stage, and the entire bound document is called the project manual, described in Section 1.7. The construction drawings plus the specifications constitute the construction document set, Figure 1.4 (see also Figure 1.11). Although hardcopy drawings and specification are common, their digital versions are being increasingly used.

Owner's Role During Design Phase
The owner's role in the design phase of the project may not appear as active as in the predesign phase, but it is important all the same. In fact, a conscientious owner will be fully involved throughout the entire project delivery process—from the predesign phase through the project closeout phase.

1.5 CSI MASTERFORMAT AND SPECIFICATIONS

The specification document for even a modest-sized project can run into hundreds of pages. It is used not only by the contractor and the subcontractors, but also by the owner, the material suppliers, and in fact, the entire construction team. With so many different people using it, it is necessary that the specifications be organized in a standard format so that each user can go to the section of particular interest without having to wade through the entire document.

The standard organizational format for specifications, referred to as MasterFormat, has been developed by the Construction Specifications Institute (CSI) and is the format most commonly used in the United States and Canada. MasterFormat is divided into two groups— (i) Procurement and Contracting Requirements group and (ii) Specifications group, Figure 1.5. The Specifications group is further divided into five subgroups, and each subgroup consists of divisions. The subgroup General Requirements comprises one division; Facilities Construction subgroup has 18 divisions; and the following three subgroups have 10 divisions each.

The total number of divisions in MasterFormat is 50, which are identified using six-digit numbers. The first two digits of the numbering system (referred to as Level 1 digits) identify the division number. The 50 division numbers are 00, 01, 02, 03, . . . , 48, and 49. A division identifies the broadest collection of related products and assemblies, such as Division 03—Concrete.

The next two digits of the numbering system (Level 2 digits) refer to various sections within the division, and the last two digits (Level 3 digits) refer to the subsections within a section. In other words, Level 2 and Level 3 digits classify products and assemblies into progressively closer affiliations. Thus, Level 1 digits in MasterFormat may be compared to chapter numbers in a book, Level 2 digits to section numbers of a chapter, and Level 3 digits to subsection numbers of a section.

A complete list of MasterFormat titles is voluminous. Figure 1.6 provides a bird's-eye view of MasterFormat, showing groups, subgroups, and divisions in each subgroup. It also provides additional details of one of the divisions, Division 04—Masonry—as brief illustration of the numbering system. Note that the Procurement and Contracting Requirements group is Division 00 and the Specifications group consists of Divisions 01 to 49.

Also note that MasterFormat deals with all types of construction (new buildings, renovations, and maintenance). Construction work and products, not directly related with buildings (services, urban infrastructural construction, equipment, etc.) are also included—in Divisions 30 to 49.

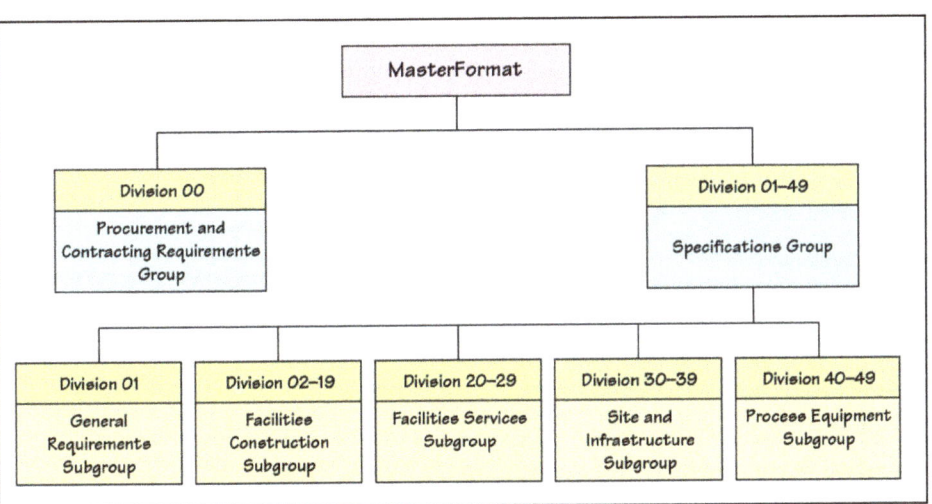

FIGURE 1.5 Structure of the MasterFormat, showing its separation into two groups—(i) Procurement and Contracting Requirements group and (ii) Specifications group. The Specifications group is further divided into five subgroups. Each subgroup is divided into a number of divisions.

PROFIT BY DESIGN

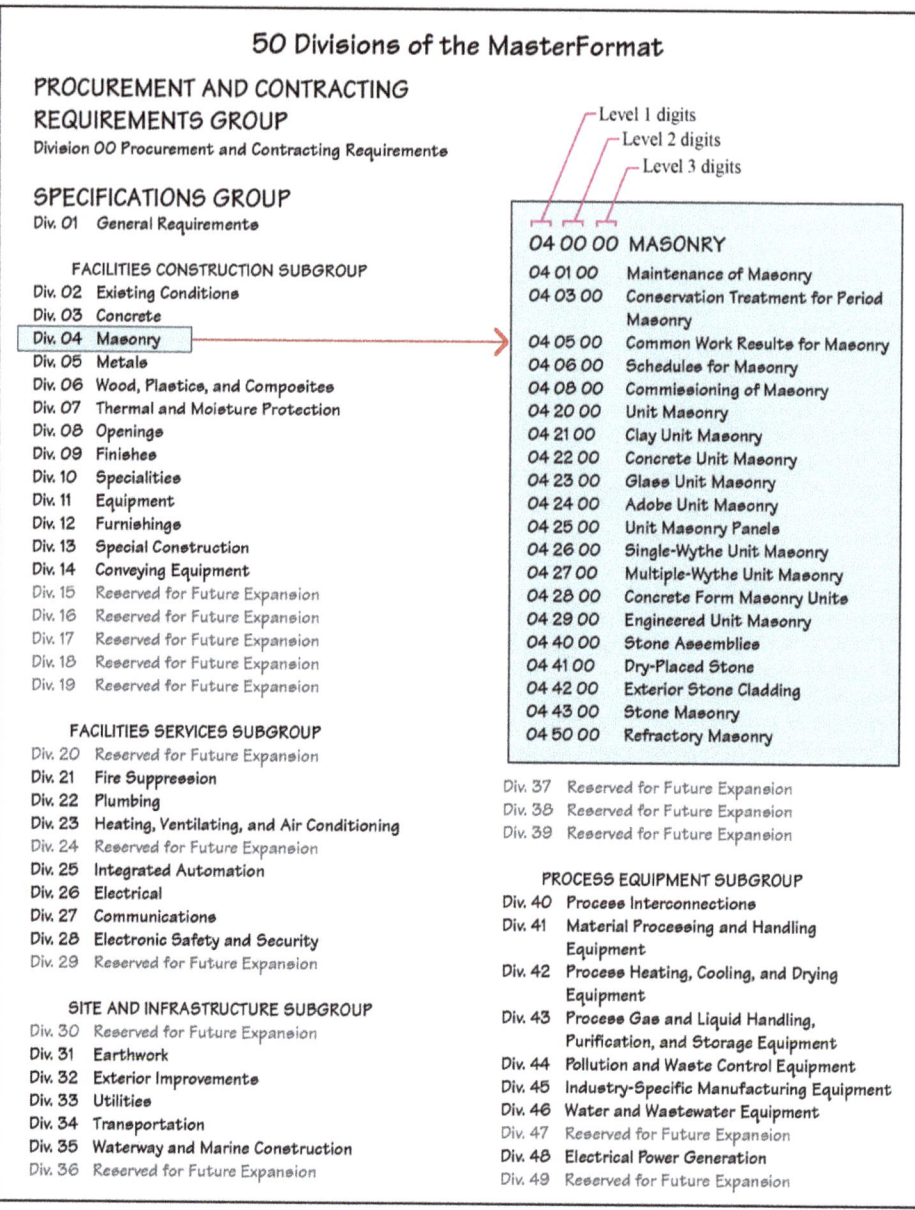

FIGURE 1.6 MasterFormat divisions. The first few sections (Level 2 details) of Masonry division have been highlighted in a box. Level 3 details would show further divisions of a section. For example, 04 23 13 covers the specifications of vertical glass unit masonry, 04 23 16 covers glass unit masonry floors, and 04 23 19 covers glass unit masonry skylights.

PROFIT BY DESIGN

Recollecting MasterFormat Division Sequence

Architectural design typically involves Divisions 02 to 14 of the Facilities Construction subgroup. Although the basis for sequencing the Divisions in this subgroup is far more complicated, the first few divisions (that are used in virtually all buildings) may be deduced by visualizing the sequence of operations required in constructing the simple building shown in Figure 1.7. The building consists of load-bearing masonry walls, steel roof joists, and wood roof deck.

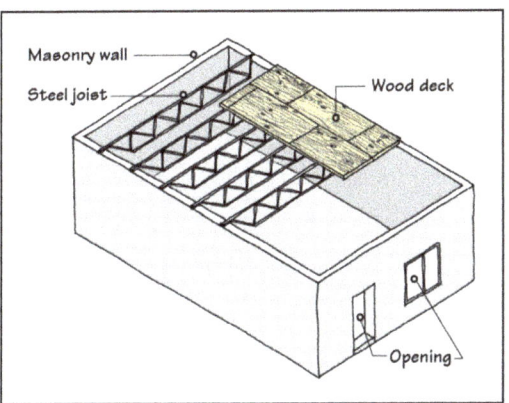

FIGURE 1.7 A simple load-bearing masonry wall building with steel roof joists and wood roof deck, used as an aid to recalling the sequence of first few divisions of the MasterFormat.

Obviously, the first operation in constructing such a building is to excavate for foundations and lay below-ground utility lines (water supply, sewage, electrical and telecommunication lines, etc.). Because excavation deals with earthwork, MasterFormat includes it in Division 31 (Site and Infrastructure subgroup). After earthwork, the next operation is to construct foundations. Because foundations are typically made of concrete, Concrete is Division 03. After the foundations have been completed, masonry work for the walls can begin. Thus, Masonry is Division 04. After the walls are completed, steel roof joists can be placed. Thus, Division 05 is Metals. The installation of wood roof deck follows that of the steel joists. Hence, Wood, Plastics, and Composites constitute Division 06.

After the roof deck is erected, it must be insulated and protected against weather. Therefore, Thermal and Moisture Protection is Division 07. Roofing and waterproofing (of basements) are part of this division, as are insulating materials and joint sealants. The next step is to protect the rest of the envelope; hence, Division 08 is Openings. All doors and windows are part of this division, regardless of whether they are made of steel, aluminum, or wood.

With the envelope protected, finish operations, such as those involving the interior dry-wall, flooring, and ceiling, can begin. Thus, Division 09 is Finishes. Division 10 is Specialties, which consists of several items that cannot be included in the previous divisions, such as toilet partitions, lockers, storage shelving, and movable partitions.

Obviously, the building must now receive all the necessary office, kitchen, laboratory, or other equipment. Thus, Division 11 is Equipment. Division 12 is Furnishings, followed by Special Construction (Division 13) and Conveying Equipment (Division 14).

Division 01 and Division 02
Before beginning with the coverage of individual materials and products, the MasterFormat covers items that apply to all of them, such as price and payment procedure, product substitution procedure, and contract modification procedure. These items are included in Division 01, titled as General Requirements, and illustrated in Figure 1.8. This illustration also provides items covered in Division 02—Existing Conditions.

Division 01 comes into effect during the construction phase, but all parties involved in the project (particularly the owner and the contractor) must know of their respective roles and obligations, detailed in this division, before signing the construction contract. By contrast Division 00, discussed in Section 1.7, comes into effect when the project is ready for soliciting bids for construction, that is, during the preconstruction phase.

MasterFormat and Construction-Related Information
Familiarity with MasterFormat is required to prepare the project manual and write the specifications for the project. It is also helpful in filing and storing construction information in an office. Material manufacturers also use MasterFormat division

numbers in catalogs and publications provided to design and construction professionals. MasterFormat is also helpful when seeking information about a construction material or system, as any serious student of construction (architect, engineer, or builder) must frequently do.

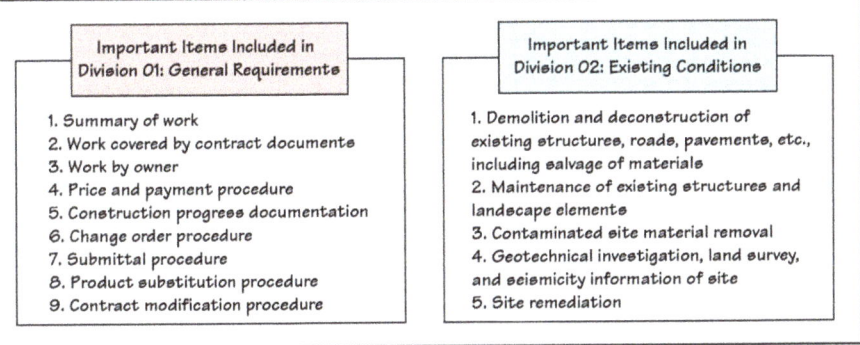

FIGURE 1.8 Important items included in MasterFormat Division 01 and Division 02.

1.6 THE CONSTRUCTION TEAM

The construction of even a small building involves so many specialized skills and trades that the work cannot normally be undertaken by a single construction firm. Instead, the work is generally done by a team consisting of the general contractor (GC) and a number of specialty subcontractors, Figure 1.9. Thus, a project may have roofing, window and curtain wall, plumbing, and heating, ventilation, and air-conditioning (HVAC) subcontractors among others, in addition to the general contractor. The general contractor's own work may be limited to certain components of the building (such as the structural components— load-bearing walls, reinforced concrete beams and columns, and roof and floor slabs), with all the remaining work subcontracted.

In contemporary projects, however, the trend is toward the general contractors not per- forming any actual construction work but subcontracting the work entirely to various sub- contractors. Because the subcontractors are contracted by the general contractor, only the GC is responsible and liable to the owner.

PROFIT BY DESIGN

In some cases, a subcontractor will, in turn, subcontract a portion of his or her work to another subcontractor, referred to as a second-tier subcontractor. In that case, the GC deals only with the subcontractor, not the second-tier subcontractor.

Whether the GC performs part of the construction work or subcontracts the entire work, the key function of the GC is the overall management of construction. This includes coordinating the work of all subcontractors, ensuring that the work done by them is completed in accordance with the contract documents, and ensuring the safety of all workers on the site. A GC with a good record of site safety not only demonstrates respect for the workers but also improves the profit margin by lowering the cost of construction insurance.

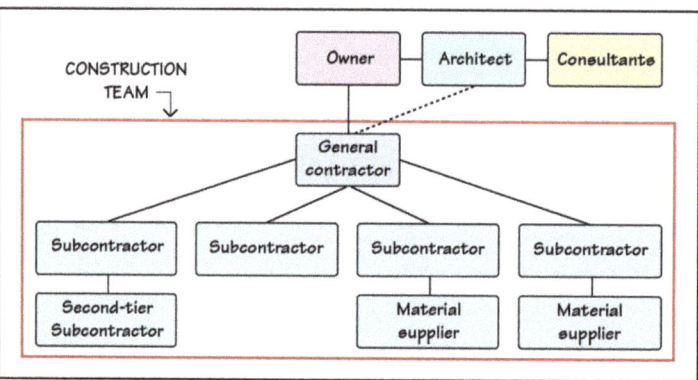

FIGURE 1.9 The construction team and their interrelationships with each other and the owner. A solid line in this illustration indicates a contractual relationship between parties. A dashed line indicates a communication link. The relationships shown here are not absolute and may change somewhat with the nature of the project.

Design and construction contracts as two-party contracts
It is important to note at this stage that all design and construction contracts are two-party contracts, such as owner-architect contract, owner-GC contract, architect-consultant con- tracts, and GC-subcontractor contracts. Multiparty design or construction contracts do not exist (except in the integrated project delivery method, described in Section 1.17).

1.7 PRECONSTRUCTION PHASE: THE BIDDING DOCUMENTS

The preconstruction phase comprises two important activities: preparation of bidding documents (also called bid package) and the selection of the GC. The bidding documents are prepared by the architect with the help of the entire design team. They are documents that are used by the GC to bid for the construction of the project. They include (i) construction documents, which comprises construction drawings and specifications (Divisions 01 to 49) and (ii) Division 00.

Division 00, titled as Procurement and Contracting Requirements, contains legal and contractual information that the GC must be aware of before preparing the bids. For the ease of grasping its contents, Division 00 may be divided into four parts: (a) bid procurement requirements, (b) contract requirements, (c) contract administration, and (d) available project information, Figure 1.10.

As shown in Figure 1.10, the bid procurement part of Division 00 refers to items that a GC will typically not deal with after signing the contract, such as instruction to bidders, prebid meetings, and bid bond information. The contract requirements part contains owner-GC agreement, conditions of contract, etc. Contract administration includes performance and payment bond details, and requirements for certificates of substantial and final completion. Available project information relates to land survey, geotechnical information, geophysical information, etc. An important component of geophysical information is the degree of seismicity of the site.

The bidding documents may also contain addenda. An addendum refers to a document that is added to the original construction documents during the bidding period because of the errors or omissions observed after the bidding documents have been released to the bidders. An addendum may also become necessary in response to questions raised during a prebid meeting by the prospective bidders.

After the contract has been awarded to the successful bidder, the bidding documents (with owner's and GC's signatures on documents where needed, and blank forms in Division 00 completed) become the contract documents. The contract documents may also include modifications to owner-GC contract after the execution of the original contract. These modifications must be mutually agreed to between the owner and the GC per contract modification procedure described in Division 01. The items included in contract documents are shown in Figure 1.11, which also illustrates the differences between construction documents, bidding documents, and contract documents.

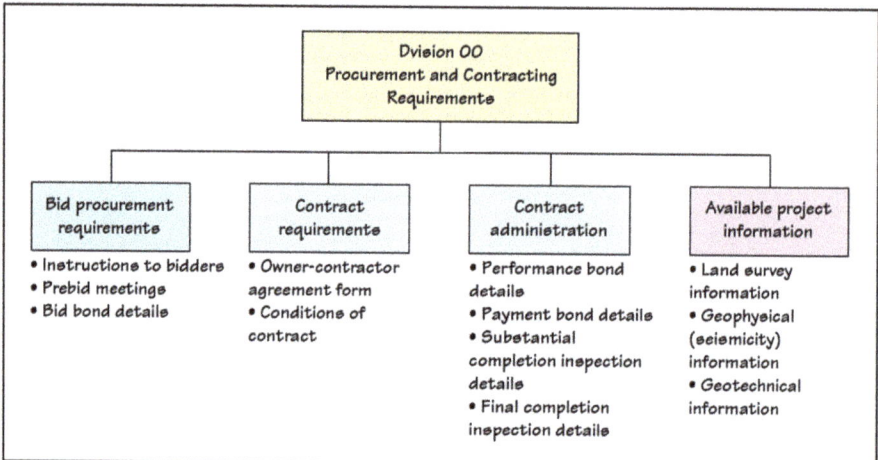

FIGURE 1.10 Important contents of MasterFormat Division 00.

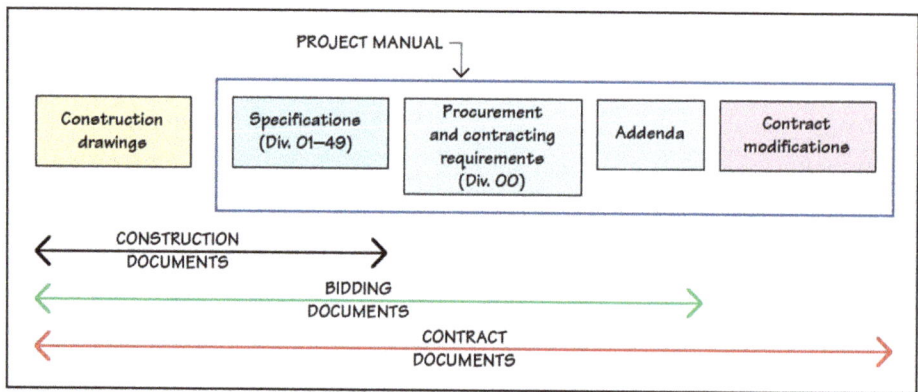

FIGURE 1.11 Differences among construction documents, bidding documents (also called "bid package"), and contract documents.

Although no owner would like to modify the contract, contract modifications are not uncommon. The reason, as stated in the introduction to this chapter, is that the construction of a typical building, unlike a manufactured product, is one-off entity, which may be subjected to unforeseen situations. Causes such as significant change in project scope (additive or deductive), design error or omission, nonavailability of materials due to national emergency, and extreme weather conditions may require contract modification.

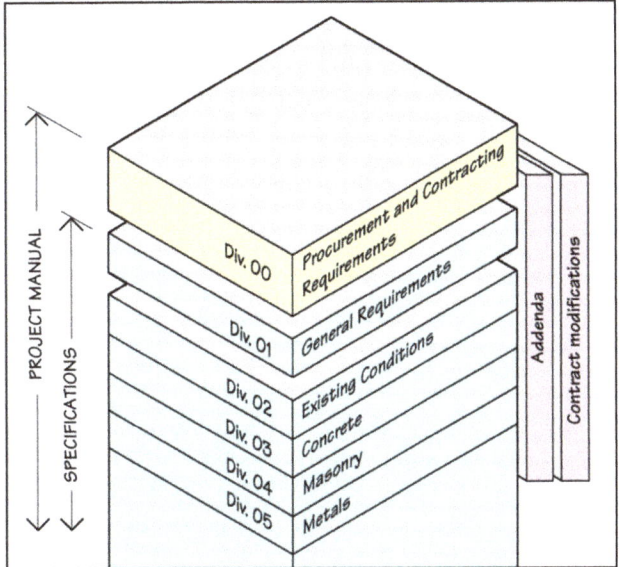

FIGURE 1.12 Contents of a typical project manual.

Project Manual

Project specifications (Division 01 to 49), Division 00, addenda, and contract modifications are bound together into a document called the project manual, Figure 1.12. In other words, the project manual comprises the contract documents minus the construction drawings.

1.8 PRECONSTRUCTION PHASE: THE SURETY BONDS

It is essential that the GCs bidding for the project are qualified by virtue of their financial resources and a successful record of contracting experience to undertake the project of the size and complexity of the owner's project. Therefore, a reliable and just process of screening the GCs must be used, which is achieved by requiring the GCs to provide bonds to the owner.

A bond is a form of surety, which ensures that if the GC fails to fulfill contractual obligations, there will be a financially sound third party—referred to as the surety (also called the guarantor or bonding company)—available to take over those unfulfilled obligations of the GC. The bond is, therefore, a form of insurance that the GC buys from a surety—a bonding company.

There are three types of surety bonds in most building projects. A few others may be required in some special projects. The three types of bonds are: (i) bid bond, (ii) performance bond, and (iii) payment bond, each with a unique purpose, as described hereunder, and illustrated in Figure 1.13.

Bid Bond
The purpose of the bid bond (also called the bid security bond) is to exclude frivolous bidders. It ensures that, if selected by the owner, the bidder (GC) will be able to enter into a contract with the owner based on the bidding requirements, and that the bidder will be able to obtain performance and payment bonds from an acceptable bonding company.

A bid bond is required at the time the GC submits the bid for the project. If the GC refuses to enter into an agreement or is unable to provide the required performance and payment bonds, the bonding company is obliged to pay a penalty (bid security amount) to the owner—usually between 5% and 10% of the project's anticipated cost.

Performance Bond
The performance bond is required by the owner before entering into an agreement with the successful GC. The performance bond ensures that if, after the award of the contract, the GC is unable to perform the work as required by the contract documents, the bonding company will provide sufficient funds for the completion of the project.

A performance bond protects the owner against default by the GC or by those for whose work the GC is responsible, such as the subcontractors. For that reason, the GC will generally require a performance bond from all major subcontractors.

Payment Bond
A payment bond (also referred to as a labor and materials bond) ensures that those providing labor, services, and materials for the project—such as the subcontractors and material suppliers—will be paid by the GC. In the absence

PROFIT BY DESIGN

of the payment bond, the owner may be held liable to those subcontractors and material suppliers whose services and materials have been invested in the project. This liability exists even if the owner has paid the GC for the work of these subcontractors and material suppliers.

Pros and Cons of Bonds

The bonds are generally mandated for a publicly funded project. In a private project, the owner may waive the bonds, particularly the bid bond. This saves the owner some money because although the cost of a bond (the premium) is paid by the GC, it is in reality paid by the owner since the GC adds the cost of the bond to the bid amount.

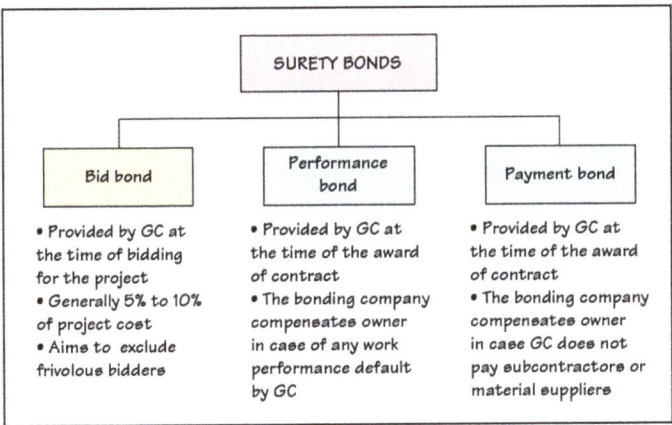

FIGURE 1.13 Details of three surety bonds used in construction projects.

Despite their cost, most owners consider the bonds (particularly the performance and payment bonds) a good value because they eliminate the financial risks of construction. The bid bond is unnecessary in an invitational bidding method where the owner knows the GC's financial standing and the ability to perform. However, where uncertainty exists, a bid bond provides an excellent prequalification screening of the GC. Responsible GCs and subcontractors generally maintain a close and continuous relationship with their bonding companies. Therefore, the bonding company's knowledge of a contractor's financial and contracting capabilities far exceeds that of most owners or architects (as the owner's representative).

1.9 PRECONSTRUCTION PHASE: SELECTING THE GENERAL CONTRACTOR AND PROJECT DELIVERY

After the bidding documents are ready, the selection of the GC is next obvious and a significant step forward. A number of selection methods exist. They differ from each other depending on:

    a. the basis of selection—open competition, limited competition, or negotiation with selected GCs,
    b. the timing of selection—stage of the project at which the selection is made—predesign phase, design phase, or preconstruction phase,
    c. the GC's role during the design phase, and
    d. the level of coordination between the design and construction teams through all phases of the project.

These methods are called the project delivery methods. Some of the most commonly used project delivery methods are:
- Design-bid-build (DBB) method
- Design-negotiate-build (DThB) method
- Construction manager at risk (CMAR) method
- Design-build (DB) method
- Integrated project delivery (IPD) method

The DBB is the oldest and most familiar method of project delivery. It has stood the test of time and enjoys the largest market share. The IPD is the latest method and still evolving in details with limited amount of industry consensus. Figure 1.14 gives the cur- rent approximate market shares of various methods [Refs. 1.2, 1.3], and the table "Project Delivery Methods at a Glance", at the end of this chapter, provides a synopsis of their pros and cons. The reader is urged to go through this table to obtain a bird's-eye view of various methods.

Regardless of the method selected, the essential features of construction and postconstruction phases are almost identical in all methods. Therefore, the activities involved in these two phases are covered first. In this coverage, we will assume that the GC has been selected and the construction has commenced. After the discussion of construction and postconstruction phases, the project delivery methods are covered in Sections 1.13 through 1.17.

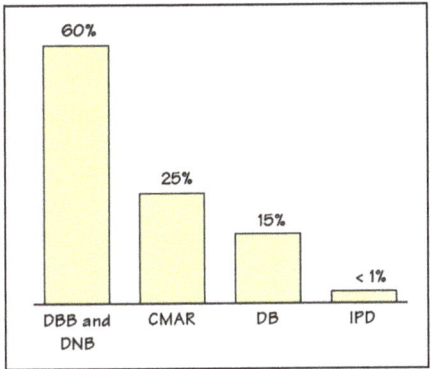

FIGURE 1.14 The current approximate market shares of various project delivery methods [Refs. 1.2, 1.3].

1.10   CONSTRUCTION PHASE: SUBMITTALS AND CONSTRUCTION PROGRESS DOCUMENTATION

The construction phase begins after the GC has been selected, contract awarded, and "notice to proceed" has been issued. The selection of a GC is a function of the chosen project delivery method. Regardless of the chosen project delivery method, the role of GC in the construction phase remains essentially the same in all of them, and the GC must conform to the work described in the contract documents.

In preparing the contract documents, the design team's aim is to communicate the design intent effectively in order to minimize missing pieces of information. However, in almost every project, there are a few items that cannot be described to absolute finality in contract documents. For these items, the design team makes its final decision based on the information sought from the GC. The entities from which the required information is obtained are called submittals. Typical submittals include material and product samples, product performance data, shop drawings, and mockups.

Shop Drawings
Shop drawings are required for components and products that must typically be made off-site (in a fabrication "workshop"). The need for shop drawings for certain items arises because the

construction drawings do not describe them to a level of detail that makes their fabrication possible. Therefore, the fabricators generate their own drawings, referred to as shop drawings, to provide the higher level of detail necessary to fabricate and assemble the components.

Shop drawings are not generic, consisting of manufacturers' or suppliers' catalogs, but are exclusively prepared for the project by the manufacturer, fabricator, erector, or subcontractors. Shop drawings are a big item for structural members, such as steel columns, steel beams, and reinforcement details in reinforced concrete members. They are also required for nonstructural components. For example, an aluminum window manufacturer must produce shop drawings to show that the required windows conform with the construction drawings and the specifications. Similarly, precast concrete panels, stone cladding, and marble or granite floor coverings require shop drawings before they are fabricated and installed.

Before commencing fabrication, the subcontractors and suppliers submit the shop drawings to the GC. The GC reviews them, marks them "approved", if appropriate, and then submits them to the architect for review and approval. Subcontractors or suppliers cannot submit shop drawings directly to the architect.

The review of all shop drawings is coordinated through the architect, even though they may actually be reviewed in detail by the appropriate consultant. Thus, the shop drawings pertaining to structural components are sent to the architect and then to the structural consultant for review and approval. The subcontractor or supplier generally begins fabrication only after receiving the architect's review of the shop drawings.

The review of shop drawings by the architect is limited to checking that the work indicated therein conforms with the overall design intent shown in the contract documents, Figure 1.15. Approval of shop drawings that are later discovered to deviate from the contract documents does not absolve the GC of the responsibility to comply with the contract documents for quality of materials, workmanship, or the dimensions of the fabricated components.

PROFIT BY DESIGN

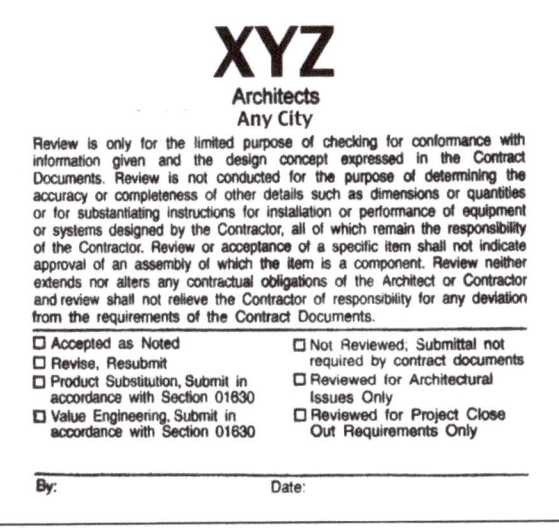

FIGURE 1.15 A typical stamp used by architects to indicate the result of review of shop drawings and other submittals.

FIGURE 1.16 A typical mockup showing various finishes on the exterior facade of a building under construction. The workmanship in the finished building will be evaluated to match that of the approved mockup.

Mockups

In addition to shop drawings, full-size mockups of one or more critical elements of the building may be required in some projects. This is done to establish the quality of materials and workmanship by which the completed work will be judged. For example, it is quite common for the architect to ask for the construction of a mockup that shows various exterior façade materials before undertaking the construction of the actual façade. Figure 1.16 shows a typical mockup of a building under construction. In some cases, the architect may require mockups of the same façade utilizing different materials, different colors, or different features to make the final design decision (see Figure 29.20).

Construction Progress Documentation

Keeping a complete and continuous documentation of construction is an essential part of a GC's work. Important documentation includes project correspondence, minutes of meetings, verbal conversations, weather conditions, change order logs, critical materials brought to the site, and site visits by third party (design team members, building inspection personnel from the city, OSHA staff, etc.). (OSHA is an acronym for Occupational Safety and Health Administration of the U.S. Government.)

In many contemporary projects, the owner requires the GC to install web-based cameras (webcam) on the site for a continuous, photographic documentation of construction progress, Figure 1.17. This digital imagery provides real-time (24 * 7) and remote access of construction progress to the owner and the design team, in addition to time-lapse videos if needed. Modern webcam technology provides high-resolution images that help detect breach of site safety conditions, theft of materials, and such other activities. Images of construction obtained through drones and helicopters are also common, but they do not provide continuous documentation.

PROFIT BY DESIGN

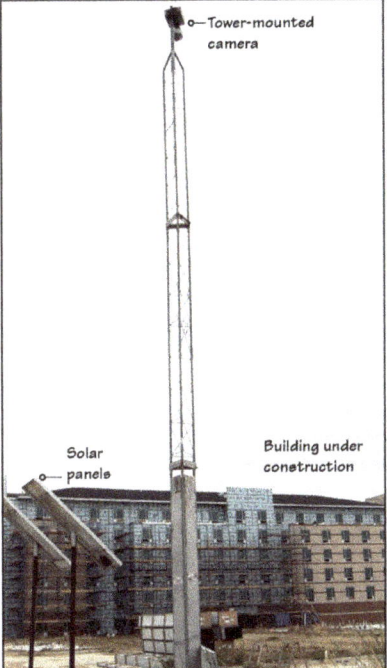

FIGURE 1.17 A tower-mounted camera takes regular photographs of the construction of the building shown. The solar panels power an array of batteries that, in turn, power the camera. The batteries are housed in a box below the panels, not visible in the photograph.

1.11 CONSTRUCTION PHASE: CONTRACT ADMINISTRATION

The GC will normally have an inspection process to ensure that the work of all subcontractors is progressing as indicated in the contract documents and that the work meets the standards of quality and workmanship. On smaller projects, this may be done by the project superintendent. On large projects, a team of quality-assurance inspectors generally assists the contractor's project superintendent. These inspectors are individuals who, by training and experience, are specialized in their own areas of construction—for example, concrete, steel, or masonry.

Additional quality control is required by the contract through the use of independent testing laboratories. For instance, structural concrete brought to the site must be verified for strength and other properties by independent concrete-testing laboratories.

Leaving quality control of materials and performance entirely in the hands of the GC is considered inappropriate. It can render the owner vulnerable to omissions and errors in the work, and it places an additional legal burden on the GC. Therefore, the owner usually retains the services of the project architect to provide a third-party level of scrutiny to administer the construction contract. If not, the owner will retain another independent architect, engineer, or inspector to provide construction contract administration services.

Architect's Observation of Construction
The architect's role during the construction phase has evolved over the years. There was a time when architects provided regular supervision of their projects during construction, but the liability exposure resulting from the supervisory role became so adverse for the architects that they have been forced to relinquish this responsibility. Instead, the operative term for the architect's role during construction is referred to as field observation of the work.

The observational role still allows the architects to verify that their drawings and specifications are transformed into reality just as they had conceived. It also provides a sufficient safeguard against the errors caused by the contractors' misinterpretation of contract documents in the absence of the architects' clarification and interpretation.

The shift in the architect's role to observer of construction also recognizes the important and entirely independent role that the GC must play during construction. This recognition provides full authority to the GC to proceed with the work in the manner that the GC deems appropriate. This reinforces the earlier statements that:
- The architect determines the what and where.
- The GC determines the how (means and methods) and when (sequence) of construction.

In other words, daily supervision or superintendence of construction is the function of the GC—the most competent person to fulfill this role. The architect provides periodic observation and evaluation of the GC's work and notifies the owner if the work is not in compliance with the intent of the contract documents. This underscores the division between the responsibilities of the architect and the GC during construction.

Note that by providing observation, the architect does not certify the GC's work. Thor does the observation relieve the GC of his or her responsibilities under the contract. The GC remains fully liable for any error that has not been discovered through the architect's observation. However, the architect may be held liable for all or part of the work observed, should the architect fail to detect or provide timely notification of work not conforming with the contract documents. This omission is known as failure to detect.

Because many components can be covered up by other items over days or hours, the architect should visit the construction site at regular intervals, as appropriate to the progress of construction. For example, earthwork covers foundations and underground plumbing, and gypsum board covers ceiling and wall framing. Observing the work after the components are hidden defeats the purpose of observation.

On some projects, a resident project architect or engineer may be engaged by the architect, at an additional cost to the owner, to observe the work of the GC. Under the conditions of the contract, the GC is generally required to provide this person with an on-site office, water, electricity, a telephone, and other necessary facilities.

Inspection of Work
There are only two times during the construction of a project that the architect makes an exception to being an observer of construction. At these times, the architect inspects the work. These inspections are meant to verify the GC's claim that the work is: (a) substantially complete and (b) fully complete, and hence is ready for the final payment. These inspections, explained in Section 1.12, are referred to as:
- Substantial completion inspection
- Final completion inspection

Payment Certifications

In addition to construction observation and inspection, there are several other duties the architect must discharge in administering the contract between the owner and the GC. These are outlined in the box "Summary of Architect's Functions as Construction Contract Administrator". Certifying (validating) the GC's periodic requests for payment against the work done and the materials stored at the construction site is perhaps the most critical of these functions.

An application for payment (typically made once a month unless stated differently in the contract) is followed by the architect's evaluation of the work and necessary documentation to verify the GC's claim. Because the architect is not involved in day-to-day supervision, the issuance of the certificate of payment by the architect does not imply acceptance of the quality or quantity of the GC's work. However, the architect has to be judicious and impartial to both the owner and the GC, and perform within the bounds of the contract.

Change Orders

There is hardly a construction project that does not require changes after construction has begun. The contract between the owner and the GC recognizes this fact and includes provisions for the owner's right to order a change and the GC's obligation to accept the change order in return for an equitable price adjustment. Here again, the architect performs a quasi-judicial role to arrive at a suitable agreement and price between the owner and the GC.

Note that the change orders refer to minor changes in the project and are unilaterally made by the owner. Where the project requires significant modifications, the contract must be modified and the modifications are to be mutually agreed upon between the owner and the GC. Thus, a construction contract differentiates between "changes" and "modifications".

1.12 POSTCONSTRUCTION PHASE: PROJECT CLOSEOUT

Once the project is sufficiently complete, the GC will ask the architect to conduct a substantial completion inspection to confirm that the work is complete in most respects. By doing so, the GC implies that the work is complete enough for the owner to occupy the facility and start using it, even though there might be cosmetic and minor work yet to be completed.

The GC's request for substantial completion inspection by the architect should include a list of incomplete portions of the work (to be completed), referred to as the punch list. The punch list, which is prepared by the GC, is used by the architect as a checklist to review all work, not merely the incomplete portions of the work. If the architect's inspection discloses incomplete items not included in the GC's punch list, they are added to the list by the architect.

The substantial completion inspection is also conducted by the architect's consultants, either with the architect or separately. Incomplete items discovered by them are also added to the punch list. If the additional items are excessive, the architect may ask the GC to complete the selected items before rescheduling the substantial completion inspection.

Certificate of Occupancy and GC's Request for Substantial Completion Inspection

The GC is required to secure a certificate of occupancy before requesting substantial completion inspection by the architect and the design team. The certificate of occupancy is provided by the authority having municipal jurisdiction over the project—usually the city where the project is permitted and built. The certificate of occupancy confirms that all appropriate inspections and approvals, required by the authority having jurisdiction, have taken place, the project is safe to use and occupy, and that the site has been cleared of the GC's temporary facilities so that the owner can occupy the building without obligations to any authority.

Substantial Completion—The Most Important Project Date

In addition to the certificate of occupancy, the GC must submit all required guaranties and warranties from the manufacturers of equipment and materials and the specialty subcontractors and installers used in the building. For instance, the manufacturers of roofing materials, windows, curtain walls, mechanical equipment, etc. warrant their products for specified time periods. These warranties are in addition to the standard one-year correction period between the owner and the GC.

The warranties are to be given to the architect at the time of substantial completion for review and transmission to the owner. Because the obligatory one-year correction period between the owner and the GC, as well as other extended-time warranties, begins from the date of substantial completion of the project, the substantial completion date is an important project closeout event. That is why the GC is allowed a brief time interval to complete the work fully after the successful substantial completion inspection.

A successful substantial completion inspection results in the GC receiving the certificate of substantial completion from the architect. An important part of this certificate is the date of substantial completion, which implies that the GC is no longer liable for the maintenance (cleaning and upkeep), utility costs, insurance, and security of the project. These responsibilities and liabilities are transferred to the owner.

Final Completion Inspection
After the GC carries out all the corrective work identified during the substantial completion inspection and so informs the architect, the architect (with the assistance of the consultants) carries out the final inspection of the project. If the final inspection passes, certification for final payment is issued by the architect, which entitles the GC to receive the final payment from the owner.

Before the certification for final completion is executed by the architect, and finally by the owner, the owner receives the record documents, keys and key schedule, equipment manuals, and other specified necessities. Additionally, the owner receives all legal documentation to indicate that the GC will be responsible for claims made by any subcontractor, manufacturer, or other party with respect to the project.

Record Documents (As-Built Documents)
As previously stated, minor design changes are often made during the construction of a project. These changes must be recorded for the benefit of the owner should the owner wish to

alter or expand the building in the future. Therefore, after the building has been completed, the GC is required to provide a set of record drawings (previously known as as-built drawings). These drawings reflect the changes that were made during the course of construction by the GC.

In addition to record drawings, record specifications, as well as a set of approved shop drawings, are usually required to complete the record document package delivered to the owner.

1.13 PROJECT DELIVERY METHOD: DESIGN-BID-BUILD METHOD

In the design-bid-build method, the GC is selected through competition. The owner obtains multiple bids for the project from which the GC, who provides the "best value for money", is selected. Within this overall approach, several versions are available to suit the requirements of the project and the particular needs of the owner. Collectively, these delivery versions are referred to as the design-bid-build (DBB) method because in this version, the design, bid, and construction phases of a project are sequential, and one phase does not begin until the previous phase has been completed, as graphically shown in Figure 1.18. Following are three commonly used versions of the DBB method of delivery.

- DBB Method—competitive sealed bidding (open bidding)
- DBB Method—competitive sealed proposal
- DBB Method—invitational bidding (closed bidding)

DBB Method—Competitive Sealed Bidding

The award of a construction contract to the GC is based on open bidding process, commonly called competitive sealed bidding. This refers to the process by which "qualified" GCs are invited to bid on the project; the "qualification" comes from the requirement of the bid bond. The invitation can be issued through advertisements in newspapers and trade publications, but web-based construction project bidding platforms, also called construction project procurement opportunities, are commonly used. The GCs regularly access these Web sites to keep abreast of the opportunities.

PROFIT BY DESIGN

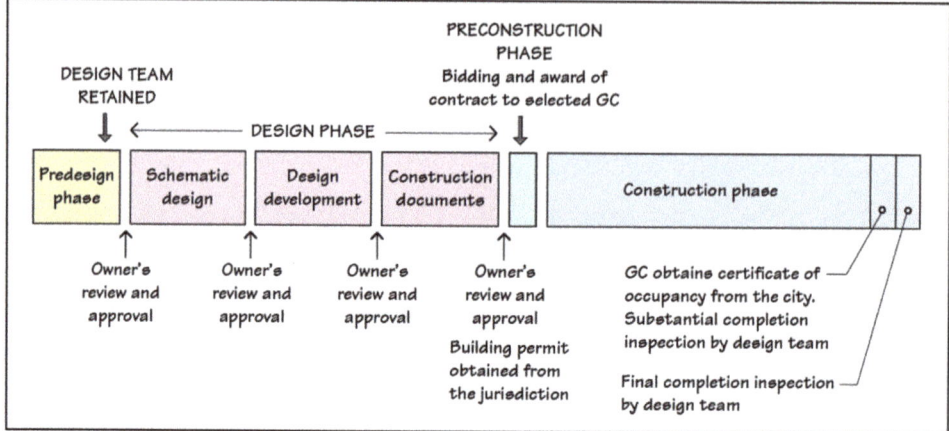

FIGURE 1.18 Sequence of operations in design-bid-build (DBB) method of project delivery. Note that design and construction phases are in sequence, and GC is selected only after the construction documents have been completed by the design team.

Because of the prequalification established through bid bond, all bidders are similarly qualified with respect to financial ability, experience, and technical expertise. Because all bidders receive the same information and are of the same standing, the competition is fair. Therefore, the contract is generally awarded to a qualified bidder with the lowest bid amount.

DBB Method—Competitive Sealed Proposal

This method is similar to competitive sealed bidding and is commonly used for publicly funded projects. The difference between competitive sealed bidding and competitive sealed proposal methods is that the owner's selection of the GC is not based on price alone but also on other criteria such as the GC's past experience, safety record, proposed personnel, and project schedule. To ensure fairness, the advertisement and bidding documents must provide the details of the selection criteria, with relative weightings assigned to each criterion.

DBB Method—Invitational Bidding

Invitational bidding, also called closed bidding, is another variation of the DBB method that is generally used for quasi-public and some private projects. In this method, the owner preselects the GCs who have demonstrated, based on their experience, resources, and financial standing, their qualifications to perform the work. The selected GCs are then invited to bid for the project, and the GC with the lowest bid is then awarded the contract. The architect (as the owner's representative) may be involved in preselection process.

Advantages of DBB Method
As stated in Section 1.9 and shown in Figure 1.14, the DBB method is the most popular method. In addition to being simple and well understood because of its long history, it has following advantages: (a) there is a single point of responsibility for construction, (b) the GC is selected through aggressive and open competition, and (c) the project's scope and cost are fully defined before construction starts.

1.14 PROJECT DELIVERY METHOD: DESIGN-NEGOTIATE-BUILD METHOD

A major disadvantage of the DBB method is the absence of the GC's preconstruction (design-phase) services. A delivery method that addresses this concern uses a negotiated contract and is called the design-negotiate-build (DThB) project delivery method.

The DThB method is used where the owner knows of one or more reputable, competent, and trusted GCs. The owner simply negotiates with them concerning the overall contract price, time required for completion, and other important details of the project. The negotiations are generally conducted with one GC at a time, and after negotiations with all selected GCs are complete, the owner analyzes the bids, selects a GC, and awards the contract.

A major advantage of the negotiated contract is that the GC can be on board during the design (or predesign) phase. This helps the owner ensure that the architect's design is realistically constructible. In many situations, the GC may advise the architect of simpler, less expensive, or more sophisticated building systems to realize the architect's design intentions.

Additionally, because the GC is the one who is most knowledgeable about construction costs, budget estimates can be obtained at various stages during the design phase. This means that value engineering can proceed throughout the design phase instead of being undertaken at the end of this phase or during construction, as in the DBB method of project delivery.

Because the vast majority of owners have to work within a limited budget, the DThB method is fairly popular for private projects. The services offered by the GC during the design phase of a negotiated contract are referred to as the GC's preconstruction services.

The negotiated contract is not devoid of competition, because the GC obtains competitive bids from numerous subcontractors and material suppliers. Because the GC is selected during the SD or DD stage, the bids from some or all subcontractors can be obtained earlier, which generally shortens the project delivery time.

1.15 PROJECT DELIVERY METHOD: CONSTRUCTION MANAGEMENT-RELATED METHODS

In the delivery methods so far discussed (DBB and DThB), the role of the architect remains essentially the same: the architect designs the project, helps the owner select the GC, and provides construction administration services during the construction phase as the owner's representative. In the 1970s, in response to cost overruns and time delays caused by lack of realism in the design of several projects, owners began to seek the assistance of the contracting community during the design phase of the project. This approach became more common as project complexities grew, giving birth to an entirely new profession called construction management.

Construction Manager as the Owner's Agent— (CMAA) Method

The project delivery method, in which a construction manager (CM) is included, is referred to as the construction manager as agent (CMAA) method. In this method, the owner retains a CM as the owner's agent to advise on such issues as cost, scheduling, site supervision, site safety, construction finance administration, and overall building construction.

Note that the CM is not a GC, but a manager who plays no entrepreneurial role in the project (unlike the GC, who assumes financial risks in the project). In most CMAA projects, the owner hires the CM as the first step. The CM may advise the owner in the selection of the architect and other members of the design team as well as the contracting team.

The birth of the CMAA delivery method does not mean that there is no construction management in DBB, or the negotiated contract method. It exists but it is done informally and shared by the design team and the GC.

The introduction of a CM on the project transfers various functions of the GC (in a traditional method) to the CM. Thus, in the CMAA method, the GC becomes redundant. Therefore, there is no GC in this method, and the owner awards multiple contracts to various trade and specialty contractors, whose work is coordinated by the CM. Thus, the structural framework of the building may be erected by one contractor, masonry work done by another, interior drywall work by yet another, and so on.

Each contractor is referred to as a prime contractor, who may have one or more subcontractors, Figure 1.19. The task of scheduling and coordinating the work of all prime contractors and ensuring site safety—undertaken by the GC in the DBB and DThB methods—is done by the CM in the CMAA method. Additionally, the CM administers the contracts between the prime contractors and the owner. Note, however, that because the CM is only an agent (employed to administer the contract on behalf of the owner), all the financial risks and other liabilities in the project are assumed by the owner.

Thus, the owner, by assuming part of the role of the GC, eliminates the GC's markup on the work of the subcontractors. The owner may also receive a reduction in the fee charged by the architect for contract administration. Although these savings are partially offset by the fee that the owner pays to the CM, there can still be substantial savings in large but technically simple projects.

PROFIT BY DESIGN

The CMAA project delivery method is particularly attractive to owners who are knowledgeable about the construction process and can participate fully in all of its aspects, from bidding and bid evaluation to the closeout phase.

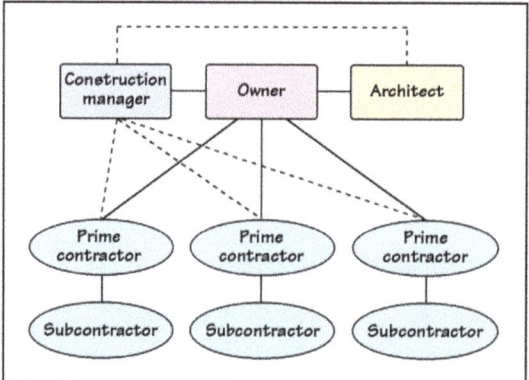

FIGURE 1.19 Contractual relationships between various parties in the CMAA method of project delivery. A solid line in this illustration indicates a contractual relationship between parties.
A dashed line indicates a communication link, not a contract.

Construction Manager at Risk (CMAR) Method

A disadvantage of the CMAA method lies in the liability risk that the owner assumes, which in the DBB method is held by the GC. This means that there is not the same incentive for the CM to optimize efficiency as when the CM carries financial risks.

Additionally, in the CMAA method, there is no single point of responsibility among the various prime contractors. Each prime contractor has a direct contract with the owner. Consequently, the CM has little leverage to ensure timely performance. The owner must therefore exercise care in selecting the CM because the cost, timeliness, and quality of the ultimate product are heavily dependent on the expertise of the CM.

In response to the preceding concerns, the CMAA method has evolved into what is known as the construction manager at risk (CMAR) method. In this method, the roles of the CM and GC are performed by one entity, but the compensation for these roles is paid separately by the owner.

PROFIT BY DESIGN

In the CMAR method, the owner contracts with a CMAR company to (a) provide preconstruction services during the design phase of the project for a professional fee and (b) work as the GC of the project. Thus, the CMAR company works with the architect during the design phase to develop construction documents that will meet the owner's budget and schedule. In doing so, the CMAR company functions as the owner's representative. The relationships between the various parties in a CMAR project delivery method are shown in Figure 1.20.

After the drawings are completed, all the work is competitively bid by subcontractors and the bids are opened in the owner's presence. The work is normally awarded to subcontractors with the lowest bids. In working as the GC, the CMAR company assumes all responsibilities for subcontractors' work and site safety. The CMAR method is being increasingly used for publicly funded projects such as schools, university residence halls, and apartment buildings.

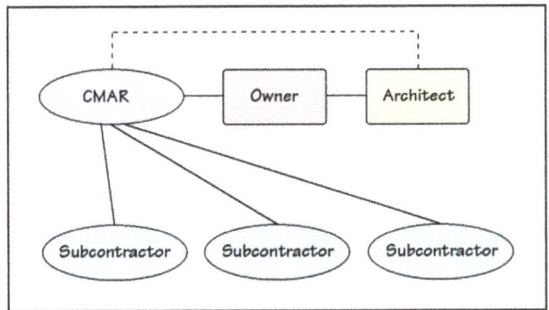

FIGURE 1.20 Contractual relationships between various parties in the CMAR method of project delivery. A solid line in this illustration indicates a contractual relationship between parties.
A dashed line indicates a communication link, not a contract.

1.16 PROJECT DELIVERY METHOD: DESIGN-BUILD METHOD

A project delivery method that integrates design and construction activities into a single entity is called the design-build (DB) method. In this method, the owner awards the contract to one firm, which designs the project and also builds it, either on a cost-plus-profit basis or on a lump-sum basis. In many ways, this method resurrects the historic master-builder method, in which there was no separation between the architect and the contractor. The design-build firm is usually a GC, which in addition to providing construction capabilities, has a design team (of architects and engineers) within the organization, or a closely allied separate design firm.

The DB method has the advantage of integrating design and construction, thus fostering teamwork between the design team and the contracting team throughout the project. It can provide a reduction in change orders for the owner, faster project completion, and a single source of responsibility. The major disadvantage is that the owner does not receive the protection provided by the checks and balances inherent in delivery methods with separate design and construction responsibilities. Consequently, once the contract has been awarded to a DB firm, the owner loses much of the control over the project. Additionally, the architect does not represent the owner, as in other delivery methods. Therefore, for the DB method of delivery to succeed, the end result must be meticulously defined prior to the award of the contract.

The DB method has been in existence for decades in single-family residential construction. It is now being increasingly accepted in commercial construction—for both private and publicly funded projects. The establishment of the Design-Build Institute of America (DBIA) has further promoted the method.

A special version of DB method, referred to as the turnkey method, consists of the DB firm arranging for the land and financing for the project in addition to designing and constructing it.

1.17 INTEGRATED PROJECT DELIVERY METHOD

The integrated project delivery (IPD) method is the ultimate in promoting harmony, collaboration, and integration among all team members who contribute to the project. While the members of the triad (owner, architect-engineer team, and contracting team) are separated into three distinct entities in the DBB or CMAR method, and into two distinct entities in the DB method, they are integrated fully into one entity in the IPD method, Figure 1.21.

PROFIT BY DESIGN

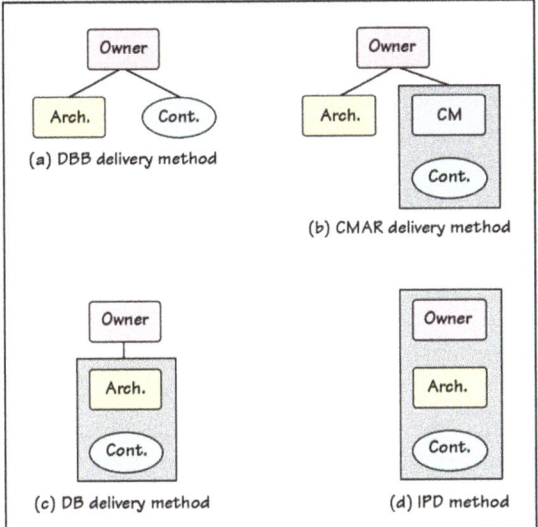

FIGURE 1.21 This illustration shows the relative integration among three major entities—owner, architect (Arch.), and contractor (Cont.)—in four major project delivery methods. Note that there is limited integration among the three entities in the DBB or CMAR method, partial integration in the DB method, and (supposedly) full integration in the IPD method. (The term architect implies the entire design team, which includes the architect and the architect's consultants.)

In fact, the IPD method involves not simply the integration of the three major entities but of all those who contribute to the project (owner, architect, engineers, GC, subcontractors, fabricators, material suppliers, etc.). All participants come on board during the design phase or as soon as their expertise is needed. The entire delivery process, from inception to completion, is open across participants, with continuous sharing of knowledge.

The central underlying philosophy of IPD is across-the-board, trust-based collaboration in a zero-blame and zero-litigation environment. Differences and disputes are resolved with-out delay, as in any well-run organization under a single command authority comprising a group of individuals representing different interests and expertise in the project. Therefore, the project's management is shared, and so are the responsibilities, risks, and rewards.

Integrated Project Delivery (IPD) and Building Information Modeling (BIM)

IPD can be used with traditional computer-aided design (CAD) technologies for design, preparation of construction documents, and actual construction and its management, but it is best suited for use with the latest technology known as building information modeling (BIM). Simply explained, BIM technology produces a virtual, three-dimensional model of the pro- posed building so that a complete digital version of the building is completed before its actual construction begins.

The virtual model is constructed through the participation and coordination of all members of the triad representing the owner, the architect-engineer team, and the contracting team, Figure 1.22. The model is built over a period of time in the same way that a real building is constructed. That is why the process using BIM is commonly referred to as virtual construction.

A virtual, three-dimensional model of the building is just one important feature of BIM. Another important feature is that the model contains information about the physical and performance characteristics of various components of the model—walls, floors, roofs, openings, finishes, and so on. Therefore, the model comprises intelligent, data-rich three-dimensional objects rather than mere two-dimensional graphics (lines, rectangles, curves, etc.).

BIM and Detection of Clashes Among Building Components

The virtual construction feature of BIM ensures that the clashes between various building systems or components are discovered during the design phase and can be eliminated as the model is constructed. For example, because of the two-dimensional nature of conventional drafting technology, unintended but serious errors, such as an HVAC duct passing through a floor beam or an underground utility pipe crossing a column footing, are not uncommon in conventional projects. When discovered during construction, such errors result in a blame game, request for information (RFI) from the GC, change orders, increased project costs, and delayed project completion. In extreme cases, litigation is a possibility. BIM eliminates such possibilities. Figures 1.23(a) and 1.23(b) illustrate the capability of BIM for detecting clashes, such as between an HVAC duct and a column, and between a duct and two beams.

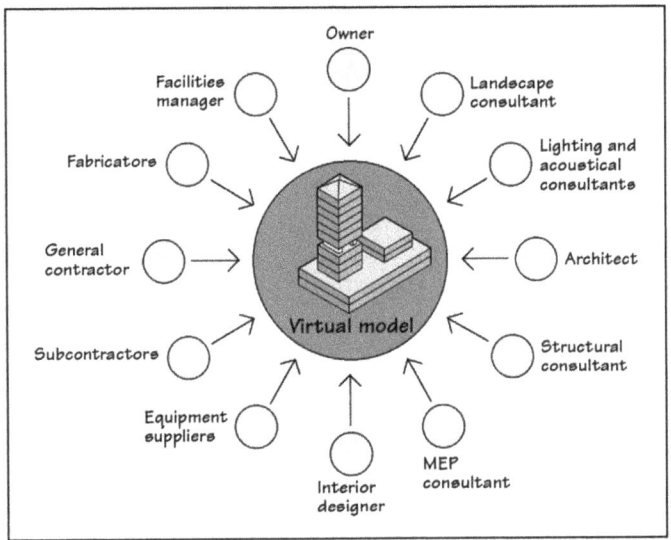

FIGURE 1.22 In an IPD method, all stakeholders in the project, such as the owner, architect, architect's consultants, general contractor, and subcontractors, contribute in constructing the virtual model.

Error checking and ensuring compatibility among the works of various design and fabrication teams are revolutionizing project delivery because of BIM. Consequently, in some projects, there may be zero (or almost zero) change orders, providing substantial savings in project costs. Because the construction of the virtual model is comprehensive, the time needed to complete the sketch design (SD) and design development (DD) stages using BIM technology is greater than that using the conventional drafting technology. However, it is more than compensated by substantial reduction in the time needed for construction documentation because the model allows the extraction of two-dimensional construction documents (plans, elevations, sections, and specifications) with the press of a button, Figure 1.24.

The shift of time and effort toward design stages (SD and DD) from the documentation (CD) stage in BIM technology provides greater control over design. It also makes it easier to make design changes as compared with conventional technology because the cost of design changes during the CD stage is far greater than during SD and DD stages.

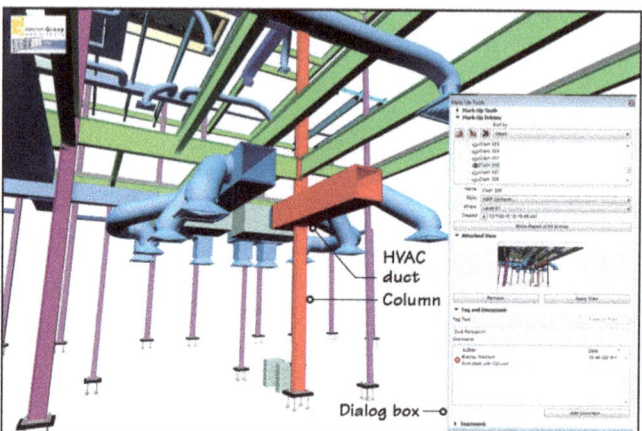

FIGURE 1.23(a) A screenshot from BIM model of a building showing the clash between a column and an HVAC duct. (Image courtesy of Hennon Group Architects and Graphisoft—the producer of ARCHICAD BIM software)

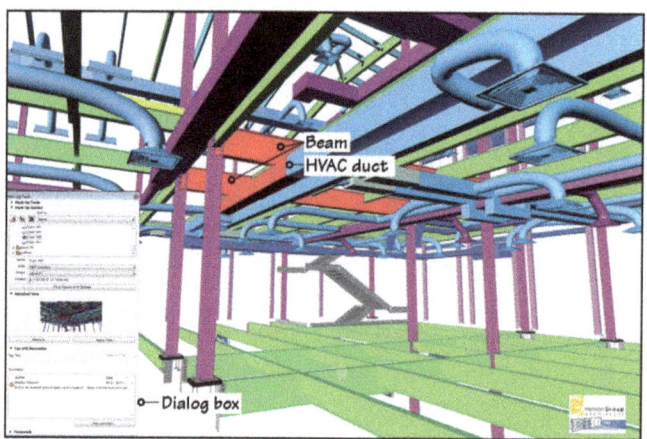

FIGURE 1.23(b) A screenshot showing the clashes between an HVAC duct and two beams. Note that the model for this image and that of Figure 1.23(a) highlights the clashing elements in red color. The dialog box in each image shows the image in miniature, the floor level where the clash occurs, and the identification mark of the clash to distinguish it from other clashes in the building. (Image courtesy of Hennon Group Architects and Graphisoft - the producer of ARCHICAD BIM software.)

PROFIT BY DESIGN

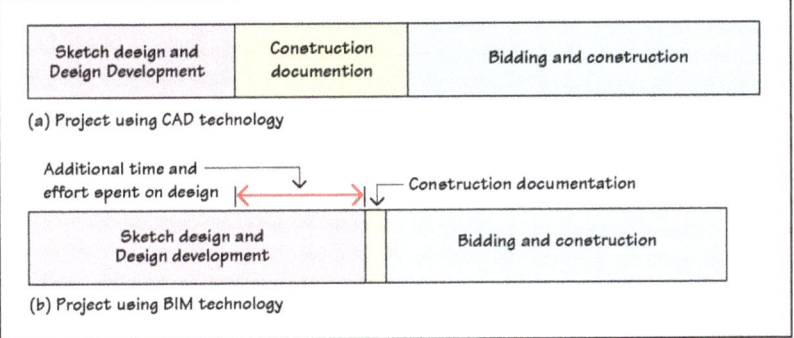

FIGURE 1.24 A comparison of the approximate overall time and effort spent in various activities in a project using CAD technology versus BIM technology.

BIM Tools and Interoperability

Various team members (shown in Figure 1.22) who contribute to the construction of the virtual model must use different software that are specific to their specialty. Thus, an archi- tect uses architectural design BIM software to construct the model (e.g., Autodesk's Revit Architecture or Graphisoft's ArchiCAD BIM), a structural engineer uses structural analysis and design software (e.g., Autodesk's Revit Structure), and so on. These software tools are known as BIM tools. In order for a BIM tool to extract, process, and insert the information into the virtual model to update or modify it, it must be capable of providing seamless two-way communication with the model and other BIM tools.

The ability to exchange information between the virtual model and BIM tools is called interoperability. Interoperability implies that a software developed by a vendor as a BIM tool (say, a code analysis tool) is considered interoperable provided that it can be used correctly, completely, and easily with other BIM tools (such as BIM software for architectural design and for structural design).

Life-Cycle Nature of BIM

The dynamic nature of BIM precludes the need to require record documents, as all changes made to the project during the design or construction phases are recorded in the model in real time. For the same reason, the model also serves as a maintenance tool for building users and facilities managers, providing a tool for record keeping throughout the life of the building, concerning factors such as life-cycle cost, energy use, and sustainability assessment.

Because BIM can track building performance, repairs, maintenance, and changes made to the building over its entire life, the owner's knowledge of and participation in virtual construction are critical. The same applies to architects and engineers, who will need to be more knowledgeable about building construction—how building assemblies go together—because they will be fully involved in the building's construction, albeit in the virtual environment.

BIM and Pre-IPD Delivery Methods

Although the development of BIM technology has helped the adoption of IPD, it should be noted that BIM is not limited to IPD but can be used with any project delivery method. Increasingly, a larger number of architecture and engineering firms are using BIM software with all types of delivery methods.

1.18 FAST-TRACK PROJECT SCHEDULING

A scheduling technique that can be used to save project delivery time with most project delivery methods is known as the fast-track scheduling technique. In this technique, the project is divided into multiple segments, and each segment of construction is awarded to different contractors through negotiations. The division of construction into segments is such that the segments are sequential. Thus, the first segment of the project may be site construction (site development, excavations, and foundations), the second segment may be structural framing (columns, beams, and floor and roof slabs), and the third segment may be the exterior enclosure, interior finishes, and project closeout that takes the project to completion.

Sequential segmenting of the project saves time because the earlier segments of the project can be constructed while the construction documents for the later segments are still in progress, resulting in overlapping design and construction processes, Figure 1.25.

PROFIT BY DESIGN

Fast-track sequencing requires a great deal of coordination between segments. It also requires a commitment from the owner that the decisions will not be delayed and, once made, will not be changed.

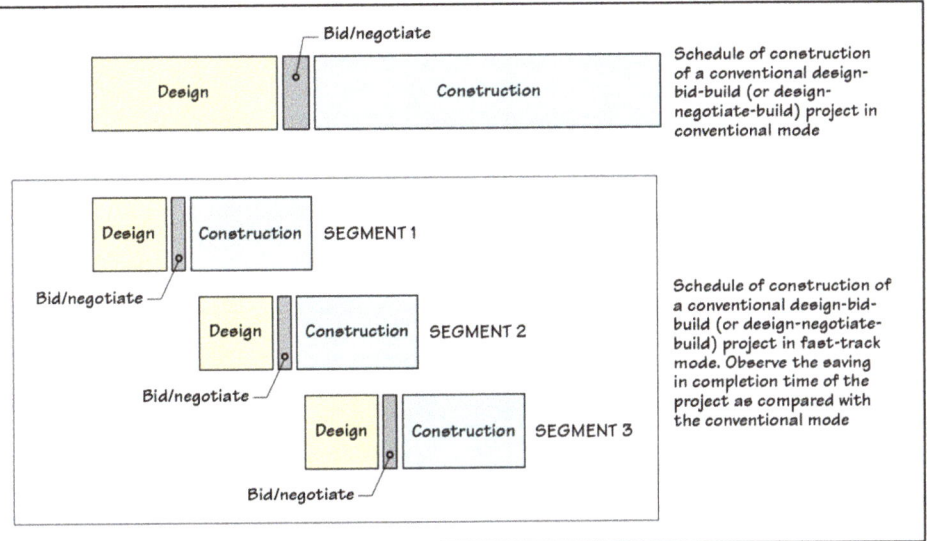

FIGURE 1.25 In fast-track scheduling, a project is segmented into parts, which overlap in time. As shown in this illustration, segmentation shortens project delivery in comparison with unsegmented scheduling. Fast-track scheduling is particularly suitable with DNB and CMAR project delivery methods because the GC is on board during the design phase.

PROJECT DELIVERY METHODS AT A GLANCE	
Project Delivery Method	Description
Design-Bid-Build (DBB) Delivery (Competitive Sealed Bids)	The oldest and most familiar project delivery method. Construction work is awarded to the general contractor (GC) with the lowest bid through open aggressive bidding. There is no design-phase assistance from the GC, and hence a lack of coordination between the design and construction processes. The exact price is unknown until bidding process is complete. Commonly used for public projects.
Design-Bid-Build (DBB) Delivery (Competitive Sealed Proposals)	Same as the DBB (competitive sealed bid) method, except that the owner's selection of the GC is based not only on cost but also on several other criteria such as the project schedule, safety record, and qualifications of the GC's personnel. Commonly used for public projects. Design-Bid-Build (DBB) Delivery (Invitational Bidding)

Design-Bid-Build (DBB) Delivery (Invitational Bidding)	Same as the above two methods, except that the competition is not open, but limited to those GCs who are preselected by the owner and invited to bid. The GC with the lowest bid is generally awarded the contract. Commonly used for private or quasi-private projects.
Design-Negotiate-Build (DNB) Delivery	Same as the DBB (invitational bidding) method, except that the competition among GCs is limited to those who are preselected by the owner. Negotiations are conducted early during the design phase with one GC at a time. The GC who provides the best value for money is awarded the contract, who also provides design-phase assistance. Commonly used for private or quasi-private projects.
Construction Manager as Agent (CMAA) Delivery	The owner hires a construction manager (CM) as his or her agent (instead of the architect), who provides design-phase assistance to the architect and also performs several functions of the GC, such as construction scheduling, coordination, and site safety. There is no GC in this method, and the work is awarded to several subcontractors (called prime contractors) under contracts with the owner. The CM is paid a fee and carries no financial risk or legal responsibility for the prime contractors' work. Commonly used for projects when the owner is experienced in contract administration.
Design-Build (DB) Delivery	In all previous methods, there is a lack of collaborative relationship between the design and construction teams—a lack that is addressed in this method because both design and construction work are awarded to one firm, called a design-build firm. The method generally saves time and cost to the owner, but to be successful, the owner's program must be precisely defined at the beginning of the project. Used for both private and public projects.
Integrated Project Delivery (IPD)	This method, which is still evolving, differs substantially from all other methods. It requires complete collaboration among the owner, architect, and GC in a zero-blame and zero-litigation environment. For successful integrated delivery, a virtual model of the project is constructed (using building information modeling, BIM) during the design phase with collaboration from all parties—owner, architect, consultants, GC, subcontractors, fabricators, material suppliers, so on.

Conclusion

If you are reading these pages first, before reviewing the content of each chapter, you were taught to launch ahead and read the conclusion prior to investing valuable time and money on another book. A proper conclusion should summarize the salient points of each chapter and pull all the parts together into some profound statement of timeless relevance.

This book addresses one thing thoroughly: design professionals should earn larger profits in the conduct of their work. The formula for generating larger profits can be quite complex to the beginner. Elements of the formula are described in this book with sufficient detail as to allow the reader to focus on specific aspects of the profit issue. Investing serious energy in any one of the subject areas discussed in this text should result in bottom line profit benefits. Combining the complete range of recommendations contained in this book will lead to significant improvements in project management, strategic planning and financial performance.

Every firm evolves its own culture and management style. Even when purchasing and implementing standardized financial management software from recognized and credible sources, variations occur in data manipulation and system function. Design professionals tend to modify and adapt commercially available business management tools with nearly the same frequency as they generate schematic design options for an anxious client. No two firms place the same emphasis on management systems and internal financial controls. With this in mind, the greatest value of this book may reside in the attention it has directed to profit as a budgeted project cost.

The chapter headings in this book identify specific areas within A/E practice that require close scrutiny and potentially rigorous restructuring in the interest of improving profitability. Listing the elements of profitability is easier than ranking them in order of relative impact. Because every firm is managed in a unique way, attention to profit may be limited to only certain items while others are overlooked. It is likely that all profit-driven design enterprises view their profit plan from a singular perspective. Firms may key on just one element of profitability and ignore the combined benefit of others. Maintaining an open mind and broader view of the many facets of professional practice that have profit impact is difficult.

Striking a balance between earning profits and producing quality design work takes time. In order to compress the learning curve and equip firm principals with background information on the profit side of this scale, the following list contains a specific set of recommendations to enable a firm to achieve higher profits. A successful and profitable A/E firm should:

1. have a well crafted business plan
2. have a profit plan as part of the business plan
3. have an enthusiastic attitude about profit
4. accept only the right commissions with the right fee
5. employ skillful negotiators
6. insist on well-written, clear and limited scoping documents
7. have concise and thorough project management plans for each project
8. practice strategic project budgeting
9. treat profit as a project cost
10. use a detailed, automated time management system
11. generate invoices more frequently
12. have an aggressive accounts receivable collections plan
13. understand earned revenue
14. understand the relevance of financial statements
15. maintain consistently high staff utilization
16. create project reserve accounts as part of project budgeting
17. use a break even analysis with each budget cycle
18. control overhead expenses
19. shift indirect expenses to reimbursable categories
20. apply pressure to reduce DSOs
21. produce realistic estimates to complete (ETCs)
22. plan for backlog growth
23. outsource reproduction, graphic services and other equipment intensive functions
24. develop and enforce a once through design process
25. subscribe to an automated financial reporting system
26. provide PMs with immediate access to project management and project performance data

27. conduct periodic internal audits
28. teach staff about utilization, budgeting, contribution, reserves, overhead reduction and billable time
29. learn to say "no" when clients offer inadequate fees
30. develop a profit sharing plan with broad staff participation
31. reduce unbilled work-in-progress
32. have a checklist for booking new work
33. use design guidelines on all projects and tasks
34. avoid scope creep
35. perform work without mistakes
36. market services but sell time

Larger A/E firms, with many projects being performed simultaneously, may realize greater benefit from implementing these recommendations. However, smaller firms may find immediate improvement in financial performance by selecting and implementing just the first 6 or 7 items listed.

The search for a formula which adequately expresses the inter-relationships and aggregate benefits of multiple profit strategies continues. Eliminating variables is far easier than defining empirical boundaries and weighting the factors within an equation. One simplified algebraic expression intended to describe maximum gross profit might be:

$$MGPf = \frac{EP+PR+PCR+PO+PCM - WO}{\text{Total Billings}} = \frac{\sum P - WO}{TB}$$

Where: $MGPf$ = Maximum Gross Profit Factor
EP = Earned Profit
PR = Profit From Reserves
PCR = Profit From Cost Reductions
PO = Profit From Outsourcing
PCM = Profit From Consultant Mark-up
TB = Total Billings
WO = Write Offs

When viewed as a formula demanding many inputs to accurately reflect total profit potential, the importance of all profits in relation to Total Billings reveals that many profit strategies are necessary. The formula also shows that profit and billings are linked in a way that require maximum billing in order to derive maximum profit.

This formula results in a ratio expressed as the summation of all profit sources, net of expected losses or write off reserves, to Total Billings. The resultant factor is a percentage of total billed revenue. Successful firms should establish a goal relating to this factor and manage firm operations to achieve the goal.

Further reading and additional reference material may be found in the bibliography at the end of this book.

Appendix

How the Federal Government Selects Architect/Engineering Firms

The Brooks Act – the Basis for Awarding A/E Contracts

The Brooks Act (Public Law 92-582), which was enacted on October 18, 1972, establishes the procurement process by which architects and engineers (A/Es) are selected for design contracts with federal design and construction agencies. The Brooks Act establishes a qualifications-based selection process, known as "QBS," in which contracts for A/Es are negotiated on the basis of demonstrated competence and qualification for the type of professional services required at a fair and reasonable price. Under Brooks Act procurement procedures, price quotations are not a consideration in the selection process.

This QBS process, as established by the Brooks Act, has long been enthusiastically supported by every professional A/E society.

There are seven basic steps involved in pursuing federal design work under the Brooks Act:

1. Public solicitation for architectural and engineering services
2. Submission of an annual statement of qualifications and supplemental statements of ability to design specific projects for which public announcements were made
3. Evaluation of both the annual and project-specific statements
4. Development of a shortlist of at least three submitting firms in order to conduct interview with them
5. Interviews with the firms
6. Ranking of at least three of the most qualified firms
7. Negotiation with the top ranked firm.

A brief explanation of each of these steps, along with a description of what is involved in each, follows. The user must be reminded that while the above Brooks Act procurement is mandated by law, agencies may modify the procedures slightly, within the confines of the act and the Federal Acquisition Regulation.

1. Public Announcement

The Brooks Act calls for public announcement of opportunities for design contracts. The government fulfills this obligation by publicizing opportunities in the Commerce Business Daily. The Commerce Business Daily, or "CBD," as it is known, is published Monday through Friday by the U.S. Department of Commerce. The CBD lists proposed government procurements, subcontracting leads, and contract awards. A proposed procurement action appears in the CBD only once.

All intended procurement actions of $25,000 or more, whether for military or civilian agencies, are published in the CBD. Also, this publication identifies contracts that have been awarded, if the contract amount exceeds $25,000 for civilian agencies and $100,000 for the Department of Defense. The CBD does not list procurements that are:

- Classified for reasons of national security
- For perishable items
- For certain utility services
- Required within 15 days
- Placed under existing contracts
- For personal professional services
- Made only from foreign sources
- Not to be given advance publicity, as determined ` by the Small Business Administration

These notices in the CBD given the location and scope of a project and may also contain such information as:

- Estimated construction contract award range
- Project schedule and the date and time limit for receiving replies
- Categories of evaluation criteria and weight factors
- Any requirements for submitting supplemental information.

Usually, opportunities for A/E services are listed under the "R" section. However, design opportunities can be included in other sections, such as those for design/build services (listed under "Y," Construction of Structures and Facilities).

2. Statement of Qualification

A/E firms with an interest in being considered for design services contracts must submit the required statements of qualifications to each agency with which the A/E wants to contract. The Standard Form 254 (SF 254), Architect-Engineer and Related Services Questionnaire, may be filed each year with a field office of each agency with which the architect intends to do business. This form can also be updated and resubmitted at any time. A completed form furnishes the federal agency with general information on the size, capabilities, personnel, and past experience of an interested firm.

Many federal agencies keep the SF 254 on file and review this file for prospective design firms if they have a small project that will not be advertised. The A/E firm can submit this form at the same time as the required project-specific form is submitted.

The next statement of qualifications that a firm is to submit is the Standard Form 255 (SF 255), Architect-Engineer and Related Services Questionnaire for Specific Project. Following the review of the notices in the CBD, if an A/E firm wants to be considered for a specific project listed in it, then it must submit Standard Form 255, Architect-Engineer and Related Services Questionnaire for Specific Project. This form is submitted in response to a specific solicitation and, when completed, contains the data relative to the specific project.

When a project is advertised in the CBD, the agency does not usually notify firms directly that have filed a SF 254. The project advertisements, or notices, that appear in the CBD are tailored to each specific project and invite interested firms to submit both the SF 254 and SF 255, along with any supplemental data requested in the announcement. Firms that have a current SF 254 on file with the listed procurement office are not required to resubmit that form; however, they must submit a SF 255, Architect-Engineer and Related Services Questionnaire for Specific Project, to be considered for each separate project.

Instructions on how to complete Standard Forms 254 and 255, which include substantial guidance on what information to add to your 254 and 255 and what information to add, are contained in the forms. For example, the instruction in Standard Form 254 stress that additional data, brochures, photos, etc. should not accompany this form unless specifically requires. On the other hand, the instructions for Standard Form 255 state that when appropriate, respondents may supplement this proposal with graphic material and photographs that best demonstrate design capabilities of the proposer for the specific project.

Completing this standard forms is an art and can be frustrating to firms that are new to the process or have been unsuccessful. Detailed insight into this process is available: the Insider's Guide to SF 254/255 Preparation written by Nancy J. Usrey and published by Mark Zweig & Associates, offers thoughtful suggestions and advice of an experienced design firm marketer. The Insider's Guide is obtained by contacting the AIA Bookstore, (202) 626-7541.

3. Evaluation of Statements

The evaluation/selection process for architectural/engineering evaluation boards composed of members who, collectively, have experienced in architecture, engineering, construction, and government and related acquisition matters. The members of the boards are usually appointed from among the professional employees of the agency or other agencies. In some situations, private practitioners sit on these boards if authorized by agency procedures. Of course, when these private practitioners sit on an evaluation board, they or their firms are not eligible for award for a design contract.

The evaluation boards then review the statements of qualifications (Standard Forms 254 and 255). The boards must evaluate them in accordance with the criteria contained in the CBD notice. For example, some of the criteria in the CBD notice may include the following: professional qualifications and experience of the firm with design of a specific type of project; experience and professional qualifications of the firm's staff to be assigned to the project; location of the main office of the proposing firm and its consultants; overall performance record of the firm; and analysis of the firm's current workload.

4. Development of a Shortlist

Following the evaluation of the statements of qualifications, the boards prepare reports that recommend the firms to be on the shortlist. The reports rank at least three of the firms for the purpose of discussing the project with them. The boards are not limited in the number of firms that they can select for these "interviews"; it is left to the discretion of the boards.

5. Interviews/Discussions with Firm

With interviews usually involve discussions on project concepts and the relative utility of alternative methods of furnishing the required services. Before the interview, some agencies send detailed selection criteria and other information about the project to the firms recommended for further consideration. Under the system established by the Brooks Act, the architect-engineer designer does not produce any design product in competing for the project.

Usually these interviews are held at the agency's office. Occasionally, and in special circumstances, phone interviews are conducted. The interviews are brief, usually lasting only 30 to 60 minutes.

6. Ranking of the "Top Three" Firms

Following the interviews, the boards' reports are presented to the agency head or a person who is designated to act in the head of the agency's behalf. The reports list, in order of preference, at least three firms that are considered to be the most highly qualified to perform the services. This is considered to be the final selection of the competing firms. If the firm listed as the most preferred is not the firm that was recommended as the most highly qualified by the evaluation board, the head of the agency must provide a written explanation for the reason for the preference. The head of the agency, or that person's designate, may not add names of other firms to the final report. The report reviews the recommendations of the evaluation board and, from that, the agency head makes the final selection.

7. Negotiation with the Top-Ranked Firm

When the final selection is made by the agency head, the contracting officer is authorized to begin negotiations with the top-ranked firm. The negotiations are conducted pursuant to the procedures set forth in the FAR. Usually, the firm is requested to submit a fee proposal listing direct and indirect costs as the basis for contract negotiations. Contract negotiations are conducted following an evaluation of the fee proposal and an audit when the proposed design fee is more than $100,000.

If a fee is not agreed upon within a reasonable time, the contracting officer will conclude negotiations with the top-ranked firm and initiate negotiations with the second-ranked firm. If a satisfactory contract is not worked out with this firm, then this procedure will be continued until a mutually satisfactory contract is negotiated. If negotiations fail with all selected firms, the contracting firms, which are ranked by competence and qualifications, are identified. The negotiation process will then continue until an agreement is reached and a contract awarded. As a practical note, it is rare that a contract is not successfully negotiated with the top-ranked firm.

Since 1939, federal construction agencies have been required by law to limit the fee payable to an architect or engineer to 6 percent of the estimated construction cost. Presently, there are at least four statutes that prescribe limitations on architect-engineer fees and apply to all civilian and military construction agencies with the exception of the U.S. Department of State.

Federal agencies have interpreted the statutory fee limitations as applying only to the part of the fee that covers the production and delivery of "designs, plans, drawings, and specifications." The agencies, therefore, consider that a 6 percent fee limitation does not apply to the cost of field investigation, surveys, topographical work, soil boring, inspection of construction, master planning, and similar services not involving the production and delivery of designs, plans, drawings, and specifications. Most direct federal awarding agencies have, as a part of their supplement to the Federal Acquisition Regulation, a list of those items exempt from the 6 percent fee limitation.

**Brooks Architect-Engineers Act:
Public Law 92-582**

TITLE IX – SELECTION OF ARCHITECTS AND ENGINEERS DEFINITIONS

SEC. 901. [40 U.S.C. 541] As used in this title –
(1)   The term "firm" means any individual, firm, partnership, corporation, association, or other legal entity permitted by law to practice the profession of architecture or engineering.
(2)   The term "agency head" means the Secretary, Administrator, or head of a department, agency, or bureau of the Federal Government.
(3)   The term "architectural and engineering services" means –
(A)   professional services of an architectural or engineering nature, as defined by State law, if applicable, which are required to be performed or approved by a person licensed, registered, or certified to provide such services as described in this paragraph;
(B)   professional services of an architectural or engineering nature performed by contract that are associated with research, planning, development, design, construction, alteration, or repair of real property; and (C)   such other professional services of an architectural or engineering nature, or incidental services, which members of the architectural and engineering professionals (and individuals in their employ) may logically or justifiably perform, including studies, investigations, surveying and mapping, tests, evaluations, consultations, comprehensive planning, program management, conceptual designs, plans and specifications, value engineering, construction phase services, soils engineering, drawing reviews, preparation of operation and maintenance manuals, and other related services.

POLICY

SEC. 902. [40 U.S.C. 542] The Congress hereby declares it to be the policy of the Federal Government to publicly announce all requirements for architectural and engineering services, and to negotiate contracts for architectural and engineering services on the basis of demonstrated competence and qualification for the type of professional services required at fair and reasonable prices.

REQUESTS FOR DATA ON ARCHITECTURAL AND ENGINEERING SERVICES

SEC. 903. [40 U.SC. 543] In the procurement of architectural and engineering services, the agency head shall encourage firms engaged in the lawful practice of their profession to submit annually a statement of qualifications, and performance data. The agency head, for each proposed project, shall evaluate current statements of qualifications and performance date on file with the agency, together with those that may be submitted by other firms regarding the proposed project, and shall conduct discussions with no less than three firms regarding anticipated concepts and the relative utility of alternative methods of approach for furnishing the required services and then shall select therefrom, in order of preference, based upon criteria established and published by him/her, no less than three of the firms deemed to be the most highly qualified to provide the services required.

NEGOTIATIONS OF CONTRACTS FOR ARCHITECTURAL AND ENGINEERING SERVICES

SEC. 904. [40 U.S.C. 544] (a) The agency head shall negotiate a contract with the highest qualified firm for architectural and engineering services at compensation which the agency head determines is fair and reasonable to the Government. In making such determination, the agency head shall take into account the estimated value of the services to be rendered, the scope, complexity, and professional nature thereof. (b)   Should the agency head be unable to negotiate a satisfactory contract with the firm considered to be the most qualified, at a price he/she determined to be fair and reasonable to the Government, negotiations with that firm should be formally terminated. The agency head should then undertake negotiations with the second most qualified firm. Failing accord with the second most qualified firm, the agency head should terminate negotiations. The agency head should then undertake negotiations with the third most qualified firm. (c)   Should the agency head be unable to negotiate a satisfactory contract with any of the selected firms, he shall select additional firms in order of their competence and qualifications and continue negotiations in accordance with this section until an agreement is reached.

1 Selling costs and proposal costs associated with a firm's marketing and sales promotion program are allowable, but advertising costs in support of these business development functions are not allowable.

PROFIT BY DESIGN

Existing Building Assessment Template

This Template is the property of The Matrix Design Companies, Inc. This is a proprietary system for Building Evaluation and Existing Conditions Assessments as they pertain to existing buildings & facilities. Use of this system may be granted only by Steven L. Biegel, AIA, under special license issued for a single application.

This Template may not be duplicated or copied without the direct written consent of The Matrix Design Companies, Inc.

This Template is licensed by agreement to PLACE Designers, Inc. PLACE Designers, Inc. may use this Building Evaluation Template for specific projects.

Copyright 2004. All rights reserved. This template complies with current standards published by ASTM. Specifically, this document is consistent with the approach defined in ASTM E2018-15 "Standard Guide for Property Condition Assessments".

1.0 Building Data
Building name:
Address:
Zoning Classification:
Use Group:
Occupant load:
Purpose of study:
Net usable floor area in square feet:
Gross floor area in square feet:
Building age/date constructed:
Codes in force when constructed/renovated:
Number of stories:
Height from level of Fire Department access:
Architect Name:
Engineers Name(s):
Dates of field survey/inspection:
Date of report preparation:

1.1. Architectural Systems

Provide a general description of the building structure. Consultant will study and assess the conditions of architectural elements and their major components including, but not limited to, the following. Include photographs as appropriate.

DO NOT DELETE any of the categories.

If not applicable, write NOT APPLICABLE and if not verified write NOT VERIFIED.

1.1.1. Roof
1.1.1.1. Type of roof
1.1.1.1.1. Life expectancy of this type
1.1.1.1.2. Remaining life
1.1.1.2. Approximate date last replaced
1.1.1.3. Presence of skylights and/or hatches
1.1.1.4. Condition of skylights and/or hatches
1.1.1.5. Present Conditions
1.1.1.5.1. Current slope and drainage characteristics, making special note of ponding water conditions.
1.1.1.5.2. Current drainage methods noting storm drain piping, gutters, and scuppers both primary and secondary/emergency.
1.1.1.5.3. Current height relationships of walls, MEP penetrations, windows, etc. versus industry/County standards for noted applications.
1.1.1.5.4. Current sheet metal flashing and membrane flashing types, gauges, and characteristics.
1.1.1.5.5. Complaints and nature of complaints
1.1.1.5.6. R values of the existing roof
1.1.1.5.7. Indicate all deficiencies in roofing system in terms of type of system, system age, energy conservation, code-related issues, maintenance procedures, slope, drainage, and summary of repair costs over the last 5 years.
1.1.1.5.8. Provide recommendations for rehabilitation, remediation, upgrading or repair of the roofing system including but not limited to drainage, slope, height adjustments and modifications, insulation, flashing types/adjustments, and membrane for its intended use.

1.1.2. Foundation / Waterproofing
1.1.2.1. Type of wall and membrane system
1.1.2.1.1. Life expectancy of this type

1.1.2.1.2. Remaining Life
1.1.2.2. Approximate date last replaced
1.1.2.3. Present Conditions
1.1.2.3.1. Current perimeter drainage characteristics, making special note of ponding and water infiltration locations
1.1.2.3.2. Current drainage methods noting storm drain piping, gutters, and scuppers both primary and secondary/emergency
1.1.2.3.3. Cracks or points of moisture infiltration
1.1.2.3.4. Current height relationships of walls, MEP penetrations, windows, etc. versus industry/County standards for noted applications
1.1.2.3.5. Current sheet metal flashing and membrane flashing types, gauges, and characteristics
1.1.2.3.6. Complaints and nature of complaints
1.1.2.3.7. R-values
1.1.2.3.8. Indicate all deficiencies in foundation/waterproofing system in terms of type of system, system age, energy conservation, code-related issues, maintenance procedures, drainage, and summary of repair costs over the last 5 years.

1.1.2.4. Provide recommendations for rehabilitation, remediation, upgrading or repair of the foundation/waterproofing system including but not limited to drainage, perimeter slope, height adjustments and modifications, insulation, flashing types/adjustments, and membrane for their intended use.

1.1.3. Perimeter Skin
1.1.3.1. Type of construction/materials
1.1.3.2. R-values
1.1.3.3. Condition and quantity of caulking, mortar, and/or grout
1.1.3.4. Condition of exterior finish surface (brick, block, metal, wood, etc.)
1.1.3.5. Approximate date and extent of last paint/point/caulk work
1.1.3.6. Provide recommendations for rehabilitation, remediation, upgrading or repair of the perimeter skin for its intended use.

1.1.4. Exterior Glazing
1.1.4.1. Glazing area (sq. ft.)
1.1.4.2. Number and size of windows
1.1.4.3. Type of windows (operable / non-operable)
1.1.4.4. Frame system (wood, aluminum, mullionless) and finish
1.1.4.5. Condition of windows
1.1.4.6. Condition of glazing tape/gaskets/caulk
1.1.4.7. Single pane/insulating glazing
1.1.4.8. Appearance of glazing (tinted and/or reflective coating)
1.1.4.9. Age of windows
1.1.4.10. Approximate date last replaced/repaired
1.1.4.11. Indicate all deficiencies in window system in terms of type of system, age, energy conservation, code-related issues, maintenance procedures and summary of repair costs over the last 5 years, availability of to match with existing type etc.
1.1.4.12. Provide recommendations for rehabilitation, remediation, upgrading or repair of exterior glazing for its intended use.

1.1.5. Interior Partitions
1.1.5.1. Condition of drywall (to be submitted on a space-by-space basis as applicable)
1.1.5.2. Extent and type(s) of finish surface materials (paint, wall covering, wood pane,
/masonry, tile, stone, etc.)
1.1.5.3. Type of paint (i.e. lead, oil-based, water-based, polymer)
1.1.5.4. Condition of finish surface materials
1.1.5.5. Approximate date and extent of last paint/point up/caulk work
1.1.5.6. Indoor air quality issue due to paint
1.1.5.7. Indicate all partition deficiencies in terms of: type of walls, age, energy conservation, code-related issues, maintenance procedures and summary of repair costs over the last 5 years, etc.
1.1.5.8. Determine fire rating of all partitions and review above-ceiling condition of same to identify any breaches in separation assembly due to post-construction penetrations.
1.1.5.9. Provide recommendations for rehabilitation, remediation, upgrading or repair of the interior partitions for their intended use.

1.1.6. Interior Glazing
1.1.6.1. Window configuration (sidelight, transom, frameless panels, etc.)
1.1.6.2. Glazing area (sq. ft.)
1.1.6.3. Number of windows/panels
1.1.6.4. Type of windows (operable / non operable)
1.1.6.5. Type of glazing (acid etched, clear or colored, patterned, decorative, tempered, laminated, etc.)
1.1.6.6. Glazing dimensions (including thickness)

1.1.6.7. Frame system (wood, aluminum, mullionless) and finish
1.1.6.8. Condition of windows (frames and glazing)
1.1.6.9. Condition of glazing tape/gaskets/caulk
1.1.6.10. Provide recommendations for rehabilitation, remediation, upgrading or repair of interior glazing for its intended use.

1.1.7. Doors / Entranceways (exterior and interior)
1.1.7.1. Type of doors and locations
1.1.7.2. Size, quantity and configuration
1.1.7.3. Frame material
1.1.7.4. R-values (include assessment of weatherstripping,, threshold, door bottom, etc)
1.1.7.5. Glass door (sq. ft.)
1.1.7.6. Hardware components and door operation
1.1.7.7. ADA compliance
1.1.7.8. Vestibules (if any)
1.1.7.9. Type of vestibules (pressurized / non-pressurized)
1.1.7.10. Floor surface characteristics (grade changes, material change, etc.)
1.1.7.11. Age of doors
1.1.7.12. Condition of doors
1.1.7.13. Approximate date last replaced
1.1.7.14. Approximate date last painted
1.1.7.15. Indicate all deficiencies in doors and entranceway in terms of ADA requirements, size, type of system, age, energy conservation, code-related issues, maintenance procedures and summary of repair costs over the last 5 years,, availability of to match with existing etc.
1.1.7.16. Review all openings in fire-rated partitions to determine that assembly has code- compliant labels and hardware (applies to opening assemblies that have been

modified since initial construction).
1.1.7.17. Provide recommendations for rehabilitation, remediation, upgrading or repair of the doors/entranceways for their intended use.

1.1.8. Ceilings & Soffits (interior and exterior)
1.1.8.1. Total ceiling/soffit area (sq. ft.)
1.1.8.2. Type and locations (suspension system and tile/panel spec/material)
1.1.8.3. Ceiling/soffit area (sq. ft.) Type A
1.1.8.4. Ceiling area (sq. ft.) Type B
1.1.8.5. Ceiling area (sq. ft.) Type C
1.1.8.6. Acoustical properties
1.1.8.6.1. Type A
1.1.8.6.2. Type B
1.1.8.6.3. Type C
1.1.8.7. Ceiling/soffit height and locations
1.1.8.8. Ceiling/soffit transitions
1.1.8.9. Condition of ceiling
1.1.8.9.1. Type A
1.1.8.9.2. Type B
1.1.8.9.3. Type C
1.1.8.10. Approximate date last replaced
1.1.8.11. Condition of paint and approximate date last painted
1.1.8.12. Indicate all deficiencies in ceiling/soffit system(s) in terms of type of system, age, code-related issues, maintenance procedures and summary of repair costs over the last 5 years, etc.
1.1.8.13. Provide recommendations for rehabilitation, remediation, upgrading or repair of the ceiling/soffit system(s) for their intended use.

1.1.9. Flooring
1.1.9.1. Total floor area (sq. ft.)
1.1.9.2. Floor substrate (concrete slab on grade, raised access floor, etc.)
1.1.9.3. Type(s) of finish (carpet, vinyl tile, rubber, cork, porcelain tile, quarry tile, thickset stone, etc)
1.1.9.4. Flooring area (type-by-type in sq. ft.)
1.1.9.5. Condition of carpet
1.1.9.6. Condition of tile and/or other finishes

1.1.9.7. Approximate date last replaced (carpet? tile? others?)
1.1.9.8. Indoor air quality issue due to condition of carpet/tile/others
1.1.9.9. Indicate all deficiencies in flooring materials in terms of wear, age, code-related issues, maintenance procedures and summary of repair costs over the last 5 years, availability of to match with existing.
1.1.9.10. Provide recommendations for rehabilitation, remediation, upgrading or repair of the flooring materials for their intended use.

1.1.10. Stairs & Ramps
1.1.10.1. Location and quantity of stairs
1.1.10.2. Width of stairs
1.1.10.3. Landing dimensions
1.1.10.4. Riser height
1.1.10.5. Condition of finishes
1.1.10.6. ADA compliance
1.1.10.7. Provide recommendations for rehabilitation, remediation, upgrading or repair of the stairs and ramps for their intended use.

1.1.11. Elevator / Escalator Systems
1.1.11.1. Description of the existing elevator/escalator system 1.1.11.1.1. Type of the existing elevator equipment (traction/hydraulic) 1.1.11.1.2. Number of elevator cab(s) / escalator(s)
1.1.11.1.3. Size of elevator cab(s) / escalator(s) 1.1.11.1.4. Capacity of elevator cab(s) 1.1.11.1.5. Age of the existing system
1.1.11.2. Appropriate and effectiveness of the existing system with building functions
1.1.11.3. Condition of the system
1.1.11.4. Condition of the equipment
1.1.11.5. Condition of the cab / door / side panel / handrail finishes
1.1.11.6. Elevator / escalator control system and its effectiveness
1.1.11.7. ADA compliance
1.1.11.8. Approximate date last replaced
1.1.11.9. Life expectancy
1.1.11.10. Safety issues

1.1.11.11. Indicate all deficiencies in the existing elevator / escalator system in terms of capacity, equipment size and installation, type of system, ADA requirements, age, energy conservation, code-related issues, maintenance issues and procedures and summary of repair costs over the last 5 years, availability of spare parts etc.
1.1.11.12. Provide recommendations for rehabilitation, remediation, upgrading or repair of the elevator(s) / escalator(s) for their intended use.

1.1.12. Potential Environmental & Hazardous Materials
1.1.12.1. Investigate for the presence of asbestos and/or lead etc.
1.1.12.1.1. Indicate suspicion of asbestos and/or lead containing products, mercury, PCBs etc. and recommend professional investigation.
1.1.12.1.2. Asbestos in roofing, roof flashing, duct wrap, pipe insulation, flooring lead paint and coatings and other building components.

1.1.12.1.3. Mercury in lamps (light bulb) and thermostat.
1.1.12.1.4. PCBs in light fixtures and ballasts

1.1.12.2. Investigate for the presence of mold, mildew, fungus, bacterial compounds or rot, radon gas etc.
1.1.12.2.1. Indicate suspicion of a mold, mildew, fungus, bacterial compounds or rot, radon gas, and recommend professional investigation.
1.2. Structural System
Consultant will study and assess the conditions which include, but are not limited to the following structural criteria and elements. Include photographs as appropriate.

1.2.1. General Criteria
1.2.1.1. Adequacy
1.2.1.1.1. Gather design criteria and the applicable codes of the existing building.
1.2.1.1.2. Consideration shall be given to investigate the adequacy of the structure for future functions to be performed, the loads imposed by equipment, occupants and their activities, life expectancy and cost of material to match with existing material for repair work.

1.2.1.2. Evaluate the possibilities of alterations, maintenance costs, and ease of demolition during future construction.
1.2.1.3. Stability
1.2.1.3.1. Overall structure stability shall be investigated to confirm the recognized engineering principles. Stability shall provide resistance against lateral loads and gravity loads etc.
1.2.1.4. Fire Resistance
1.2.1.4.1. Fire resistance rating of all structural members shall be investigated for future function to be performed.
1.2.1.5. Security
1.2.1.5.1. Structure specific security criteria shall be investigated for future function to be performed. The risk assessment shall consider risk factors, severity level etc.
1.2.1.6. Material Strength
1.2.1.6.1. Exploratory field work and testing is required in the absence of original contract documents, or when information is required to define in-place construction. Materials such as concrete, steel, masonry and wood etc.
1.2.1.7. Provide recommendations for rehabilitation, remediation, upgrading or repair of general structural criteria for the structures intended use.

1.2.2. Roof
1.2.2.1. Ponding of water on roof
1.2.2.2. Clogging of scuppers and other overflow mechanisms
1.2.2.3. Adequacy of roof top unit /skylight/hatch support framing
1.2.2.4. Exposed steel above roof to be galvanized
1.2.2.5. Joist bridging
1.2.2.6. Vertical /horizontal bridging of trusses
1.2.2.7. Roof framing member (beams, girders, slab etc.) conditions such as cracks, spalling, excessive deflection etc.
1.2.2.8. Expansion joint locations and condition
1.2.2.9. Beam/truss bearing conditions
1.2.2.10. Water leakage
1.2.2.11. Vibration due to roof mounted equipments
1.2.2.12. Provide recommendations for rehabilitation, remediation, upgrading or repair of the structural roof for its intended use.

1.2.3. Floors

1.2.3.1. Floor framing member (beams, girders, slab etc.) condition such as crack, spalling, and excessive deformation of framing members.
1.2.3.2. Severity of cracks on floor
1.2.3.3. Beam/truss/joist bearing conditions
1.2.3.4. Floor opening framing members
1.2.3.5. Equipment pads size and condition
1.2.3.6. Vibration due to floor mounted equipments
1.2.3.7. Wheel loads on floors
1.2.3.8. Provide recommendations for rehabilitation, remediation, upgrading or repair of the floors for their intended use.

1.2.4. Foundation & Foundation Drainage System
1.2.4.1. Effects on the foundation from adjoining property, buildings and facilities must be examined.
1.2.4.2. Proper drainage of water from the building
1.2.4.3. Water seepage through basement walls.
1.2.4.4. Cracks on floor due to differential settlement of footings
1.2.4.5. Frost depth
1.2.4.6. Provide recommendations for rehabilitation, remediation, upgrading or repair of the foundation for its intended use.

1.2.5. Walls
1.2.5.1. Variations of hydrostatic pressure and surcharge on retaining walls
1.2.5.2. Back fill material and water proofing of retaining walls
1.2.5.3. Blocked weep Holes
1.2.5.4. Cracks on exterior walls due to lack of control joints and concentrated loads
1.2.5.5. Provide recommendations for rehabilitation, remediation, upgrading or repair of structural walls for their intended use.

1.3. Mechanical Systems

Consultant will study and assess mechanical systems and their major components including, but not limited to, the following. Include photographs as appropriate.

1.3.1. Heating System
1.3.1.1. Description of the existing heating system

1.3.1.2. Heating plants
1.3.1.3. Boiler(s) (year, make, model, capacity, gas fired / electric / oil fired)
1.3.1.4. Type of systems (two pipe / four pipe)
1.3.1.5. Piping Arrangement (single loop / primary or secondary loop)
1.3.1.6. Return (direct / reverse)
1.3.1.7. Circulating Pumps (year, make, model, capacity, HP, GPM, /head)
1.3.1.8. Piping
1.3.1.9. Pipe insulation
1.3.1.10. Valves
1.3.1.11. Expansion tank (year, make, model, size)
1.3.1.12. Air separator (year, make, model, size)
1.3.1.13. Other type(s) of heating systems
1.3.1.14. Radiant heating
1.3.1.15. Under-floor heating
1.3.1.16. Indicate all deficiencies in heating system in terms of equipment size, equipment installation, water distribution, type of system, system age, energy conservation, code-related issues, maintenance procedures and summary of repair costs over the last 5 years, availability of spare parts etc.

1.3.1.17. Provide recommendations for rehabilitation, remediation, upgrading or repair of heating system(s) for their intended use.

1.3.2. Air Conditioning System
1.3.2.1. Description of the existing air conditioning system
1.3.2.2. Chilled water plant
1.3.2.3. Air cooled / water cooled (year, make, model, capacity)
1.3.2.4. Type of chiller (centrifugal / reciprocating / screw / scroll etc.) (year, make, model, capacity)
1.3.2.5. Piping Arrangement
1.3.2.5.1. Single loop / primary or secondary loop
1.3.2.5.2. Return (direct / reverse)
1.3.2.6. Cooling tower (year, make, model, capacity)
1.3.2.7. DX system (year, make, model, capacity)
1.3.2.8. Self-contained unit (year, make, model, capacity)
1.3.2.9. Location of all units
1.3.2.10. Type of systems (two pipe / four pipe)
1.3.2.11. Circulating pumps (year, make, model, capacity,

HP, GPM/head)
1.3.2.12. Piping
1.3.2.13. Pipe insulation
1.3.2.14. Valves
1.3.2.15. Expansion tank (year, make, model, size)
1.3.2.16. Air separator (year, make, model, size)
1.3.2.17. Indicate all deficiencies in cooling system in terms of equipment size, equipment installation, water distribution, type of system, system age, energy conservation, code-related issues, maintenance procedures and summary of repair costs over the last 5 years, availability of spare parts etc.
1.3.2.18. Provide recommendations for rehabilitation, remediation, upgrading or repair of air conditioning system for its intended use.

1.3.3. Air Distribution System
1.3.3.1. Description of the existing air distribution system
1.3.3.2. Type of system (constant volume / VAV / VVT)
1.3.3.3. VAV / VVT (fan power / non fan power)
1.3.3.4. Total number of VAV / VVT boxes
1.3.3.5. VAV / VVT (year, make, model, capacity)
1.3.3.6. Floor-wise air distribution arrangement (for multi-storied buildings)
1.3.3.7. Zone-wise air distribution arrangement (for single / two storied buildings)
1.3.3.8. Identify all air handlers with corresponding serving areas
1.3.3.9. Type and condition of diffusers
1.3.3.10. Type and condition of return air grilles
1.3.3.11. Type of duct (round / rectangular / oval)
1.3.3.12. Insulation type and condition
1.3.3.13. Type of return air system (ducted / ceiling plenum)
1.3.3.14. Assess indoor air quality
1.3.3.15. Record all complaints from building occupants / building engineer 1.3.3.15.1. Frequency of complaints
1.3.3.15.2. Severity of complaints
1.3.3.16. Indicate all deficiencies in air distribution system in terms of equipment size, equipment installation, air flow (CFM) through the terminal units, type of system, system age, energy conservation, code-related issues, maintenance

procedures and summary of repair costs over the last 5 years, availability of spare parts etc.

1.3.3.17. Provide recommendations for rehabilitation, remediation, upgrading or repair of air distribution system for its intended use.

1.3.4. Make up / Fresh Air Intake System
1.3.4.1. Description of the existing make up/fresh air intake system
1.3.4.2. Make up / fresh air intake fan (year, make, model, capacity)
1.3.4.3. Age of the fan
1.3.4.4. Approximate date last replaced
1.3.4.5. Condition of fan(s)
1.3.4.6. Intake damper size/type
1.3.4.7. Any issues regarding damper location(s) in terms of indoor air quality and/or other concerns
1.3.4.8. Indicate all deficiencies in make-up/fresh air intake system in terms of equipment size, equipment installation, air flow (CFM), type of system, system age, energy conservation, code-related issues, IAQ issues, maintenance procedures and summary of repair costs over the last 5 years, availability of spare parts etc.
1.3.4.9. Provide recommendations for rehabilitation, remediation, upgrading or repair of make-up / fresh air intake system for its intended use.

1.3.5. Exhaust / Relief Air System
1.3.5.1. Description of the existing exhaust / relief air system
1.3.5.2. Exhaust air fan(s) (year, make, model, capacity)
1.3.5.3. Relief air fan(s) (year, make, model, capacity)
1.3.5.4. Age of the fan(s)
1.3.5.5. Approximate date last replaced
1.3.5.6. Condition of fan(s)
1.3.5.7. Damper size / type
1.3.5.8. Any issues regarding exhaust and relief air damper locations in terms of indoor air quality and/or other concerns
1.3.5.9. Indicate all deficiencies in exhaust / relief air system in terms of equipment size, equipment installation, air flow (CFM), type of system, system age, energy conservation, code-related issues, IAQ issues, other concern, maintenance procedures and summary of repair costs over the last 5 years,

availability of spare parts etc.
1.3.5.10. Provide recommendations for rehabilitation, remediation, upgrading or repair of exhaust / relief air system for its intended use.

1.3.6. Water Distribution System (chilled, hot, condenser etc.)
1.3.6.1. Description of the existing water distribution system
1.3.6.2. Type of system (two pipe / four pipe)
1.3.6.3. Return (direct / reverse)
1.3.6.4. Loop (single vs. primary and secondary)
1.3.6.5. Pipe material
1.3.6.6. Condition of piping in the space
1.3.6.7. Condition of insulation
1.3.6.8. Condition of valves
1.3.6.9. Life expectancy and age of piping systems
1.3.6.10. Approximate date last replaced
1.3.6.11. Report any issue regarding pipe supports
1.3.6.12. Record all complaints from building occupants/building engineer in terms of leakage 1.3.6.12.1. Frequency of complaints
1.3.6.12.2. Severity of complaint
1.3.6.13. Indicate all deficiencies in water distribution system in terms of pipe size, installation, water flow (CFM) through the terminal units, type of system, system age, energy conservation, code-related issues, maintenance procedures and summary of repair costs over the last 5 years, availability of spare parts etc.
1.3.6.14. Provide recommendations for rehabilitation, remediation, upgrading or repair of water distribution system for its intended use.

1.3.7. Automatic Temperature / Humidity Control System
1.3.7.1. Description of the existing automatic temperature / humidity control system
1.3.7.2. Type of system (electric / pneumatic / DDC etc.)
1.3.7.3. Age of the system
1.3.7.4. Approximate date last replaced
1.3.7.5. Life expectancy of the system
1.3.7.6. Condition of all components
1.3.7.7. Effectiveness and appropriateness of the system
1.3.7.8. Energy conservation issues with existing system

1.3.7.9. Record all complaints from building occupants / building engineer in terms of temperature, humidity, IAQ, etc.
1.3.7.9.1. Frequency and nature of complaints
1.3.7.9.2. Severity of complaints
1.3.7.10. Indicate all deficiencies in the existing control system in terms of effectiveness, appropriateness, installation, system age, energy conservation, IAQ issue(s), code- related issues, maintenance procedures and summary of repair costs over the last 5 years, availability of spare parts etc.
1.3.7.11. Provide recommendations for rehabilitation, remediation, upgrading or repair of automatic temperature / humidity control system for its intended use.

1.3.8. Plumbing System
1.3.8.1. Description of the existing plumbing system
1.3.8.2. Domestic water heating plant
1.3.8.3. Boiler(s) / water heater (year, make, model, capacity, gas fired / electric / oil fired)
1.3.8.4. Piping arrangement (single loop / primary or secondary loop)
1.3.8.5. DWH circulating pumps (year, make, model, capacity, HP, GPM/head)
1.3.8.6. Piping
1.3.8.7. Pipe insulation
1.3.8.8. Valves
1.3.8.9. Age of the existing DWH system
1.3.8.10. Condition of the system
1.3.8.11. Approximate date last replaced
1.3.8.12. Life expectancy
1.3.8.13. Type of plumbing fixtures
1.3.8.14. Age of plumbing fixtures
1.3.8.15. Condition of plumbing fixtures
1.3.8.16. ADA compliance
1.3.8.17. Indicate all deficiencies in plumbing system in terms of equipment size, equipment installation, water distribution, type of system, system age, energy conservation, water temperature control, code-related issues, ADA issues, maintenance procedures and summary of repair costs over the last 5 years, availability of spare parts etc.
1.3.8.18. Provide recommendations for rehabilitation, remediation, upgrading or repair of plumbing system for its intended use.

1.4. Electrical Systems

Consultant will study and assess electrical systems and their major components including, but not limited to, the following. Include photographs as appropriate.

1.4.1. Primary Electrical System
1.4.1.1. Description of the existing electrical system
1.4.1.1.1. Electrical power provider (PEPCO / Allegheny Power, etc.)
1.4.1.1.2. Electric panels (year, make, model, capacity)
1.4.1.1.3. MCCs (year, make, model, capacity)

1.4.1.1.4. Age of the existing system
1.4.1.1.5. Condition of the system
1.4.1.1.6. Approximate date last replaced
1.4.1.1.7. Life expectancy
1.4.1.2. Type of wires (aluminum / copper / other)
1.4.1.2.1. Age of the existing wires
1.4.1.2.2. Condition of existing wires
1.4.1.2.3. Approximate date last replaced
1.4.1.2.4. Life expectancy of existing wires
1.4.1.3. Grounding
1.4.1.3.1. Type(s) (standard building / isolated)
1.4.1.4. Distribution
1.4.1.4.1. Type(s) (ductbank, conduit, cable tray, etc)
1.4.1.5. Transformer(s)
1.4.1.5.1. Xyz
1.4.1.6. Indicate all deficiencies in primary electrical system in terms of equipment/components size, capacity, equipment installation, distribution, type of system, system age, energy conservation, code-related issues, maintenance issues and procedures and summary of repair costs over the last 5 years, availability of spare parts etc.
1.4.1.7. Provide recommendations for rehabilitation, remediation, upgrading or repair of primary electrical system for its intended use.

1.4.2. Emergency Power System
1.4.2.1. Emergency Generator
1.4.2.1.1. Description (year, make, model, output relative to building loads, redundancy)
1.4.2.1.2. Fuel storage tank (year, make, model, capacity)

1.4.2.1.3. Age of the existing system
1.4.2.1.4. Condition of the system
1.4.2.1.5. Load shed sequence
1.4.2.1.6. Approximate date last replaced
1.4.2.1.7. Life expectancy
1.4.2.1.8. Conduits (concealed / exposed)
1.4.2.2. Uninterrupted Power System
1.4.2.2.1. xyz
1.4.2.3. Automatic Transfer Switch (ATS) (year, make, model, capacity)
1.4.2.3.1. Age of the existing ATS
1.4.2.3.2. Condition of ATS
1.4.2.3.3. Approximate date last replaced
1.4.2.3.4. Life expectancy of ATS
1.4.2.3.5. Condition of the conduits
1.4.2.4. Indicate all deficiencies in emergency power system in terms of equipment/components size, capacity, equipment installation, distribution, type of system, system age, energy conservation, code-related issues, maintenance issues and procedures and summary of repair costs over the last 5 years, availability of spare parts etc.
1.4.2.5. Provide recommendations for rehabilitation, remediation, upgrading or repair of emergency power system for its intended use.

1.4.3. Lighting Systems
1.4.3.1. Description of the existing lighting systems
1.4.3.2. Type of light fixtures (year, make, model)
1.4.3.3. Number of fixtures per floor (for various types)
1.4.3.4. Age of the existing fixtures
1.4.3.5. Condition of the fixtures

1.4.3.6. Lighting control system description and locations
1.4.3.7. Approximate date last replaced
1.4.3.8. Life expectancy
1.4.3.9. Energy efficiency of the fixtures
1.4.3.10. Indicate all deficiencies in lighting system in terms of component size, capacity, fixture installation, illumination (foot candles), switching distribution, type of system, age, energy conservation, code-related issues, maintenance issues and procedures and summary of repair costs over the last 5 years, availability of spare parts etc.

1.4.3.11.	Provide recommendations for rehabilitation, remediation, upgrading or repair of lighting system for its intended use.

1.5.	Fire Prevention Systems

Consultant will study and assess the condition of the fire prevention system and its major components including, but not limited to, the following. Include photographs as appropriate.

1.5.1.	Fire Alarm System
1.5.1.1. Type of existing fire alarm system
1.5.1.2. Age of the existing system
1.5.1.3. Appropriate and effectiveness of the existing system with building functions
1.5.1.4. Condition of the system
1.5.1.5. Approximate date last replaced
1.5.1.6. Life expectancy
1.5.1.7. Location of pull stations and appropriateness
1.5.1.8. Location of the enunciator and appropriateness
1.5.1.9. Locations of egresses and appropriateness
1.5.1.10.	Indicate all deficiencies in the existing fire alarm system in terms of component size, capacity, installation, type of system, age, energy conservation, code-related issues, maintenance issues, procedures, and summary of repair costs over the last 5 years, availability of spare parts etc.
1.5.1.11.	Provide recommendations for rehabilitation, remediation, upgrading or repair of fire alarm system for its intended use.

1.5.2.	Sprinkler System
1.5.2.1. Type of the existing system (dry / wet / other)
1.5.2.2. Age of the existing system
1.5.2.3. Appropriate and effectiveness of the existing system with building functions
1.5.2.4. Condition of the system
1.5.2.5. Approximate date last replaced
1.5.2.6. Life expectancy
1.5.2.7. Indicate all deficiencies in the existing sprinkler system in terms of component size, capacity, installation, type of system, age, energy conservation, code-related issues, maintenance issues, procedures and summary of repair costs over the last 5 years, availability of spare parts etc.
1.5.2.8. Provide recommendations for rehabilitation,

remediation, upgrading or repair of sprinkler system for its intended use.

1.6. Communications

Consultant will study and assess communications systems including, but not limited to, the following. Include photographs as appropriate.

1.6.1. Telephone System
1.6.1.1. Description of the existing telephone system
1.6.1.2. Age of the existing system
1.6.1.3. Appropriate and effectiveness of the existing system with building functions
1.6.1.4. Condition of the system

1.6.1.5. Approximate date last replaced
1.6.1.6. Life expectancy
1.6.1.7. Indicate all deficiencies in the existing telephone system in terms of component size, capacity, installation, type of system, age, energy conservation, code-related issues, maintenance issues, procedures and summary of repair costs over the last 5 years, availability of spare parts etc.
1.6.1.8. Provide recommendations for rehabilitation, remediation, upgrading or repair of telephone system for its intended use.

1.6.2. Network System
1.6.2.1. Description of the existing network system
1.6.2.2. Age of the existing system
1.6.2.3. Appropriate and effectiveness of the existing system with building functions
1.6.2.4. Condition of the system
1.6.2.5. Approximate date last replaced
1.6.2.6. Life expectancy
1.6.2.7. Indicate all deficiencies in the existing network system in terms of component size, capacity, installation, type of system, age, energy conservation, code-related issues, maintenance issues, procedures and summary of repair costs over the last 5 years, availability of spare parts etc.
1.6.2.8. Provide recommendations for rehabilitation, remediation, upgrading or repair of network system for its intended use.

1.6.3. Optic Fiber
1.6.3.1. Description of existing optic fiber
1.6.3.2. Age of the existing lines
1.6.3.3. Appropriate and effectiveness of the existing lines with building functions
1.6.3.4. Condition of the lines
1.6.3.5. Approximate date last replaced
1.6.3.6. Life expectancy
1.6.3.7. Indicate all deficiencies in the existing optic fiber lines in terms of component size, capacity, installation, type of system, age, energy conservation, code-related issues, maintenance issues, procedures and summary of repair costs over the last 5 years, availability of spare parts etc.
1.6.3.8. Provide recommendations for rehabilitation, remediation, upgrading or repair of optic fiber system for its intended use.

1.6.4. Cabling Plant
1.6.4.1. Description of the existing cabling plant
1.6.4.2. Age of the existing cabling plant
1.6.4.3. Appropriate and effectiveness of the existing cabling plant with building functions
1.6.4.4. Condition of the cabling plant
1.6.4.5. Approximate date last replaced
1.6.4.6. Life expectancy
1.6.4.7. Indicate all deficiencies in the existing cabling plant in terms of component size, capacity, installation, type of system, age, energy conservation, code-related issues, maintenance issues, procedures and summary of repair costs over the last 5 years, availability of spare parts etc.
1.6.4.8. Provide recommendations for rehabilitation, remediation, upgrading or repair of cabling plant for its intended use.

1.6.5. Satellite / Cable TV
1.6.5.1. Description of existing satellite / cable TV
1.6.5.2. Age of the existing equipment
1.6.5.3. Appropriate and effectiveness of the existing equipment with building functions

1.6.5.4. Condition of the equipment
1.6.5.5. Approximate date last replaced

1.6.5.6. Life expectancy
1.6.5.7. Indicate all deficiencies in existing satellite / cable TV in terms of component size, capacity, installation, type of system, age, energy conservation, code-related issues, maintenance issues, procedures and summary of repair costs over the last 5 years, availability of spare parts etc.
1.6.5.8. Provide recommendations for rehabilitation, remediation, upgrading or repair of satellite / cable TV for its intended use.

1.6.6. Radio System
1.6.6.1. Description of the existing radio system
1.6.6.2. Age of the existing system
1.6.6.3. Appropriate and effectiveness of the existing system with building functions
1.6.6.4. Condition of the system
1.6.6.5. Approximate date last replaced
1.6.6.6. Life expectancy
1.6.6.7. Indicate all deficiencies in the existing radio system in terms of component size, capacity, installation, type of system, age, energy conservation, code-related issues, maintenance issues, procedures and summary of repair costs over the last 5 years, availability of spare parts etc.
1.6.6.8. Provide recommendations for rehabilitation, remediation, upgrading or repair of radio system for its intended use.

1.7. Site Conditions
Consultant will study and assess site conditions including, but not limited to, the following. Include photographs as appropriate.

1.7.1. Parking Lot / Garage
1.7.1.1. Description of the existing parking lot / garage
1.7.1.1.1. Total area (sq. ft.)
1.7.1.1.2. Total number of parking spaces including handicap spaces
1.7.1.1.3. Size, type and proximity to entrance of handicap spaces
1.7.1.2. Condition of the parking lot / garage
1.7.1.3. Approximate date last repaired / resurfaced
1.7.1.4. Vehicular circulation issues

1.7.1.5. Pedestrian circulation issues
1.7.1.6. Signage issues
1.7.1.7. Appropriate number of spaces to the building occupant / patron load
1.7.1.8. Code related issues in terms of handicap spaces and access to building
1.7.1.9. ADA compliance
1.7.1.10.   Security / controlled access system (type, location, effectiveness, issues)
1.7.1.11.   Parking attendant structure
1.7.1.12.   Indicate all deficiencies in the existing parking lot / garage in terms of ADA requirements, age of the surfaces, code-related issues, vehicular circulation issues, pedestrian circulation issues, signage, maintenance issues and procedures and summary of repair costs over the last 5 years etc.
1.7.1.13.   Provide recommendations for rehabilitation, remediation, upgrading or repair of parking lot / garage for its intended use.

1.7.2.   Parking Lot / Site Lighting System(s)
1.7.2.1. Description of the existing parking lot / garage lighting
1.7.2.2. Condition and type of parking lot / garage lighting fixtures
1.7.2.3. Approximate date parking lot/garage lighting system was last upgraded

1.7.2.4. Level and direction of illumination (LEED compliance)
1.7.2.5. Description of the existing site / entry lighting
1.7.2.6. Condition and type of site/entry lighting fixtures
1.7.2.7. Approximate date site/entry lighting system was last upgraded
1.7.2.8. Level and direction of illumination (LEED compliance)
1.7.2.9. Indicate all deficiencies in the existing parking lot / garage and site / entry lighting systems in terms of ADA requirements, age, energy conservation issues, code- related issues, illumination issues, LEED compliance, maintenance issues and procedures and summary of repair costs over the last 5 years etc.
1.7.2.10.   Provide recommendations for rehabilitation, remediation, upgrading or repair of parking lot / site lighting systems for their intended use.

1.7.3. Sidewalks & Curb Cuts

1.7.3.1. Location and description of sidewalk(s) and curb cut(s)
1.7.3.2. Material and condition of sidewalk(s) and curb cut(s)
1.7.3.3. Length and width of sidewalk (in ft.) and curb cut(s)
1.7.3.4. Approximate date the existing sidewalk(s) and curb cut(s) were last repaired / resurfaced
1.7.3.5. Circulation issues
1.7.3.6. Indicate all deficiencies in the existing sidewalk(s) and curb cut(s) in terms of ADA requirements, age of the surfaces, code-related issues, vehicular circulation issues, pedestrian circulation issues, signage, maintenance issues and procedures and summary of repair costs over the last 5 years etc.
1.7.3.7. Provide recommendations for rehabilitation, remediation, upgrading or repair of sidewalk(s) and curb cut(s) for their intended use.

1.7.4. Stairs & Ramps

1.7.4.1. Location and quantity of stairs
1.7.4.2. Width of stairs
1.7.4.3. Landing dimensions
1.7.4.4. Riser height
1.7.4.5. Condition of surfaces
1.7.4.6. ADA compliance
1.7.4.7. Provide recommendations for rehabilitation, remediation, upgrading or repair of the stairs and ramps for their intended use.

1.7.5. Storm Water Management

1.7.5.1. Condition of existing system
1.7.5.2. DPS requirements
1.7.5.3. Upgrading requirements
1.7.5.4. Indicate all deficiencies in the existing storm water management system, code- related issues, maintenance issues and procedures and summary of repair costs over the last 5 years etc.
1.7.5.5. Provide recommendations for rehabilitation, remediation, upgrading or repair of storm water management system for its intended use.

1.7.6. Retention Facilities

1.7.6.1. Xyz

1.7.7. Access from Public Transportation
1.7.7.1. Description of existing access from public transportation
1.7.7.2. Condition of structures and surfaces along path of travel
1.7.7.3. ADA compliance

1.7.7.4. Indicate all deficiencies in the existing access from public transportation in terms of ADA requirements, code-related issues, illumination issues, maintenance issues and procedures and summary of repair costs over the last 5 years etc.
1.7.7.5. Provide recommendations for rehabilitation, remediation, upgrading or repair of access from public transportation.

1.7.8. Utility Locations & Terminations
1.7.8.1. Xyz
1.8. Special Areas
Consultant will study and assess the condition of special areas including, but not limited to, the following. Include photographs as appropriate.

1.8.1. Kitchens & Pantries
1.8.1.1. Description of the existing spaces (size, location, equipment, fixtures, millwork, finishes, colors, etc.)
1.8.1.2. Age and condition of the existing equipment, fixtures, millwork, finishes, etc.
1.8.1.3. ADA compliance
1.8.1.4. Appropriate and effectiveness of the existing facility / components with building functions
1.8.1.5. Indicate all deficiencies in the existing kitchens and pantries in terms of capacity, energy conservation, ADA compliance, code-related issues, maintenance issues, etc.
1.8.1.6. Provide recommendations for rehabilitation, remediation, upgrading or repair of kitchens and pantries for their intended use.

1.8.2. Fitness & Locker Rooms
1.8.2.1. Description of the existing spaces (size, location, equipment, lockers, fixtures, toilet / shower partitions and accessories, millwork, finishes, colors, etc.)

1.8.2.2. Age and condition of the existing equipment, lockers, fixtures, toilet / shower partitions and accessories, millwork, finishes, etc.
1.8.2.3. ADA compliance
1.8.2.4. Appropriate and effectiveness of the existing facility / components with building functions
1.8.2.5. Indicate all deficiencies in the existing fitness and locker rooms in terms of capacity, ADA compliance, code-related issues, maintenance issues, etc.
1.8.2.6. Provide recommendations for rehabilitation, remediation, upgrading or repair of fitness and locker rooms for their intended use.

1.8.3. Restrooms
1.8.3.1. Description of the existing spaces (size, location, fixtures, toilet partitions and accessories, millwork, finishes, colors, etc.)
1.8.3.2. Age and condition of the existing fixtures, toilet partitions and accessories, millwork, finishes, etc.
1.8.3.3. ADA compliance
1.8.3.4. Appropriate and effectiveness of the existing restrooms with building functions
1.8.3.5. Indicate all deficiencies in the existing restrooms in terms of capacity, ADA compliance, code-related issues, maintenance issues, etc.
1.8.3.6. Provide recommendations for rehabilitation, remediation, upgrading or repair of restrooms for their intended use.
1.9. Miscellaneous Systems & Equipment
Consultant will study and assess the condition of miscellaneous systems and equipment including, but not limited to, the following. Include photographs as appropriate.

1.9.1. Security System & Equipment
1.9.1.1. Description of the existing security system and equipment
1.9.1.2. Age of the existing security system and equipment
1.9.1.3. Appropriate and effectiveness of the existing security system and equipment with building functions
1.9.1.4. Condition of the security system and equipment
1.9.1.5. Approximate date last replaced
1.9.1.6. Life expectancy

1.9.1.7. Indicate all deficiencies in the existing security system and equipment in terms of component size, capacity, installation, type of system, age, effectiveness, code- related issues, maintenance issues, procedures and summary of repair costs over the last 5 years, availability of spare parts etc.
1.9.1.8. Provide recommendations for rehabilitation, remediation, upgrading or repair of security system and equipment for their intended use.

1.9.2. Furniture
1.9.2.1. Description of the existing furniture (general, systems and custom)
1.9.2.2. Age of the existing furniture
1.9.2.3. Appropriate and effectiveness of the existing furniture with building and occupant functions
1.9.2.4. Condition of the furniture
1.9.2.5. Approximate date last replaced
1.9.2.6. Life expectancy
1.9.2.7. Indicate all deficiencies in the existing furniture in terms of size, condition, installation, type of system, age, code-related issues, maintenance issues, procedures and summary of repair costs over the last 5 years, availability of spare parts etc.
1.9.2.8. Provide recommendations for rehabilitation, remediation, upgrading or repair of furniture for its intended use.

1.9.3. Audiovisual Systems & Equipment
1.9.3.1. Description of the existing audiovisual systems and equipment
1.9.3.2. Age of the existing audiovisual systems and equipment
1.9.3.3. Appropriate and effectiveness of the existing audiovisual systems and equipment with occupant requirements
1.9.3.4. Condition of the audiovisual systems and equipment
1.9.3.5. Approximate date last replaced
1.9.3.6. Life expectancy
1.9.3.7. Indicate all deficiencies in the existing audiovisual systems and equipment in terms of component characteristics, installation, type of system, age, code-related issues, maintenance issues, procedures and summary of repair costs over the last 5 years, availability of spare parts etc.
1.9.3.8. Provide recommendations for rehabilitation, remediation, upgrading or repair of audiovisual systems and

equipment for their intended use.

1.9.4. Food Service Equipment
1.9.4.1. Description of the existing food service equipment
1.9.4.2. Age of the existing food service equipment
1.9.4.3. Appropriate and effectiveness of existing food service equipment with building functions
1.9.4.4. Condition of the food service equipment
1.9.4.5. Approximate date last replaced
1.9.4.6. Life expectancy
1.9.4.7. Indicate all deficiencies in the existing food service equipment in terms of equipment size, capacity, installation, type, age, energy conservation, condition, code-related

issues, maintenance issues, procedures and summary of repair costs over the last 5 years, availability of spare parts etc.
1.9.4.8. Provide recommendations for rehabilitation, remediation, upgrading or repair of food service equipment for its intended use.

1.9.5. Medical Equipment
1.9.5.1. Description of the existing medical equipment
1.9.5.2. Age of the existing medical equipment
1.9.5.3. Appropriate and effectiveness of the existing medical equipment with building functions
1.9.5.4. Condition of the medical equipment
1.9.5.5. ADA compliance
1.9.5.6. Approximate date last replaced
1.9.5.7. Life expectancy
1.9.5.8. Indicate all deficiencies in existing medical equipment in terms of equipment size, capacity, installation, type, age, code-related issues, maintenance issues, procedures and summary of repair costs over the last 5 years, availability of spare parts etc.
1.9.5.9. Provide recommendations for rehabilitation, remediation, upgrading or repair of medical equipment for its intended use.

1.9.6. Signage
1.9.6.1. Description of existing signage (exterior, building-mounted, directional, room (permanent and otherwise), building directory, workstation, etc.)
1.9.6.2. Age of existing signage components

1.9.6.3. Sizes of existing signage components
1.9.6.4. Materials / finishes of existing signage components
1.9.6.5. Locations of existing signage components
1.9.6.6. Appropriate and effectiveness of existing signage with building functions
1.9.6.7. Condition of signage
1.9.6.8. Life expectancy (illuminated type)
1.9.6.9. ADA compliance (Braille, raised letters, mounting height and location, etc.)
1.9.6.10. Indicate all deficiencies in existing signage in terms of size, installation, type of system, age, energy conservation (illuminated type), code-related issues, maintenance issues, procedures and summary of repair costs over the last 5 years, availability of spare parts etc.
1.9.6.11. Provide recommendations for rehabilitation, remediation, upgrading or repair of signage for its intended use.

1.10. Phasing Plan

1.10.1. Recommended Phasing Scenario(s)
1.10.1.1. Consultant shall provide one or more recommended phasing plans /scenarios. Scenarios shall:
1.10.1.1.1. Identify impact on the functions of the building
1.10.1.1.2. Identify if building renovation can be accomplished without shutting down operations
1.10.1.1.3. Identify if building renovation can only be accomplished by shutting down entire operation
1.10.1.1.4. Include estimated amount of space that must be vacant during the course of work if applicable
1.10.1.1.5. Identify if computer, electrical or mechanical rooms will be affected and if so, strategy for eliminating or reducing impact on building occupants
1.10.1.1.6. Identify to what extent surrounding property will be needed for construction staging
1.10.1.1.7. Identify if underground utility or other work will impact public access to building

1.10.2. Duration of Phases
1.10.2.1. Provide sequence of phases
1.10.2.2. Provide construction time frames for each phase

1.10.3. Impact on Building Occupants and Surrounding Area
1.10.3.1. In conjunction with recommended phasing scenarios, provide: 1.10.3.1.1. Strategies for temporary relocation of personnel work spaces
1.10.3.1.2. Strategies for temporary relocation of building amenities (cafeteria, fitness rooms, copy center, etc.)
1.10.3.1.3. Identify noise, vibration and/or odor creating operations, define level of anticipated disruption, and make recommendations for mitigating impact on building occupants
1.10.3.1.4. Identify potential disruption on surrounding area and make recommendations for mitigating impact.
1.11. Indirect Costs
Consultant shall discuss indirect costs which include, but are not limited to the following:
1.11.1.1. Moving
1.11.1.2. Temporary heating / air conditioning / ventilation
1.11.1.3. Temporary supply of domestic water (hot and cold)
1.11.1.4. Temporary power
1.11.1.5. Temporary parking spaces
1.11.1.6. Weekends / non regular hour construction work
1.11.1.7. Noise control
1.11.1.8. Smoke / welding fumes control
1.11.1.9. Dust control
1.11.1.10. Special rigging with street closure (helicopter / large crane)
1.11.1.11. Necessary duct modification / replacement / new installation above the existing ceiling, if the ceiling / lighting systems are in appropriate condition, add the tasks for removing and reinstalling the ceiling and lighting system as indirect cost elements.
1.11.1.12. Necessary pipe modification / replacement / new installation above the existing ceiling, if the ceiling / lighting systems are in appropriate condition, add the tasks for removing and reinstalling the ceiling and lighting system as indirect cost elements.

1.12. Space measurement summary
Consultant must verify the existing building spaces and fill the

PROFIT BY DESIGN

following charts. If building is one floor only Total Building Chart (the last one) must be filled, otherwise for the first floor use the Ground Floor Chart and for typical floors use the Typical Floor Chart.

1.12.1. Floor: Typical Floor (SAMPLE)

No.	Space category	Area		
SF	Multiplier	Formula for area		
A	Programmable Area	10,983	1.00	Total from Space Tabulation Charts
B	Internal walls	1,296	0.12	
C	Assignable Area	12,279	1.12	A+B
d1	Internal corridors	1,858	0.17	
d2	Non-programmable areas	80	0.01	
D	Internal circulation	1,938	0.18	d1+d2
E1	Net Usable Area	12,839	1.17	A+d1
E2	Usable Area	14,217	1.30	C+D
f1	Lobby	399		
f2	Mech. room	0		
f3	Equipment room	0		
f4	Mail room	0		
f5	Telephone/IT room	0		
F	Building Common area	399	0.04	Σf
g1	Janitor's closet	20		
g2	Elect. & Tel. room	90		
g3	Mech. room	90		
g4	Rest room	493		
g5	Corridors	1,845		
G	Floor Common Area	2,538	.23	Σg
h1	Shafts	78		
h2	Elevator banks	267		
h3	Stairs	391		
H	Major Vertical Penetrations	736	0.07	Σh
I	Rentable Area	17,154	1.56	E2+F+G
J	Gross Measured Area	17,890	1.63	I+H
K	Exterior walls	486	0.04	
L	Gross Building Area	18,595	1.67	J+K

PROFIT BY DESIGN

1.12.2. Floor: Ground Floor

No.	Space category	Area		
SF	Multiplier	Formula for area		
A	Programmable Area	10,351	1.00	Total from Space Tabulation Charts
B	Internal walls	931	0.09	
C	Assignable Area	11,282	1.09	A+B
d1	Internal corridors	1,858	0.18	
d2	Non-programmable areas	80	0.01	
D	Internal circulation	1,938	0.19	d1+d2
E1	Net Usable Area	12,210	1.18	A+d1
E2	Usable Area	13,220	1.28	C+D
f1	Lobby	1,197		
f2	Mech. room	199		
f3	Equipment room	0		
f4	Mail room	0		
f5	Telephone/IT room	0		
F	Building Common area	1,396	0.13	Σf
g1	Janitor's closet	20		
g2	Elect. & Tel. room	90		
g3	Mech. room	90		
g4	Rest room	493		
g5	Corridors	1,845		
G	Floor Common Area	2,538	.24	Σg
h1	Shafts	78		
h2	Elevator banks	267		
h3	Stairs	391		
H	Major Vertical Penetrations	736	0.07	Σh
I	Rentable Area	17,154	1.66	E2+F+G
J	Gross Measured Area	17,890	1.73	I+H
K	Exterior walls	486	0.04	
L	Gross Building Area	18,595	1.79	J+K

1.12.3. Floor: Total Building

No.	Space category	Area	Formula for area	
SF	Multiplier			
A	Programmable Area	43,300	1.00	Total from Space Tabulation Charts
B	Internal walls	4,820	0.11	
C	Assignable Area	48,120	1.11	A+B
d1	Internal corridors	7,433	0.17	
d2	Non-programmable areas	320	0.01	
D	Internal circulation	7,753	0.19	d1+d2
E1	Net Usable Area	50,733	1.18	A+d1
E2	Usable Area	55,873	1.30	C+D
f1	Lobby			
f2	Mech. room			
f3	Equipment room			
f4	Mail room			
f5	Telephone/IT room			
F	Building Common area	2,593	0.06	Σf
g1	Janitor's closet			
g2	Elect. & Tel. room			
g3	Mech. room			
g4	Rest room			
g5	Corridors			
G	Floor Common Area	10,150	.23	Σg
h1	Shafts			
h2	Elevator banks			
h3	Stairs			
H	Major Vertical Penetrations	2,943	0.07	Σh
I	Rentable Area	68,616	1.59	E2+F+G
J	Gross Measured Area	71,559	1.66	I+H
K	Exterior walls	1,732	0.04	
L	Gross Building Area	73500	1.79	J+K

PROFIT BY DESIGN

PROFIT by Design
Basic Paradigms & Conventions
Summary & Applications

Steven L. Biegel, AIA, NCARB, LEED AP
ARCHITECT

- **Time Management / Time Sheets**
- **Forecasting & Scheduling**
- **Utilization**
- **Client Contact & Communication**
- **Scope Creep & Additional Services**
- **Budgeting Reserves**

PROFIT BY DESIGN

Profit by Design

Elements of A/E firm Profitability

- Equity
- Professional liability
- Successful management
- Professional skill & judgment
- Entrepreneurial risk
- Extra time
- Innovation

PROFIT by Design

Terminology

- Earned Revenue
- Cash Flow
- Billings
- Overhead
- Allowable Costs
- Direct Costs
- InDirect Costs
- Accounts Receivable
- DSOs (Days Sales Outstanding)
- WIP (Work-In-Progress)

- Reserves
- Backlog
- Collections
- Utilization
- Business Plan
- Front Side/Back Side
- Contribution
- Bookings/Sales
- Revenue Recognition
- EBITDA

PROFIT BY DESIGN

PROFIT by Design

Firm Profitability (Pre-Tax)

▪ All As & Es	6.05%
▪ Top 25% of As & Es	12.72%
▪ Top 25% of As Only	14.49%
▪ Top 10% of Es Only	19.21%
▪ Top 10% of As Only	22.19%

Source: SMPS

PROFIT by Design

Gross Revenue = Total fees earned and recognized through performance of services for a customer.

Net Revenue = Gross revenue minus expenses for supplies, consultants and external services.

PROFIT BY DESIGN

PROFIT by Design

Gross Profit = Total revenue earned and recognized above all direct and indirect expenses (including consultant services).

Net Profit = Gross profit minus costs for interest, taxes, depreciation, amortization, reinvestment, staff retention (bonuses).

PROFIT by Design

Revenue Recognition = Fees earned at the time when sales are consummated or services provided that create an obligation on the part of the customer to make payment for the sales or services.

PROFIT BY DESIGN

PROFIT by Design

EBITDA = Earnings (net) before interest, taxes, depreciation, and amortization. Calculated by adding interest expenses and depreciation / amortization expenses to pre-tax, pre-bonus profit.

PROFIT by Design

Utilization = Ratio expressing efficiency of labor devoted to earning revenue. Usually expressed as total direct project hours divided by total of all person hours "paid for" within a specific time period. For example:

10 Employees @ 40/hrs/wk = (400 hrs)

Total Direct Project Hours = 297 (Time Sheets)

$$\text{Utilization} = \frac{297}{400} = 74.25\%$$

PROFIT BY DESIGN

PROFIT by Design

DSOs (Days Sales Outstanding)

From the time hours are posted on the time sheet . . .
The revenue has been earned and compensation is due.

Client may not be aware of fees owed for 30-45 days. Client may take 90-120 days to pay!

Typical DSO calculation:

Average Days of Project WIP = 15 days

Actual Days to Collect after Bill = 63 days

Total DSO = 78 days

PROFIT by Design

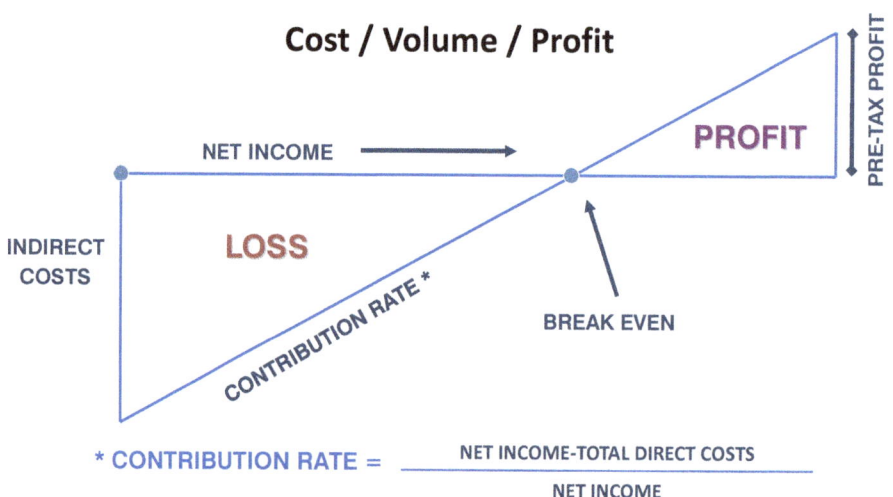

$$\text{* CONTRIBUTION RATE} = \frac{\text{NET INCOME - TOTAL DIRECT COSTS}}{\text{NET INCOME}}$$

PROFIT BY DESIGN

PROFIT by Design

Contribution (also called Gross Profit Margin) =
The percentage of net service revenue remaining after all direct project costs (including direct labor and other direct costs) have been covered. Calculated by dividing net service revenue less direct costs by net service revenue.

PROFIT by Design

Practice Sectors / Regulations

Private Sector	Unregulated
Institutional Sector	Somewhat Regulated
Federal Sector	Highly Regulated

Risk / Reward

Private Sector	High Risk/High Reward
Institutional Sector	Modest Risk/Modest Reward
Federal Sector	Low Risk/Low Reward

PROFIT BY DESIGN

PROFIT by Design

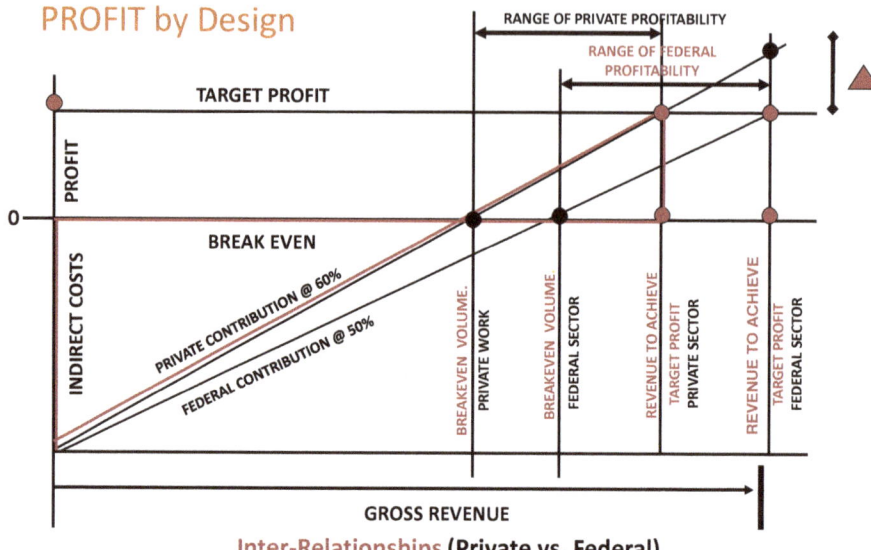

Inter-Relationships (Private vs. Federal)

PROFIT by Design

Typical Project Costs

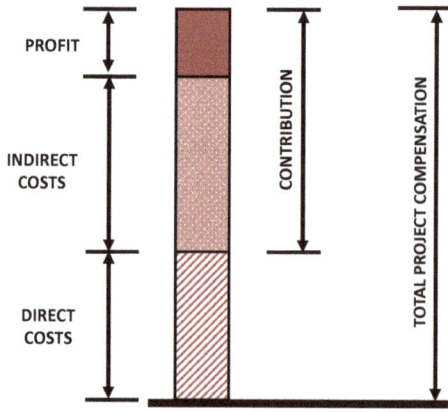

Appendix

PROFIT BY DESIGN

PROFIT by Design

Factors Impacting Contribution and Profit

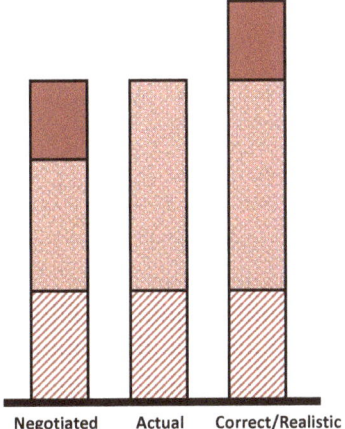

Case A:
Inadequate
O.H.
Allowance

PROFIT by Design

Factors Impacting Contribution and Profit

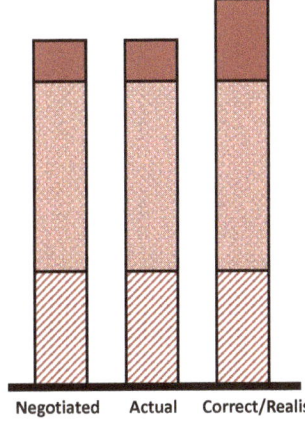

Case B:
Inadequate
Project Profit
Allowance

PROFIT BY DESIGN

PROFIT by Design

Factors Impacting Contribution and Profit

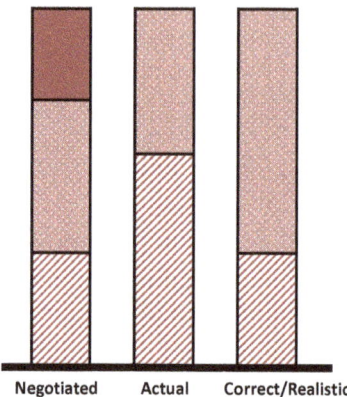

Case C:
Excessive
Direct
Costs

PROFIT by Design

Factors Impacting Contribution and Profit

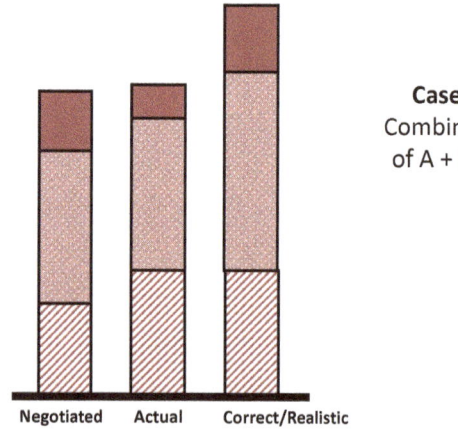

Case D:
Combination
of A + B + C

PROFIT BY DESIGN

PROFIT by Design

Work-In-Progress (WIP)

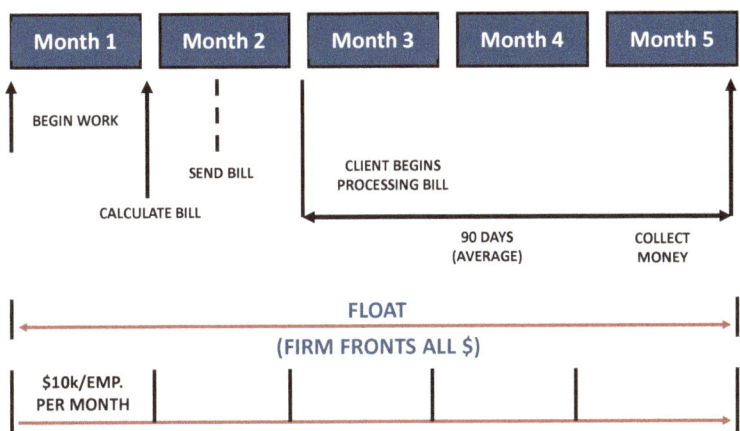

PROFIT by Design

Goals to Assure Profit

- Selective about type of work/client
- Negotiate best possible fee
- Keep scope limited/well defined
- Utilization must be high
- Overhead must be low/controlled
- Good, clear contracts
- Recognize revenue immediately
- Strive for "once through process"
- No mistakes
- Keep DSOs Down (Collect $)

PROFIT BY DESIGN

- Time Management / Time Sheets
- Forecasting & Scheduling
- Utilization
- Client Contact & Communication
- Scope Creep & Additional Services
- Budgeting Reserves

BUDGETING RESERVES

TOTAL NEGOTIATED DESIGN FEE=   **$50,000**

TOTAL NUMBER OF HOURS SUPPORTED BY FEE @ $150/HR= 333

PM ALLOCATES TIME:

RESERVES	**50 hrs**
SCHEMATIC DESIGN	40 hrs
DESIGN DEVELOPMENT	80 hrs
CDs	163 hrs
TOTAL	**333 hrs**

PROFIT BY DESIGN

PROFIT by Design

Business Plan

- Financial Goals (Annual)
- Marketing Goals
- Staff Development Goals
- Design/Recognition Goals

Plan should clearly describe yearly goals and contain concise narrative stating "How" these goals will be achieved.

PROFIT by Design

"Commodity Business"

- Architects *market* professional services
- Architects *sell* professional time
- Architecture is a commodity business with staff hours as the commodity

PROFIT BY DESIGN

PROFIT by Design

"Profit by Design"

- We are in business to make money

- We make money by working efficiently

- Demand for our services is driven by both quality and cost . . . (mostly cost).

- We grow a business (including reputation) in order to one day sell that business.

PROFIT by Design

Key Contract Provisions & Documents

- Essential Documents

- Key Provisions

- Due Diligence

PROFIT BY DESIGN

PROFIT by Design

Essential Documents

- Corporate Documents
- Purchase Agreement
- Financing Agreements
- Employment Agreements
- Buy/Sell Agreement
- Non-Compete Agreement

PROFIT by Design

Key Provisions – Purchase Agreement

- Master document incorporating other agreements
- Warranties and representations
- Cross indemnification
- Insurance
- Consents

PROFIT BY DESIGN

PROFIT by Design

Key Provisions – Buy/Sell Agreement

- Buy/Sell Formula
- Termination Provisions
- Valuation Guidelines

PROFIT by Design

Warranties & Representations

- Ownership
- Accounts receivable & accounts payable
- Taxes
- Litigation
- Pension plan & employee benefits
- Many others

PROFIT BY DESIGN

PROFIT by Design

Due Diligence

- Auditing accounts
- Taxes
- Review of contracts & leases
- WIP & project status
- Notifications

PROFIT by Design

Valuing & Pricing the Firm

- The Formulas
- Looking past the formulas
- Tax Planning
- Financing the purchase

PROFIT BY DESIGN

PROFIT by Design

The Formulas

- Future Revenues
- X times net (after tax) profits
- Book value plus goodwill
- Employee replacement cost
- X times net revenue
- Percent of backlog less WIP

PROFIT by Design

Looking Past the Formulas

- Synergy
- Hidden assets
- Key executives
- Access to clients
- Reputation

PROFIT BY DESIGN

PROFIT by Design

Tax Planning

- IRS oversight
- Tax free exchanges
- Ordinary income v. long term capital gains
- Deductibility
- Sub-chapter S corporation

PROFIT by Design

Tax Strategies

- Pension Plans
- ESOP's
- Non-Compete Payments
- Consulting Fees
- Real Estate

PROFIT by Design

Financing the Purchase

- Owner Financing
- Accounts Receivable
- ESOP's
- Bank Loans
- Equity Financing

PROFIT by Design

Elements of a Successful Merger

- Understanding each sides objectives
- Be realistic
- Remember where the value is
- War Stories from the front

PROFIT BY DESIGN

Strategy for Growth by Acquisition
The 4 "Ps"

People   (Find the Most Talented People)

Portfolio   (Acquire an Expertise Beyond Current Set)

Proximity   (Find a Location Near a Market Hot Spot)

Profit   (Take the Firm from 0 Profit to 20% or Beyond)

Predictable Results

Pre-Purchase Profit is low and flat, usually due to excess overhead and reluctance to change management style.

Post Merger (or Purchase) results show stronger initial profit due to increased billings and reduced overhead, followed by a drop in profit as new financing and new marketing efforts are initiated (expensive). Then, future profits increase and normalize.

PROFIT BY DESIGN

ISSUES / BEFORE

Settles Associates, Inc. Acquisition (2004)
Arlington, Virginia

- Declining Revenues
- Declining Staff Resources
- Declining Backlog
- Increasing Debt & Payables
- Bank No Longer Extending Credit
- Motivated Seller (Owner for 37 Years)
- Solid Regional Reputation
- Existing Government Contracts
- Strong Federal Interiors and Commercial Interiors Portfolio

RESULTS / AFTER

Matrix Settles, Architecture, Planning, Interior Design

- Reduced Overhead
- Increased Marketing Resources & Efforts
- Revenues from $1.3 mil to $5.5 mil
- Staff Grew from 12 to 38 Professionals
- Elevated Professional Staff (More Principals)
- Empowered Staff (with Stock Ownership)
- Incentive Compensation Plans

PROFIT BY DESIGN

ISSUES / BEFORE

TM/R Engineering, Inc.   Start-Up MEP Firm   (2005)
Arlington, Virginia

- Frustrated Senior Mechanical Engineer Not Content with Present Employment Situation
- Desire to Create MEP Firm and Build Capable Staff
- Needed Start-Up Funds
- Needed Infusion of Work
- Needed Office Space, Equipment & Furniture
- Immediately Began Billing in First Month of Operation
- Began Hiring Credible MEP Staff Immediately

RESULTS / AFTER

TM/R Engineering   Today

- Provided Capital / Infrastructure / Backlog of Work
- Helped Recruit Staff
- Encouraged Diversification of Client Base
- Grew from 1 to 17 Professionals
- Grew from $0 to $2.1 mil (in 3 years)

PROFIT BY DESIGN

ISSUES / BEFORE

Taylor Fierce Architecture, Inc.   Alliance (2006)
Los Angeles, California

- Small, Newly Established Firm with Noble Design Intentions
- Underfinanced
- Small Projects with Small Fees
- Unreliable Cash Flow
- No Existing Line of Credit to Support Growth
- Needed Outside Management Expertise
- Needed Financing
- Needed Professional Marketing Assistance

RESULTS / AFTER

Taylor Fierce Architecture, Inc.   Today

- Management Advice
- Established Line of Credit
- Secured New, Modern Space
- Marketing to New Sectors
- Cross Selling in Unfamiliar Markets
- Grew from 6 to 19 Professionals
- Grew from $600K to $2.4 mil in Revenues

PROFIT BY DESIGN

ISSUES / BEFORE

Ian MacKinlay Architecture, Inc. Acquisition (2007)
San Francisco, California

- Seasoned Sole Proprietor Desires to Sell Firm
- Internal Sale to Employees Not Feasible
- Declining New Business Due to Age of Senior Partner
- Declining Revenues
- Declining Backlog
- Highly Specialized Forensic Architecture Expertise
- Strong National Reputation & 20 Year History
- High Billable Hourly Rates for Research, Reports & Testimony
- Strong Existing Client Relationships

RESULTS / AFTER

Matrix IMA   Today

- Diversified Practice
- Empowered Principals
- Exported Forensic Practice to DC
- Consolidated Staff to Balance Revenue and Cash Flow
- Leveled Business Peaks & Valleys
- 16 Professionals down to 12
- $1.9 million to $2.1 million
- Maintained High Billable Rates

PROFIT BY DESIGN

Spencer Partnership Architects, Inc.   Acquisition (2008)
Houston, Texas

- 41 Year Old Firm with Outstanding Reputation
- Strong Expertise in K-12 and High Rise Condo Projects
- Declining Revenues
- Declining Staff Resources
- Declining Backlog
- Increasing Debt and Payables
- Motivated Seller (Retirement Desired in 3-5 Years)
- Loyal and Experienced Staff
- Needs Financing and Strong Marketing Partner

Comparison

- Matrix Settles
- TM/R Engineering
- Taylor Fierce
- Matrix IMA
- Matrix Spencer

After 4 Years

- 12 to 38 Professionals
- 0 to 17 Professionals
- 6 to 19 Professionals
- 16 to 12 Professionals
- 12 to 40 Professionals

- Total = 98 Professionals and Growing (5 Offices)

PROFIT BY DESIGN

Comparison

After 4 Years

- Matrix Settles
- TM/R Engineering
- Taylor Fierce
- Matrix IMA
- Matrix Spencer

$5.5 mil annual
$2.1 mil annual
$2.5 mil annual
$2.1 mil annual
$6.0 mil annual

Bibliography

Coxe, Weld, Managing Architectural and Engineering Practice, Van Nostrand Reinhold Company, 1980.

The American Institute of Architects, Financial Management for Architects, AIA Press, 1980.

Boston Society of Architects, Client's Guide to Architectural Services, AIA Press, 1978.

The American Institute of Architects, Compensation Guidelines for Architectural and Engineering Services, AIA Press, 1978.

Bolick, Erma H. and McMahan, Nanette L., Architectural Accounting, Erma H. Bolick, 1971.

COFPAES (Committee on Federal Procurement of Architect-Engineering Services), An Analysis of the Impact of Federal Government Overhead and Profit Allowances on Architect-Engineer Firms, Case and Company, Inc., 1976.

COFPAES (Committee on Federal Procurement of Architect-Engineering Services), Report to GSA on Allowable Costs and Audits, AIA Press, 1976.

National Society of Professional Engineers (NSPE), The Overhead Rates – Management Control Issues for Design Professionals, NSPE/PEPP, 1982.

Goodowens, James B., A User's Guide to Federal Architect-Engineer Contracts, second edition, American Society of Civil Engineers (ASCE), 1996.

Zweig White, 2001 Successful Firm Survey, Zweig White, 2001.

Knackstedt, Mary V., The Interior Design Business Handbook, third edition, John Wiley & Sons Inc., 2002.

Rubeling, Albert W., Jr., How to Start and Operate Your Own Design Firm, McGraw-Hill, Inc., 1994.

Callan, John & Rice, Hugh L., Construction Accounting Deskbook, third edition, Aspen Law & Business, 2002.

Ludy, Perry J., Profit Building, Berrett-Koehler Publishers, Inc., 2000.

Rasmussen, Nils H. & Eichorn, Christopher J., Budgeting, John Wiley & Sons, Inc. 2000.

Rizzo, Michael R., How to Make Profits with Service Contracts, American Management Association, 1987.

Sweet, Justin, Legal Aspects of Architecture, Engineering and the Construction Process, forth edition, West Publishing Company, 1989.

Greenstreet, Bob & Karen, The Architect's Guide to Law and Practice, Van Nostrand Reinhold Company, Inc., 1984.

Mason, Kevin, Architect's Business Problem Solver, McGraw-Hill Companies, 2000.

Spector, Tom, The Ethical Architect-the dilemma of contemporary practice, Princeton Architectural Press, 2001.

Daniels, Aubrey C., Performance Management, third edition, Performance Management Publications, 1989.

Franklin, James R., Architect's Professional Practice Manual, McGraw-Hill Companies, 2000.

Rose, Stuart W., Ph.D., Mandeville-A Guide For The Marketing of Professional Services, Professional Development Resources, Inc., 1995.

PROFIT BY DESIGN
About the Author

Steven L. Biegel, AIA, is a Principal and Director of Architecture for PLACE Designers, Inc. with offices in Round Rock and Houston, Texas.

Steven manages and directs a highly talented staff who are involved in multi-family, mixed-use, high-rise condos, and commercial retail centers in Texas, Florida and elsewhere in the US.

Director of Architecture – PLACE Designers, Inc. Round Rock, Texas	2018
CEO – The Matrix Design Companies, Inc. Fairfax, Virginia	2004
V.P. – Einhorn, Yaffee Prescott, LLC Washington, DC	1999
V.P. – URS Greiner, Inc. Washington, DC	1996
CEO – Lawrence & Lawrence, P.C. Warrenton, Virginia	1985
V.P. – The National Institute of Building Sciences Washington, DC	1981
Director of Energy – The American Consulting Engineers Council Washington, DC	1979
Director of Federal Liaison – The American Institute of Architects Washington, DC	1977
Design Fellowship – The National Endowment for the Arts	1979
Syracuse University – B. Arch	1978

Adjunct Professor of Architecture – American University
Adjunct Professor of Architectural History – University of Virginia

www.ingramcontent.com/pod-product-compliance
Lightning Source LLC
Chambersburg PA
CBHW042030050526
44107CB00128B/1491/J